Also by Arthur Wenk

Non-fiction

A Brief History of Classical Music: A Tale of Time, Tonality and Timbre (2017)

Camerata: A Guide to Organizing and Directing Small Choruses (2014)

A Guide to the Bookstores of Toronto (1996)

Musical Resources for the Revised Common Lectionary (1994)

Analyses of Nineteenth- and Twentieth-Century Music: 1940-1985 (1987)

Une esquisse de la pensée musicale (1985)

La musique et les grandes époques de l'art (1984)

Claude Debussy and Twentieth-Century Music (1983)

Introduction to Nineteenth-Century Music (1977)

Claude Debussy and the Poets (1976)

Fiction

Quarter Note Tales #4: An Axel Crochet Trilogy (2013)

Axel Crochet: Musicologist-at-Large (2011)

New Quarter Note Tales (2010)

The Quarter Note Tales (2006)

The Matrix of Western Culture:

Perspectives on History, the Arts and Ideas

Arthur Wenk

© 2017 Arthur Wenk

Visit the author's website at www.arthurwenk.ca

Cover Design by Fiverr International

In memory of Carol

Contents

Contents v

Preface xi

Introduction xii

Prologue: Purposes of Art 1

  Lascaux Cave Paintings, ca. 17,000 BC PLATE 1 1

  Imhotep, Pyramid of King Djoser, ca. 2700 BC PLATE 2 3

Ancient Greece 6

  Context 6

  Homer, The Odyssey, 800-600 BC 8

  Pythagoras, fl. ca. 500 BC 11

  Parthenon, 448-432 BC PLATE 3 14

  Herodotus, Histories, 450s BC 17

  Sophocles, Oedipus Rex, 428 BC 19

  Plato, The Republic, 360 BC 22

  Aristotle, Nichomachean Ethics, ca. 330 BC 24

  Euclid, Elements, 300 BC 27

  Connections: Proportion 31

Ancient Rome 33

  Context 33

  Julius Caesar, Commentaries on The Gallic Wars, ca. 50-40
  BC 35

  Virgil, The Aeneid, 19 BC 39

  Paul of Tarsus, Epistle to the Romans, 60 AD 42

  Colosseum, 80 AD PLATE 4 44

  Ptolemy, Almagest, ca. 150 AD 47

Connections: Virtus 50

5th To 10th Centuries... 51

Context.. 51

St. Augustine, The City of God, ca. 420 54

Gregory of Tours, Ten Books of History, 594 56

Beowulf, ca. 700 59

The Book of Kells, ca. 800 PLATE 5 61

Plainsong, Kyrie Orbis Factor, 9th century 64

Connections: Dichotomy 66

11th Century... 67

Context... 67

St. Anselm, Proslogion, ca. 1078................................... 69

Bayeux Tapestry, ca. 1100 PLATE 6 72

Song of Roland, ca. 1100.. 75

Rise of Polyphony, Alleluia Justus ut palma, ca. 1100......... 77

Connections: Faith 80

12th Century... 81

Context... 81

St. Sernin de Toulouse, ca. 1080-1120 PLATE 7................. 83

Peter Abelard, Sic et non, 1121 86

Chrétien De Troyes, Lancelot, The Knight of the Cart, 1168 88

Leonin, Viderunt omnes, 12th century 92

Connections: Rediscovery 95

13th Century... 96

Context... 96

Notre Dame Cathedral, 1163-ca. 1270 PLATE 8 98

vi

Fibonacci, Liber abaci, 1202... 101

Gottfried Von Strassburg, Tristan, 1210............................. 104

Perotin, Sederunt principes, 13th century............................. 106

Thomas Aquinas, Summa Theologica, 1274........................ 109

Connections: Consolidation... 113

14th Century 114

Context... 114

Giotto, Entrance of Christ into Jerusalem, 1306 PLATE 8 . 116

William of Ockham, Sum of Logic, 1323 119

Machaut, Ma fin est mon commencement, ca. 1360 121

Chaucer, The Canterbury Tales, 1380-1390....................... 126

Connections: Self-awareness... 129

15th Century 130

Context... 130

Robert Campin, Merode Altarpiece, ca. 1425-1438 PLATE 10
.... 132

Villon, Ballade des dames du temps jadis, 1461 135

Ockeghem, Missa prolationum, mid-15th century 137

Leonardo da Vinci, Notebooks (died 1519)........................ 140

Connections: Janus 143

16th Century 144

Context... 144

Michelangelo, Sistine Chapel Ceiling, 1511 PLATE 11 147

Erasmus, In Praise of Folly, 1511 149

Machiavelli, The Prince, 1513... 152

Luther, 95 Theses, 1517.. 154

Castiglione, The Book of the Courtier, 1528....................... 157

Copernicus, On the Revolutions of the Heavenly Spheres, 1543 159

Lassus, De Profundis, 1584 162

Shakespeare, Hamlet, ca. 1600 165

Connections: Humanism 169

17th Century 170

Context 170

Monteverdi, Orfeo, 1607 172

Descartes, Discourse on the Method, 1637 175

Velásquez, Las Meninas, 1656 PLATE 12 178

Molière, Le Misanthrope, 1666 180

Newton, Principia Mathematica, 1687 183

Hobbes, Leviathan, 1651 186

Locke, Second Treatise on Government, 1689 189

Connections: Rules 192

18th Century 193

Context 193

Euler, The Seven Bridges of Königsberg, 1735 ... 195

Bach, B Minor Mass, ca. 1748 198

Fielding, Tom Jones, 1749 201

Jefferson, Monticello, 1772 PLATE 14 204

Smith, The Wealth of Nations, 1776 207

Kant, Groundwork for a Metaphysics of Morals, 1785 209

Connections: Rationalism 211

19th Century 213

Context 213

Gauss, Theory of the Motion of the Heavenly Bodies, 1809 216

Austen, Pride and Prejudice, 1815............................ 219

Beethoven, Symphony No. 9, 1824 222

Turner, The Slave Ship, 1839 PLATE 15.................... 225

Kierkegaard, Either/Or, 1843.................................... 228

Marx, The Communist Manifesto, 1848..................... 230

Darwin, On the Origin of Species, 1859.................... 233

Connections: Rebellion... 236

20th Century 237

Context... 237

Freud, The Interpretation of Dreams, 1899 239

Picasso, Les Demoiselles d'Avignon, 1906-1907 PLATE 16 242

Einstein, General Theory of Relativity, 1915 245

Joyce, Ulysses, 1922... 247

Heisenberg, Uncertainty Principle, Quantum Mechanics, 1927 251

Bartók, Music for String, Percussion and Celesta, 1936 254

Sartre, Being and Nothingness, 1943........................ 258

Connections: Uncertainty 261

Through the Matrix.. 262

The Monomyth 262

Symbolism, Realism, Abstraction 268

Art, Literature and Music.. 269

God: Faith and Reason... 270

Conclusion 274

Repertoire 275

Plates 278

Bibliography 294

    Print Materials 294

    Internet Materials 315

Notes 317

Index 329

Preface

This book had its origins in a course I was assigned to teach at Université Laval in the 1980s: *La Musique et les grandes époques de l'art*. I was supposed to expose the self-evident underlying connections among all the arts from the Stone Age to the present in one unforgettable semester. Never mind that many cultural historians questioned the very existence of such connections. The course catalogue brooked no dispute.

I would have been delighted to take such a course, but to presume to teach it seemed like an act of unforgivable hubris. Nonetheless, the task had been assigned and I undertook it conscientiously. I insisted, however, on compiling a repertoire that would include just one work of French literature, one work of art, and one piece of music for each century, to combat the tendency in such courses to engage in empty generalizations. Eventually the Presses de l'Université Laval assigned an editor to improve my French and published my lectures in the form of a textbook.

Ten years ago, when the Jubilee United Church lecture series offered me an opportunity to rework and expand this material, in English this time, I extended the compass of the project to embrace history and the social sciences, science and mathematics, and philosophy and theology.

In order to produce the present volume, I undertook to consult at least two more books, preferably published since 2000, for each topic. I am grateful to the Interlibrary Loan departments at the Fort Myers Regional Library in Florida and the Ramara Township Public Library in Ontario for acquiring these books for me.

I am especially grateful to Nicholas Altenbernd, who employs a keener eye for detail than anyone I have ever known, for bringing his skills to bear on this manuscript.

Introduction

Aristotle has been described as the last person to know everything there was to be known. One should not underestimate the breadth of this knowledge: Aristotle's writings embraced physics, metaphysics, poetry, theater, music, logic, rhetoric, politics, government, ethics, biology and zoology. Nowadays the very idea of knowing everything seems beyond our comprehension. Many of us know more than most people in some narrow field and we may know more than nearly everybody in some tiny area of specialization. At the same time, we recognize vast areas in which we know little or nothing and we suspect that our ignorance extends to even vaster areas that we cannot even describe. Know everything? The very idea seems preposterous.

But if we cannot know everything, we can at least know something. Statistics, a powerful tool not available to Aristotle, tells us that a carefully selected sample allows us to make valid generalizations about a population. If we cannot be acquainted with all the individual trees, we can still gain knowledge of the forest through examination of particular specimens.

Imagine a grid with time on one axis and six categories of culture—Art, Literature, Music, Philosophy & Theology, Science & Mathematics, History & Social Sciences—on the other. We begin with large chunks of time for Ancient Greece, Ancient Rome, and the 5th through 10th centuries. Thereafter the century provides a convenient, if arbitrary, chronological unit. Then imagine filling each cell with a single representative work. A latitudinal view across the matrix allows one to ground general observations for each century in concrete examples. A longitudinal view down the matrix allows for an historical perspective of each cultural category.

I have undertaken to produce a framework that one could conceivably hold in mind all at once. One could have made other choices: those who prefer Proust to Joyce to represent the 20th century, those who cannot abide the thought of the 18th century without Mozart or the 19th without Wagner, may wish to create a different matrix with more satisfactory selections.

In composing the hundred-odd 700-800 word essays that make up this book, I have been ever conscious of an imaginary specialist in any given field who, if kindly disposed, might look upon this work and say, "Actually, it's a bit more complicated than that." Of course it is! Every subject treated here merits a book-length treatment, the very books I have consulted in composing these brief essays. I hope that readers may be inspired to seek out works listed in the bibliography to learn more about any subject that intrigues them. My object has been to offer both a personal view of the "big picture" as well as a tool, in the form of a matrix, enabling others to create their own.

The prologue offers speculations on the purposes of art by examining two ancient art forms, the cave paintings of Lascaux and the step pyramid of King Djoser. The first three chapters treat extended periods of time to examine the cultures of Ancient Greece, Ancient Rome, and the period from the 5th through 10th centuries known as the Early Middle Ages. Thereafter each chapter focuses on one century, beginning with an historical context for the discussions on individual works and ending with some provisional suggestions for joining these works under the umbrella of a key principle. The final chapter offers several longitudinal perspectives through the matrix.

Just as geometry leaves certain key concepts like "point" and "line" undefined, I have made no effort to offer a definition of "western culture." For the purposes of this book, western culture may be defined inductively by the choice of works cited in the repertoire. What pattern emerges from the resulting matrix? I have tried to demonstrate that each era displays characteristics that can be traced across culture. To this end, I conclude each chapter with a few paragraphs of "Connections," proposing a key-word that may serve to identify the principle underlying the culture of that era.

The several paragraphs of "Context" that open each chapter offer a basic framework for the discussion to follow. Those seeking a fuller historical treatment are directed to Norman Davies' magisterial *Europe: A History* or any of the specialized monographs referenced in the notes. I propose both the structure of the matrix and the cross-cultural connections as subjects for debate. Some readers may wish to substitute a different metaphor for an era; others may reject the thesis of underlying principles altogether. By basing my discussion on specific examples, I hope to provide a firm foundation for the debate.

Harold Bloom, in *The Western Canon*, describes the way writers speak to each other across generations. I would suggest that not just writers but all artists in some fashion speak to each other, if not within the same generation, at least within the same century. I believe that that our appreciation of Notre Dame Cathedral is deepened by coming to understand Gottfried von Strassburg, Perotin, Thomas Aquinas and Fibonacci; that we can make better sense of Velásquez by coming to know Molière, Monteverdi, Descartes, Newton, Hobbes and Locke; that our understanding of Fielding is enhanced by becoming acquainted with Jefferson, Bach, Kant, Euler and Smith. "Don't take any course where they make you read *Beowulf*," the Woody Allen character tells the Diane Keaton character in *Annie Hall*. On the contrary, reading *Beowulf* offers a terrific experience that contributes to, and benefits from, a knowledge of Gregory of Tours, and both works benefit from familiarity with the Book of Kells, St. Augustine, and plainsong. "Only connect," E. M. Forster wrote. In this book, I have tried to draw connections between aspects of western culture extending over more than three millennia.

Quotations from works of literature or by historical figures or their contemporaries appear in italics. Readers may access full-color versions of the plates for this book at http://arthurwenk.ca/books.htm. A copy of the matrix on which this book is based may be found just before the Index.

Prologue: Purposes of Art

Lascaux Cave Paintings, ca. 17,000 BC PLATE 1

A Rich, Stable Culture

The Lascaux cave paintings offer our earliest examples of human culture. Many of the works that we shall encounter in future centuries in the fields of mathematics, history or philosophy depend upon the invention of writing that occurred only much later. We have no reason to doubt that the civilization that produced the cave paintings also enjoyed music, dance, theater and story-telling, but nothing remains to inform us of these activities. Yet this civilization which lasted more than 20,000 years should not be considered primitive.

"The Paleolithic civilization in Europe and Asia should be compared with the most advanced civilizations of the past and of today. The greatest flowering of that civilization was the paintings in the caves. We should study them, not as ethnography, but the same way that we study Greek tragedy or the temples of Angkor Wat, expecting to find on the cave walls the history and beliefs of a great people along with the deepest philosophy and the most profound understanding of which humanity is capable. ... The qualities that define classicism—dignity, strength, grace, ease, confidence, and clarity—are also the principal qualities of the cave paintings."[1]

Shamanic Visions

Could the cave paintings have emerged from a superstitious belief in the power of magic to bring about desired results? Images in some sites have been defaced by pointed instruments, as if asserting the power of the hunter over actual beasts. Other images depict female animals as pregnant, perhaps to assure the tribe's

1

food supply. This early hypothesis maintained that Paleolithic hunters made no clear distinction between image and reality, so that the representations of the animals might in some way partake of the reality of the beasts themselves.

A more recent perspective imagines the paintings to have been a record of shamanic visions, the experiences of "people with special powers and skills ... believed to have access to this alternative reality."[2] "Why do the animals appear to be floating rather than standing on the ground? Why don't the animals appear in natural surroundings with trees, grass, rivers, and other features of the landscape? The painters didn't care at all about the relative size of the animals. A tiny mammoth might have a huge bison looming over him. How can that be? ... But all of these apparent anomalies make sense if the animals on the cave walls are not real animals after all, despite the realism of the art. ... They were animals first seen as visions in a hallucination. ... In many cases their purpose was to reproduce the experience of being in a trance."[3]

Complex Relationship with Animals

Nowadays, as we circumscribe certain areas to be preserved as "wilderness" and protect the habitats of animals we consider worth saving, we can scarcely conceive a wilderness world composed entirely of animal habitats. "Today it is almost impossible for us to imagine what a vast profusion of animals there actually was. Every species native to Europe today was there, along with species that are now extinct."[4] The aurochs depicted in our illustration belongs to a now-extinct species of wild cattle, known from fossil evidence to have lived in the area at the time.

A hunter society dependent upon animals for food, clothing and bone implements enjoyed a complex relationship with animals. "For the men of prehistory ... insofar as we are able to judge them, animals were in principle no less like them than other human beings. … We are certain that [Paleolithic man] confronted the animal not as though he were confronting an inferior being or a thing, a negligible reality, but as if he were confronting a mind similar to his own."[5] More than one writer has commented on how people are represented in the cave paintings. "Whereas the Upper Paleolithic painters left us admirable representations of the animals they hunted, they used childish techniques to represent men. … The representation of a man only mattered in relation to the animal."[6] Whatever the undeclared purpose of the Lascaux cave paintings, they give evidence of a society that held art in high esteem.

With global warming rapidly reaching irreversibility, and between 200 and 2000 extinctions occurring every year, we may want to reflect on what we can learn from a society that flourished for 20,000 years in harmony with nature.

Imhotep, Pyramid of King Djoser, ca. 2700 BC
PLATE 2

Pyramid

If the Lascaux cave paintings reflect the Paleolithic preoccupation with hunting, the pyramids embody the Egyptian fascination with death. Around 2650 BC Imhotep, the first architect whose name has been preserved, built a stepped pyramid as a tomb for King Djoser. The earliest large stone monument in the world, the pyramid was constructed by building six rectangular tombs with sloping sides—called mastabas—one on top of another. "It can be said without exaggeration that his pyramid complex constitutes a milestone in the evolution of monumental stone architecture in Egypt and in the world as a whole. Here limestone was first used on a large scale as a construction material, and here the idea of a monumental royal tomb in the form of a pyramid was first realized."[7]

The pyramid we see today, eroded and sand-covered, retains but a suggestion of its former glory. "At high noon forty-five centuries ago, when the pyramids were complete with their freshly smoothed white limestone casings, their brilliance must have been blinding. Only in this light can we appreciate the intensity with which the pyramids symbolized the sun god. This powerful special effect was extinguished when the outer casings of most pyramids were robbed long ago."[8]

Like an iceberg, the Egyptian pyramid held much of its volume beneath the surface. "The above-ground elements of Djoser's pyramid complex are only one part of the story. Below, the Egyptians created an underground structure on a scale previously unknown, quarrying out more than 3 ½ miles of shafts, tunnels, chambers, galleries and magazines. ... A great Central Shaft, 23 ft. square and 92 feet deep, was dug for the burial chamber."[9]

Death and Deity

The Egyptians considered life and death to be parts of a larger unity, with earthly life "merely an episode on the way to eternity. ... The pyramids and their temples, and the burials of kings, nobles and commoners, express the unique ancient Egyptian idea of death. For them death was not the end, but just one of the transformations in life's natural cycle. The final change in status depended on the first duty in the housekeeping of death—the treatment of the corpse. ... Mummification was not so much the preservation of the body as it had been during life, but the transfiguration of the corpse into a new body 'filled with magic,' a simulacrum or statue in wrappings and resin."[10]

"Resources were not only needed to sustain the king and his officials in life. From the earliest dynasties, it was believed that at the death of a king his divinely created spirit, the *ka*, would leave his body and then ascend to heaven, where it would accompany his father, the sun god, Ra, on the boat on which Ra travelled through each night before reappearing in the east. However, certain formalities had to take place if the king was to reach his destination safely. The body of the king had to be preserved, its name recorded on the tomb, and the *ka* had to be provided with all it needed for the afterlife. It could not survive without nourishment."[11]

Functional Art

According to Egyptian belief, a Pharaoh's tomb did more than commemorate his life; it contained all the elements necessary for a satisfactory afterlife. This was functional art, intended to protect the spirit of the dead king and to serve his needs, including food, servants, beasts of burden, and hieroglyphic inscriptions to identify the dead and represent him in his favourite activities.

"To suppose that the pyramid's only function in ancient Egypt was a royal tomb would be an oversimplification. The pyramid complex consisted of a group of buildings, of which the pyramid was only one element, even if it was the most important one. The pyramid complex was the site of the dead pharaoh's mystical transfiguration, rebirth, and ascent to heaven, as well as his residence in the beyond, from which he ruled over all the people of his time."[12]

The shape of the pyramid offers an insistent reminder of the contrast in status between the god-king at the top and the laborers at the bottom who provided the thousands of hours necessary for its construction.

Ancient Greece

Context

Persian Wars

Military encounters between the Greek city-states and the Persian Empire extended over nearly half a century and included unexpected victories for the Greeks over the far greater Persian forces, the Persian revenge that resulted in the destruction of the Athenian acropolis, and finally a diplomatic resolution that ended further conflict. The single most significant event in the forging of classical Greek identity was "the war between the Greeks and the vast Persian Empire, a conflict which ended in 479 BC with a glorious, if costly, Greek victory."[13] "The Persian Wars gave a permanent sense of identity to the Greeks who escaped Persian domination."[14]

Deisidaimonia

Religion for the Athenians went considerably beyond token reverence to a pantheon of gods. "Theirs was a spirit-saturated, anxious world dominated by an egocentric sense of themselves and an overwhelming urgency to keep things right with the gods. ... Spirit shadows, divinities, and heroes from the mythical past were a constant presence, fully inhabiting the landscape at every turn. Life was fragile, uncertain, never consistently happy, and full of surprises, except for the looming certainty of death."[15]

Such religious zeal bordered on what might be called superstition. "The profound, compulsive religiosity of the Athenians, an aspect that earned them a reputation for being among the most 'deisidaimoniacal,' or 'spirit-fearing,' people in all of Greece, stands in contrast to our idealizing vision of a city inhabited by philosophical rationalists. ... That some Athenians might call out the name "Athena!" upon hearing the hoot of an owl, avoid stepping on gravestones or visiting women about to give birth, and kneel to pour oil on smooth stones at crossroads to avert their power may come as a surprise to the modern reader. ... Our own separation of the philosophical from the spiritual greatly obscures our comprehension of the Athenians as they were."[16]

"The Greeks did not even have a separate word for religion, since there was no area of life that it did not permeate. Religion was embedded in everything. At Athens, it has been estimated that there were around 130 to 170 festival days per year, meaning more than a third of the calendar was devoted to observing religious feasts."[17]

Polis

In the fifth century BC, a citizen's foremost loyalty extended not to the agglomeration of territories that make up modern Greece but rather to the *polis*, that community founded on the identity of a protecting god. Fifth-century Athens saw the birth of democracy, not representative democracy as we know it but direct democracy with an assembly including as many as 30,000 citizens. "The complexity of the city's affairs can be gathered from the fact that there were no less than 600 administrative posts to be filled each year. All, with the exception of the ten generals, were chosen by lot from those citizens aged 30 or more who had good credentials. ... With the ban on reselection for most posts, this meant that virtually everyone was involved in administration or government at some point in their lives."[18]

Public participation of the citizenry became a deep value and the Athenians despised those who withdrew from public life. "Athenian democracy, which lasted for 185 years, was far from perfect. ... And yet the citizens really did rule. They enjoyed equality before the law. ... Most importantly, they held public servants to account. Dishonest or bungling officials could be dismissed, or even executed."[19]

The division of Ancient Greece into a collection of independent city-states was a source of both strength and weakness. Independence meant that each *polis* could experiment with the form of government that best suited it. Independence also meant the continual need to band together when faced with a foreign challenge and the potential for internal conflict, as when Athens and Sparta clashed in the Peloponnesian Wars.

Homer, *The Odyssey*, 800-600 BC

Poem of Stories

The tales contained in *The Odyssey* belong to an oral tradition that pre-dated Homer. "Homer did not himself invent the characters and incidents of the poem but rather organized and recorded a set of stories that had been sung by wandering bards for countless generations."[20] How did the stories come to be written down? The Phoenicians brought their alphabet to Greece in the 9th or 8th century BC, an alphabet consisting entirely of consonants derived from Egyptian hieroglyphs, to which the Greeks added vowels. So, the actual system of writing could be considered a relatively recent innovation at the time of Homer.

"Above all, it is a poem of stories and story-telling within its own narrative. Telemachus hears stories—mostly about Odysseus—from Nestor in Pylos (Book 3), from Menelaus and Helen in Sparta (4); Odysseus recounts his own adventures to the Phaeacians (9-12), and in the Underworld, for instance, others (from his mother to Agamemnon) recount theirs to him (12); Athena, in human form, tells stories, part-false, part-true, about her personae and Odysseus (first to Telemachus, 1); Odysseus in his beggar's disguise tells false tales—sometimes about Odysseus himself—

to a series of attentive listeners, from Athena (Book 13) to his father (24)."[21]

Identity

The theme of identity—declared, concealed, or disguised—runs throughout the epic. Identity in ancient times could be a matter of life or death. Was an approaching stranger a friend to be welcomed or a foe to be killed? Was the tribe that you approached more likely to offer safety or peril?

- "Helen tells of the time when Odysseus gained entrance into Troy by disguising himself as a beggar, striking down many Trojans and gaining much valuable information."[22]
- Athena repeatedly appears to Odysseus in disguise: as a warrior, as a young shepherd boy, and as a tall and beautiful woman.
- When Cyclops demands that Odysseus identify himself, the hero says that his name is "Nobody." Later this ruse allows Odysseus to escape after blinding the Cyclops, for when the other Cyclops come to his assistance, he shouts that "Nobody" is hurting him.
- At the end of the epic Odysseus returns home, disguised as a beggar, in order to survey the situation before declaring his identity.

Hospitality

The conventions concerning the treatment and behavior of a guest constituted a code of conduct that made travel abroad feasible. Three aspects of the hospitality code include the welcome, the proper length of stay, and the parting gift presented by the host to the guest. In Book 6 of *The Odyssey*, Nausicaa, daughter of the Phaeacian king, discovers ship-wrecked Odysseus, "*a terrible sight, all crusted, caked with brine,*" naked but for a leafy olive branch. Instead of taking fright and running away, the girl instructs her attendants to take care of the stranger.

But here's an unlucky wanderer strayed our way
And we must tend him well. Every stranger and beggar
Comes from Zeus, and whatever scrap we give him
He'll be glad to get. So, quick, my girls,
Give our newfound friend some food and drink
And bathe the man in the river,
Wherever you find some shelter from the wind. (6.227)

She leads Odysseus back to the palace where her father gives instructions to "*Seat the stranger now, in a silver-studded chair.*" (7.192) Despite not knowing the stranger's identity, the king offers Odysseus a hero's welcome. At the king's insistence, Odysseus extends his visit long enough to recount his adventures; this visit serves as a framing device for a long series of flashbacks. When it comes time for the hero to depart, the king offers him not only a fast ship but a vast treasure of gifts.

Compare the Phaeacian hospitality to Odysseus' treatment by Circe recounted in Book 10. Circe drugs Odysseus' men to erase their memories and turns them into pigs--surely an abuse of the hospitality code--then detains the company against their will for an entire year. When she finally lets Odysseus go, for a parting gift Circe offers advice: in order to get past the Sirens, block the crew's ears with beeswax. If you absolutely must listen to the Sirens' song, have the crew tie you to the mast.

The conventions of the hospitality code shape the climax of the book when Odysseus, returning home, routs the suitors to his wife who have installed themselves as unwelcome intruders in his estate, guests who have long overstayed their welcome. Homer, along with his audience, clearly considers the observation of these conventions to be a virtue and their abuse to merit retribution.

Homer's epic connects us with a time when people came to understand themselves through stories, and illustrates the process by which story-telling becomes literature.

Pythagoras, fl. ca. 500 BC

"Everything Is Number"

"The study of numbers in the abstract begins in sixth century BC Greece with Pythagoras and the Pythagoreans. ... Never before or since has mathematics had such an essential part in life and religion as it did with the Pythagoreans. ... They theorized that everything, physical and spiritual, had been assigned its allotted number and form, the general thesis being 'Everything is number.'"[23]

We have no writings of Pythagoras since he taught entirely orally and forbade his followers from sharing his lessons with outsiders. Yet Pythagoras exerted a tremendous influence on mathematical thought. The Pythagoreans "have been responsible for a mingling of mathematics, philosophy of life, and religion unparalleled in history. ... Pythagoras is in fact credited with having coined the words 'philosophy' (love of wisdom) and 'mathematics' (that which is learned)."[24]

The organization of the classical curriculum may also be traced to the school of Pythagoras. "The Pythagorean philosophy rested on the assumption that whole number is the cause of various qualities of man and matter. This led to an exaltation and study of number properties, and arithmetic (considered as the theory of numbers), along with geometry, music and spherics (astronomy) constituted the fundamental liberal arts of the Pythagorean program of study. This group of subjects became known, in the Middle Ages, as the *quadrivium*, to which was added the *trivium* of grammar, logic, and rhetoric."[25]

Music

No examples of actual music from ancient Greece have survived, but Pythagoras is credited with discovering that the most harmonious sonorities are produced by strings sounding in small whole-number ratios: 2:1 for the octave, 3:2 for the perfect fifth, and 4:3 for the perfect fourth, intervals designated as consonances throughout the Middle Ages.

Music for the Pythagoreans went far beyond mere sounding notes. "The Pythagorean views on astronomy could be considered an extension of this doctrine of harmonic intervals. Pythagoras held that each of the seven known planets, among which he included the sun and the moon, was carried around the earth on a crystal sphere of its own. Because it was surely impossible for such gigantic spheres to whirl endlessly through space without generating any noise by their motion, each body would have to produce a certain tone according to its distance from the center. The whole system created a celestial harmony, which Pythagoras alone among all mortals could hear. This theory was the basis for the idea of the 'music of the spheres,' a continually recurring notion in medieval astronomical speculation."[26]

"Logical Scandal" of $\sqrt{2}$

The Pythagoreans' delight in proportions naturally extended to geometry, notably the theorem associated with the name of Pythagoras: in any right triangle, the sum of the squares of the legs equals the square of the hypotenuse. The smallest triangle using whole numbers to illustrate this theorem is the 3-4-5 right triangle, since $3^2 + 4^2 = 5^2$ $(9 + 16 = 25)$.

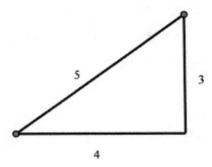

No such delight attended the discovery that √2 was irrational, that it could not be represented as a ratio of whole numbers. "The discovery of the irrationality of √2 caused consternation in the Pythagorean ranks. Not only did it appear to upset the basic assumptions that everything depends on the whole numbers .... So great was the 'logical scandal' that efforts were made for a while to keep the matter secret."[27]

The proof that √2 is irrational requires us to assume the contrary. If this assumption leads to a contradiction, then we can reject the assumption and go with what we wanted to prove in the first place. This method of proof is called *reductio ad absurdum*. (You may think of it as two negatives producing a positive.)

Assume $\sqrt{2}$ is rational.	assumption
$\sqrt{2} = \dfrac{a}{b}$, a fraction reduced to lowest terms	definition of rational
$2 = \dfrac{a^2}{b^2}$	square both sides
$2b^2 = a^2$	multiplication
a^2 is an even number	definition of even
Therefore, a is an even number, call it $2k$	if the square of an integer is even, then the integer itself must be even
then $a^2 = 4k^2$	square both sides
$2b^2 = 4k^2$	substitution

$b^2 = 2k^2$	division
Therefore, b is an even number, call it $2h$	definition of even
$\sqrt{2} = \dfrac{2k}{2h}$	substitution
But this contradicts the assumption that $\sqrt{2}$ was a fraction *reduced to lowest terms*, therefore the assumption is wrong and $\sqrt{2}$ is irrational.	QED (*quod erat demonstrandum:* "which was to be proved"): the mathematician's way of saying "Ta-da!"

Never has pure number been more fruitfully exalted than in the work of Pythagoras and his followers.

Parthenon, 448-432 BC PLATE 3

Celebration of War

A decade after their defeat at Marathon in 490 B.C., a vast Persian army and navy overran Athens seeking revenge. The Persians plundered the existing temples on the Acropolis. "It was an atrocity beyond comprehension for the Greeks. Hellenes had long followed a code by which the holy places of enemies were respected and spared during war. After all, their destruction was certain to incur divine wrath. But the Persians worshipped other gods and showed no respect for the Olympians."[28]

When an alliance of Greek city-states finally achieved security from the Persian threat in 449 BC, "Pericles lost no time in turning to a long-deferred goal: the rebuilding of the Acropolis. With peace at hand, the unspent balance in the league's treasury was no longer needed to fund the war. …Every structure would be made from bright white Pentelic marble and enhanced with a dazzling profusion of carved decoration. It would cost a fortune."[29]

Where did the money come from? "The Parthenon would be, among other things, a new home for the treasury of the allied Greek states, Pericles having shrewdly maneuvered the relocation of the funds from Delos to Athens in 454/453 B.C. ... Thus, a staggering treasure came under Athenian control. It permitted the polis to build a peerless navy for defense of the Athenian League but also to advance Athenian self-interest, expanding its international trade and beautifying the Acropolis beyond all imagining."[30]

"Pericles' rivals attacked the building works as a colossal waste of money and (even more to the point) as an insult to the Athenians' 'allies,' whose contributions to a common defence budget were being squandered on titivating the city of Athens."[31] Construction of the Parthenon proceeded, despite the complaints, eventually producing an icon of western culture.

Celebration of Mathematics

The Pythagorean exaltation of small whole numbers as the basis for everything finds monumental expression in the proportions of the Parthenon. "The ratio of the temple's height to its width on the east and west faces is 4 to 9; that of its width to its length is also 4 to 9, and that of the column diameter to the interval between columns is 9 to 4. The seventeen columns on the long sides are twice plus one the eight columns on the east and west, which again reduces to a 9 to 4 relation. With but a single module and ratio, the architect could calculate mentally all the proportions and dimensions of his building."[32] "The result is a kind of buoyancy, a sublime integration of disparate members that is organic, almost as alive as the Parthenon seems to breathe and flex supporting its Pentelic load."[33]

Ironically, in order to preserve the illusion of perfect proportion, an imperfection, called *entasis*, had to be introduced. It turns out that fluted columns, such as those employed in the Parthenon, look concave. In order to make them appear regular, the columns had to be made very slightly convex. "Thus, on all four sides of the Parthenon we see upwardly curving surfaces and lines."[34]

Celebration of Athena

The Parthenon was dedicated to the goddess Athena, patron of the city of Athens, who supposedly sprang fully armed from the forehead of Zeus. As a temple to Athena, the Parthenon housed a statue of the goddess by the sculptor Phidias. The greatest popular adoration of Athena came in the Panathenaic Games, held every four years. "The musical and athletic contests of the Panathenaia were also part of the larger, overarching religious program. Athletic games were not the secular enterprises we know today, centered on the glory of the individual winner. The goal of the festival was to give honor to the goddess, to please Athena, and to remember the ancestors."[35]

"The rites and competitions of the Panathenaia, in substance and exclusivity, enabled Athenian citizens to articulate the very essence of who they were. In no other setting, perhaps not even warfare, would they have so keenly felt the awareness of being bound together as families and tribes descending from a common point in the epic past."[36] The Panathenaic procession was commemorated in stone in the form of decorative friezes, once adorning the exterior of the Parthenon itself, now re-named the "Elgin marbles" and housed in the British Museum.

The Parthenon stands as a visible symbol of a society in which war and religion coexisted alongside philosophy, mathematics and drama.

Herodotus, *Histories*, 450s BC

Historia

Our word "history" comes from the Greek *historia* which originally meant any inquiry or investigation. The work of Herodotus "ranges over many fields and includes geography, anthropology, ethnology, zoology, even fable and folklore"[37]

The success of the Athenians against the far greater forces of the Persians in the battles of Marathon, Thermopylae and Salamis lay at the foundation of the city's self-identity. Herodotus' "lifetime's preoccupation was to explain the most incomprehensible drama of his lifetime. How had the Greeks managed to overcome the might of Persia?"[38]

Persian Wars

Darius I of Persia, having conquered all of his nearest neighbors, sought to incorporate Greece within his kingdom, a blatant act of hubris from Herodotus' perspective. Herodotus recounts three pivotal battles, separated by nearly a decade. The first took place on the plains of Marathon in 490 BC. Knowing that the Persians tended to place the bulk of their strength in the center of the battle line, the Greek general Miltiades concocted the ingenious strategy of arranging strong forces at the ends of his line with the intent of breaking through the Persian flanks and encircling and defeating their main force.

Herodotus writes: *"The Athenians advanced at a run towards the enemy, not less than a mile away. The Persians, seeing the attack developing at the double, prepared to meet it, thinking it suicidal madness for the Athenians to risk an assault with so small a force—rushing in with no support from either cavalry or archers. Well, that was what they imagined; nevertheless, the Athenians ... fought in a way not to be forgotten; they were the first Greeks, so far as we know, to charge at a run, and the first who dared to look without flinching at Persian dress and the men who wore it; for until that day came, no Greek could hear even the word Persian without terror.*"[39] The Athenians fell back, pursued by the enraged Persians. Then the strong Athenian flanks closed in on the Persians, encircled and slaughtered them.

Darius himself had died by the time of the Battle of Thermopylae ten years later. This time the Spartans, who had refused to participate in the Battle of Marathon, distinguished themselves by holding off a vastly superior Persian army at a mountain pass. *"On the Spartan side it was a memorable sight; they were men who understood war pitted against an inexperienced enemy, and amongst the feints they employed was to turn their backs in a body and pretend to be retreating in confusion, whereupon the enemy would pursue them with a great clatter and roar; but the Spartans, just as the Persians were on them, would wheel and face them and inflict in the new struggle innumerable casualties.*"[40]

A decisive sea battle took place at Salamis. As before, the Persians outnumbered the Athenians. This time the Athenians lured the Persian ships into a narrow harbor, and jammed them up so that the resulting engagement was for all intents and purposes a land battle, but the motion of the ships prevented the celebrated Persian archers from getting a proper aim. *"There were also Greek casualties, but not many; for most of the Greeks could swim, and those who lost their ships, provided they were not killed in the actual fighting, swam over to Salamis. Most of the enemy, on the other hand, being unable to swim, were drowned.*"[41] So devastating was the defeat that the Persian forces turned back, recrossed the Hellespont, and, for the time being, left the Greek city-states alone.

Lessons of History

What lessons do we learn from history according to Herodotus? An excess of pride (*hubris*)—in this case on the part of the Persians--eventually leads to destruction (*nemesis*). Herodotus quotes Artabanus: "*It is always the great buildings and the tall trees which are struck by lightning. It is God's way to bring the lofty low. ... For God tolerates pride in none but Himself.*"[42]

At the time Herodotus was writing, in the middle of the 5th century BC, Athens and Sparta were on the brink of what became known as the Peloponnesian Wars. Herodotus hoped, through his writing, to bring them in touch with a time a few generations earlier when the two city-states had been allies against the Persians. In this effort, he failed. The subsequent devastating war between the Greek city-states invites one to reflect on George Santayana's words, written twenty-five centuries later, "Those who cannot remember the past are condemned to repeat it."

Contrary to the modern insistence on specialization, Herodotus embraced every area of human knowledge in his quest for understanding.

Sophocles, *Oedipus Rex*, 428 BC

Irony of Free Will

In modern times, we remain firmly attached to the concept of free will, stubbornly rejecting any notion of determinism. In *Oedipus Rex,* Sophocles questions whether one can avoid one's destiny. In the story, King Laius of Thebes, informed by an oracle that he will be murdered by his son, Oedipus, resolves to have the baby killed. But the king's servant, drawing the line at murder, instead abandons the child to the elements. Through the intervention of sympathetic shepherds, the infant ends up in the court of King Polybus of Corinth, to be raised as his son. Oedipus also receives news from an oracle that he is fated to "murder his father and mate with his mother." Attempting to thwart his fate, and believing Polybus to be his father, Oedipus avoids returning to Corinth and travels instead to Thebes, where he ends up murdering his actual father on the road and marrying his mother.

"Certain of Oedipus's past actions were fate-bound; but everything that he does on the stage from first to last he does as a free agent. ... What fascinates us is the spectacle of a man freely choosing, from the highest motives, a series of actions which lead to his own ruin. ... What causes his ruin is his own strength and courage, his loyalty to Thebes, and his loyalty to the truth. In all this we are to see him as a free agent."[43]

Warning against Rationalism

Oedipus takes pride in his intellectual powers. "Oedipus became tyrannos by answering the riddle of the Sphinx. It was no easy riddle, and he answered it, as he proudly asserts, without help from prophets, from bird-signs, from gods; he answered it alone, with his intelligence. ... And the answer to the Sphinx's riddle was—Man, 'the measure of all things.'"[44] But by the end of the play, Oedipus has discovered his actual identity. "He is not the measurer but the thing measured, not the equator but the thing equated. He is the answer to the problem he tried to solve."[45]

"The tragedy of the piece is based not on Oedipus' fulfillment of the prophecy, but in his own discovery of the truth about his life. His relentless search for the truth about himself is continually discouraged by others, particularly those who either know the truth or who fear it. But Oedipus will not be put off, saying 'I must know it all, I must see the truth at last' and 'I am at the edge of hearing horrors, yes, but I must hear!' When he discovers the truth, his wife and mother Jocasta kills herself and Oedipus puts out his own eyes with the pins from her dress. ... All of this has come about not because of the prophecy itself, but because of Oedipus' desire to know the truth and because of the rational, intelligent and purposeful way he has gone about discovering it. ... The belief in humanity as the rational author of its own destiny was, Sophocles understood, an arrogant and dangerous delusion. ... Sophocles' *Oedipus* was a cry of anguish, a warning against the elevation of rationalism."[46]

Peripeteia and Identity

The perfection of the play, according to Aristotle, lies in its structure, since recognition of truth coincides with *peripeteia,* or reversal of fortune—the revelations that allow Oedipus to figure out his doom. Aristotle writes in his *Poetics*: "*A reversal is a change to the opposite in the actions being performed, as stated—and this, as we have been saying, in accordance with probability or necessity. For example, in the* Oedipus *someone came to give Oedipus good news and free him from his fear with regard to his mother, but by disclosing Oedipus' identity he brought about the opposite result. ... Recognition ... is a change from ignorance to knowledge. ... Recognition is best when it occurs simultaneously with a reversal, like the one in the* Oedipus.*"[47]

"The state of Oedipus is reversed from 'first of men' to 'most accursed of men.' ...As the images unfold, the enquirer turns into the object of enquiry, the hunter into the prey, the doctor into the patient, the investigator into the criminal, the revealer into the thing revealed, the finder into the thing found, the savior into the thing saved ('I was saved, for some dreadful destiny'), the liberator into the thing released ('I released your feet from the bonds which pierced your ankles' says the Corinthian messenger), the accuser becomes the defendant, the ruler the subject."[48]

Fate vs. free will becomes for Sophocles an issue not subject to a simple either/or resolution: man is neither a prisoner of destiny nor its master.

Plato, *The Republic*, 360 BC

Theory of Forms

Plato's longest lasting influence on philosophy and theology came in his Theory of Forms, the idea that what we experience in the material world are physical versions of perfect abstract ideas. Individual chairs, for example, represent manifestations of the perfect idea of a chair. "Not only do these ideal forms exist in our minds, they actually exist in another world. ... The real world that is available to our senses is therefore a corrupted shadow of the ideal."[49]

While we may harbor doubts about Plato's model, we commonly refer to, and argue about, capital-letter abstractions such as Truth, Beauty, Good and Evil as if they possessed reality beyond the merely conceptual.

Allegory of the Cave

"Nothing in intellectual history is more powerful than Plato's metaphor of the cave, which suggests that we can only perceive the world indirectly, seeing reality only by means of its firelit shadows on the wall."[50] "Plato portrays the initial and unenlightened condition of human consciousness as like that of prisoners confined since childhood in a dark cave. ... Behind them, out of their view, is a fire in front of which some people manipulate puppets and other figures. All that the prisoners can see are the shadows these cast on the wall in front of them."[51] A chosen few, the philosophers, emerge from the cave to perceive the actual, sunlit world.

Those who manage to escape their chains and emerge from the cave into sunlight understand, for the first time, the limitations of their earlier understanding. "There they see just how far removed from reality they previously were. In the cave, they knew only shadows that were only copies of ordinary objects; in the light of the sun they are able to see the objects themselves and finally the sun itself, which gives being to all else."[52] "The Allegory of the Cave ... is supposed to illustrate the Platonic journey that only a few can complete, from ignorant perception to true opinion, to knowledge of mathematics, of Platonic Forms and finally the Form of the Good."[53] Essentially Plato argues that anyone who fails to accept his Theory of Forms, which he identifies with the sunlight of truth, is no better than a prisoner in the cave of ignorance.

Ideal Society

Though we may consider democracy to be the best—or perhaps the least bad—form of government, Plato considered it abhorrent. "In 399 BC, Socrates was tried and executed for corrupting the youth of Athens. To Plato this charge was absurd and monstrous—a sign of the rotten state of Athenian politics."[54] That this should have taken place in a democracy helps to explain Plato's aversion to that form of government, where rhetoric and persuasion too often prevail over reason and wisdom. *"Finally I came to the conclusion that the condition of existing states is bad ... and that the troubles of mankind will never cease until either true and genuine philosophers attain political power or the rulers of states by some dispensation of providence become genuine philosophers."*[55] "No doubt with the fate of Socrates in mind, he argues that if a society has no use for the genuine philosopher, it is not philosophy which is at fault, but rather the society which has no understanding of it nor any use for it."[56]

In *The Republic* Plato finds the ideal form of government to be a philosopher-king, a reluctant ruler motivated by love of knowledge instead of desire for material gain. In this scheme, extremes of wealth or poverty would be prevented by the Guardians, trained to find happiness in service to the community. The philosopher-king himself would be educated in arithmetic, plane and solid geometry, astronomy and harmony in preparation for dialectic, the exercise of pure thought. We note Plato's emphasis on avoiding excess and seeking moderation as the ideal.

Plato's ideal government includes a number of aspects at which we would hesitate: forced eugenics, communal child care in place of families, and severe censorship. But Plato finds rule by a philosopher-king preferable to rule by the wealthy, the military, the masses, or a tyrant. "If the truth is available, Plato seems to ask, why would people want to live—and why should they be allowed to live—outside the truth? Whereas Plato elevates living in light of the truth over freedom, we tend to consider freedom itself to be the highest value, even if it sometimes means living under falsehoods."[57]

Plato exhorts us to consider a reality much richer than just the product of our own sensory experience.

Aristotle, *Nichomachean Ethics*, ca. 330 BC

Eudaimonia and Virtue

Aristotle, in the generation after Plato, began by studying at the elder philosopher's Academy, then set up a school of his own, called the Lyceum. "It is not implausible to count Aristotle's school as the first university: it apparently had an exceptional library; rooms for collecting specimens and doing scientific research; and, for classes, there were morning and afternoon lectures by Aristotle, who was engaged in the ambitious project of giving an account of everything that was then known."[58] The *Nichomachean Ethics,* from around 330 BC, may be considered as Aristotle's lecture notes.

Aristotle maintains that the highest good lies in the fulfillment of purpose, something sought only for its own sake. For Aristotle happiness, or *eudaimonia*, resides in the excellent performance of that which distinguishes human beings, namely the ability to reason. (You may have noticed the tendency of philosophers to consider philosophy the highest value.)

"Having analysed a *eudaimon* life as a life throughout which a person exercises the virtues, Aristotle begins an examination of the virtues. In general the virtues of a thing are relative to its function: they are those characteristics that make it good and carry out its function well."[59] "For Aristotle, then, the question of how to be happy is the question of how to live well as a human being, and living well is inseparable from attaining the virtue or virtues that make possible the best activity."[60]

Doctrine of the Mean

Aristotle situates ethical virtue between the extremes of excess and deficiency. For example, courage, the first of Aristotle's eleven moral virtues, is the mean between rashness and coward-ice. In Book 3, Chapter 7 we read: *"He who exceeds in confidence when it comes to frightening things is reckless. ... He who exceeds in being fearful is a coward. ... The coward, therefore, is someone of faint hope, for he fears everything. ... The coward, the reckless, and the courageous are concerned with the same things, then, but they differ in relation to them. For the former two exceed and are deficient respectively, whereas the latter holds to the middle and in the way he ought. ... Courage is a mean with respect to what inspires confidence and fear."*[61]

We must understand this point of balance not as the mean of the thing itself but the mean relative to us. Aristotle observes that a balanced diet for an athlete would differ from that of a non-athlete. Finding this middle ground is essential to reaching *eudaimonia*, or happiness, the ultimate form of godlike consciousness. This middle ground is often referred to as The Golden Mean. In Book 2, Chapter 6 Aristotle says, *"Thus every knower of the excess and the deficiency avoids them, but seeks out the middle term and chooses this—yet not a middle belonging to the thing in question but rather the one relative to us."*[62]

Contemplation

For Aristotle, contemplation—the activity of the intellect—is both the highest virtue and the goal of a good life. Aristotle argues "that each object contains not just a static essence, but the essence of what it can become, which he termed its natural end or *telos*. ... The fulfilment of a natural end or *telos* is a unifying principle in Aristotle's thinking about a whole range of subjects. He sees the aim of a good life to be the fulfilment of its *telos*, which is to engage in excellent activity such as intellectual contemplation or virtuous actions."[63] *"Happiness must reside in action or activity in accord with virtue. But which virtue? ... Intellectual or contemplative virtue. ... It is the practice of contemplative virtue ... that is most godlike for a human being."*[64]

Aristotle sums up his arguments in Chapter 10: *"The intellect is the most excellent of the things in us, and the things with which the intellect is concerned are the most excellent of the things that can be known. ... The most pleasant of the activities in accord with virtue is agreed to be the one that pertains to wisdom. ... What is proper to each is by nature most excellent and most pleasant for each. And so for a human being, this is the life that accords with the intellect."*[65]

Aristotle argues for an ultimate goal to life and for our obligation to pursue it.

Euclid, *Elements*, 300 BC

Postulates

Euclid's *Elements* stands as one of the earliest, and certainly the longest-lasting, textbooks ever written. "Few, if any, of the theorems established in the *Elements* are of his own discovery; Euclid's greatness lies not so much in the contribution of original material as in the consummate skill with which he organized a vast body of independent facts into the definitive treatment of Greek geometry and number theory. ... One result follows another in strict logical order, with a minimum of assumptions and very little that is superfluous.

As a point of departure Euclid lays out a handful of basic postulates. "Euclid was aware that to avoid circularity and provide a starting point, certain facts about the nature of the subject had to be assumed without proof. These assumed statements, from which all others are to be deduced as logical consequences, are called the 'axioms' or 'postulates.' In the traditional usage, a postulate was viewed as a 'self-evident truth.' ... They are in a sense the 'rules of the game' from which all deductions may proceed."[66]

1. A straight line can be drawn from any point to any other point.

2. A finite straight line can be produced continuously in a line.

3. A circle may be described with any center and distance.

4. All right angles are equal to one another.

5. Given a straight line and a point not on that line, there exists only one line passing through the point that is parallel to the given line.

Proof (Sum of Angles in Δ)

Given the basic postulates and a small number of definitions, Euclid proceeded to prove hundreds of theorems, using the results of one theorem to prove the next. Consider Euclid's proof of a familiar theorem, that the sum of the interior angles of any triangle is equal to 180° (or as Euclid would put it, equivalent to two right angles).

In order to follow the proof, we need to recall several theorems that Euclid had already proven concerning parallel lines. When two parallel lines are cut by a transversal, the angles marked in the diagram are all equal.

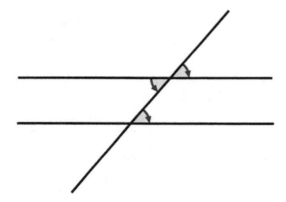

Here is Euclid's proof of Proposition XXXII.

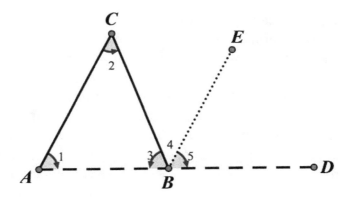

To prove: *If any side (AB) of a triangle (ABC) be produced (to D), the external angle (CBD) is equal to the sum of the two internal non-adjacent angles (A, C), and the sum of the three internal angles is equal to two right angles* (i.e., 180°).

Proof: *Draw BE parallel to AC. Now since BC intersects parallels BE and AC, the alternate angles EBC and ACB are equal. Again, since AB intersects the parallels BE and AC, the angle EBD is equal to BAC. Hence the whole angle CBD is equal to the sum of the two angles ACB and BAC. To each of these add the angle ABC and we have the sum of the three angles ACB, BAC and ABC. But the sum of CBD and ABC is two right angles. Hence the sum of the three angles ACB, BAC and ABC is two right angles.*

The proof might be easier to read if we label the angles with numbers. Because of parallel lines cut by a transversal, angle 1 = angle 5 and angle 2 = angle 4. This means that the sum of angles 1, 2, and 3 is the same as the sum of angles 3, 4 and 5 = 180°.

An Infinite Number of Primes

A prime number can be evenly divided only by itself and one. The first several prime numbers are 2, 3, 5, 7 and 11. All the rest of the whole numbers—the composites—can be represented as a product of primes. Thus, 6 = 2 x 3 and 35 = 5 x 7. Are there infinitely many primes? Like the proof of the irrationality of √2, this proof, a *reductio ad absurdum*, requires us to assume the opposite of what we want to prove and then show that this leads to a contradiction. Assume the opposite, therefore, that there is some greatest prime. Call it P. "Euclid then constructed a new number by the following process: He multiplied together all the primes from 2 up to (and including) P, and then he added 1 to the product. The new number is therefore

2 x 3 x 5 x 7 x 11 ... x P + 1.

By the original assumption, this number must be composite (not a prime), because it is obviously larger than P, which was assumed to be the largest prime. Consequently, this number must be divisible by at least one of the existing primes. However, from its construction, we see that if we divide this number by any of the primes up to P, this will leave a remainder of 1. The implication is, that if the number is indeed composite, some prime larger than P must divide it. However, this conclusion contradicts the assumption that P is the largest prime, thus completing the proof that there are infinitely many primes."[67]

Euclidean geometry represents a triumph of logical thought, with each new deductive proof serving as the basis for the next, the resulting edifice resting on a foundation of simple postulates.

Connections: Proportion

The word proportion has two related senses: either balance (the harmonious relation of parts to each other or to the whole) or ratio (the relation of one part to another or to the whole). Each of the works in our repertoire for Ancient Greece displays aspects of proportion. In *The Odyssey* we note a sense of balance in the observation of hospitality conventions in Odysseus's treatment by the Phaeacians and imbalance in his treatment by Circe. Proportion in the sense of mathematical ratio appears both in Pythagoras's discoveries regarding harmonious intervals in music and in the horror the Pythagoreans experienced in contemplating $\sqrt{2}$, a number that could *not* be represented as a ratio of whole numbers. The Parthenon relies on mathematical proportions to create its overall harmonious effect. (We tend not to focus on the immoderate cost of the project.) Herodotus comments on the results of imbalance, warning that hubris—an excess of pride-- often leads to nemesis.

The plays of Sophocles carefully observe the sense of balance inherent in the dramatic unities as described in Aristotle's *Poetics.* Unity of time meant that the action had to take place within twenty-four hours. Unity of place insisted on a single setting for the drama--in the case of *Oedipus Rex*, in front of the king's palace in Thebes. Unity of action forbade subplots or intervention by outside forces: the plot should be structurally self-contained. Events occurring offstage, as well as all acts of violence, had to be reported by messengers instead of being directly depicted. The tragedy of *Oedipus Rex* includes Jocasta hanging herself and Oedipus blinding himself, but neither action occurs on stage. In fact, virtually the entire story has already taken place by the time the play proper begins. Moreover, in Sophocles' portrayal both fate and Oedipus's reasoned attempt to defy it resemble the working out of a deductive proof.

Plato's Ideal Forms suggest a perfect harmony among the parts and the whole, and his ideal government aims to preserve moderation and avoid excess. Aristotle makes proportion in the sense of balance one of the cornerstones of human happiness. He defines moderation as the appropriate mean between extremes. Euclid's *Elements* constantly deal with the relations of the parts to the whole, either in geometry or in number theory. In both cases, deductive reasoning links the general to the particular. The sense of perfect proportion that we associate with classical architecture, as manifested in the Parthenon, runs throughout the culture of ancient Greece.

Ancient Rome

Context

Army and Administration

The glory of the Roman Empire rested on the success of its army. While the army did not actually run the empire, by the time of Augustus it consumed about 70% of the state's resources. In its heyday, the army represented a prestigious career choice for Roman citizens, who could expect a share in the booty from battles as well as generous compensation. The army would essentially co-opt the aristocracy in conquered lands, under the aegis of a Roman provincial governor. A census would establish the level of taxation, after which the local ruling class would be given responsibility for managing the details.

"Like the stones of a Roman wall, which were held together both by the regularity of the design and by that peculiarly powerful Roman cement, so the various parts of the Roman realm were bonded into a massive monolithic entity by physical, organizational, and psychological controls. The physical bonds included the network of military garrisons which were stationed in every province, and the network of stone-built roads which linked the provinces with Rome. The organization bonds were based on the common principles of law and administration, and on the universal army of officials who enforced common standards of conduct. The psychological controls were built on fear and punishment—on the absolute certainty that anyone or anything that threatened the authority of Rome would be utterly destroyed."[68]

Roman Law

"Roman Law ... was the most original product of the Roman mind. In almost all their other intellectual endeavors the Romans

33

were the eager pupils of the Greeks, but in law they were, and knew themselves to be, the masters. In their hands law became for the first time a thoroughly scientific subject, an elaborately articulated system of principles abstracted from the detailed rules which constitute the raw material of law."[69]

"Law was established through a variety of means, for example, via statutes, magisterial decisions, emperor's edicts, senatorial decrees, assembly votes, plebiscites and the deliberations of expert legal counsel and so became multi-faceted and flexible enough to deal with the changing circumstances of the Roman world, from republican to imperial politics, local to national trade, and state to inter-state politics."[70] The cumulative nature of Roman law meant a gradual accretion of legal writing eventually requiring a professional class of jurists charged with scrutinizing the body of laws. "The Romans have handed down to us not only many legal terms still-used today in the field of law but also their passion and expertise for precise and exact legal terminology in order to avoid ambiguity or even misinterpretation of the law."[71]

Rise of Christianity

The interval from 27 BC to 180 AD, a period of relative peacefulness, has been called the *Pax Romana*, or "Roman peace." "The spread of Christianity was greatly facilitated by the *Pax Romana*. Within three decades of Christ's crucifixion, Christian communities were established in most of the great cities of the eastern Mediterranean. St. Paul, whose writings constitute the greater part of the New Testament, and whose journeys were the first pastoral visit of a Christian leader, was largely concerned with the Greek-speaking cities of the East."[72] But Christians encountered persecution for their refusal to participate in public worship of the Roman gods. Nero made Christians the scapegoats for the Great Fire in Rome in 64. Carrying on their activities in secret only made the Christians further subject to suspicion.

A major turning point occurred in the fourth century with the acceptance of Christianity by the emperor Constantine. "The crucial moment in Constantine's life came during a dream when he beheld a vision containing the Christian monogram *Chi Rho*, accompanied by words of light reading *Hoc signo victor eris* (In this sign thou shalt conquer). ... His subsequent victory over Maxentius and his much larger army at Milvian Bridge, left him fully convinced of the omnipotence of the god of the Christians."[73]

The Edict of Milan in 312, extending toleration to the Christians, fostered the growth of the new church. But Constantine went still further by banning pagan faiths, essentially making Christianity the new official state church. The emperor took a personal interest in resolving disputes over the nature of Jesus—Was he human? Was he divine? What role did he play in the Holy Trinity? Constantine convened the Council of Nicaea in 325 to answer these questions unequivocally (and dogmatically). With Constantine, Christianity went from being a persecuted sect to a semiofficial organ of the state, with the state assuming the cost of maintaining the clergy, with bishops granted the same juridical authority as magistrates, and Sunday being recognized as a holiday.[74]

Julius Caesar, *Commentaries on The Gallic Wars*, ca. 50-40 BC

Propaganda

The Roman Republic, since the 6th century BC, had substantial measures in place to prevent tyranny. To avoid putting too much power in the hands of one man, two consuls ruled the republic, and to avoid the concentration of power, their term was limited to a single year. A dictator could be appointed in the case of emergency, but he could hold power for only six months.

But as history repeatedly shows us, a single individual sufficiently endowed with charisma, ambition and wit can thwart the most well-conceived controls. Such a man was Julius Caesar, who wrote ten books of *Commentaries on the Gallic Wars* to turn his military victories to full advantage. "The *Commentaries* were works of propaganda and showed everything he did in the most favorable light. Yet in the end he had to stick closely to facts— particularly those facts that were of most concern to a Roman audience—if the *Commentaries* were to achieve their aim of winning over public opinion."[75] Caesar's *Commentaries* recount how the Roman army could defeat numerically superior, and notoriously ferocious, forces through a combination of military strategy and tight discipline.

Perpetual Warfare

Julius Caesar spent his adult life in a state of more or less perpetual warfare. "Warfare in Caesar's time was a bloody, face-to-face affair in which men hacked, stabbed, and killed their opponents. It was also a normal and natural part of life."[76] "Although the modern reader may sometimes balk at the catalogue of unabashed imperialism, massacre, mass execution and enslavement contained in the *Commentaries*, a contemporary Roman would not have found these things shocking."[77]

Battle of Alesia: Circumvallation and Contravallation

The Frankish leader Vercingetorix assembled tribes from throughout Gaul, and thought he had a plan to defeat the Romans by attacking them while Caesar was in northern Italy, counting on the Alps to prevent his quick return. "The solution was typical of Caesar. Everyone knew that the mountains of the Massif Central were covered in six feet of snow and impassible, therefore Caesar led his small force of infantry and cavalry directly across them: The Gauls were caught totally unprepared as they believed these peaks guarded them like a wall. Not a single traveler had ever crossed them in winter. "[78]

Next Vercingetorix, adopting a "scorched earth" policy, "ordered all the towns, farms, hamlets, and barns anywhere near Caesar to be burned along with any stores of grain the Gauls could not carry away. By doing so, Caesar's army would starve, while Roman foraging parties would have to scatter far and wide to seek supplies, making them easy targets for the Gaulish cavalry to pick off."[79]

But then Vercingetorix made a fatal error by withdrawing his army into a seemingly impregnable position at Alesia. "Vercingetorix had led his army into a citadel surrounded by rivers and steep cliffs. There was no way for Caesar to storm the fortress, but there was also no way for the Gauls to escape if Caesar could find a way to entrap them. He immediately ordered his engineers to begin construction of an enormous wall over ten miles long that would completely encircle Alesia. The astonished Gauls looked on in dismay as they realized Caesar's intentions. At alarming speed, a twelve-foot-high palisade backed by deep trenches on both sides and manned by guarded towers every eight feet sprang up around the town."[80]

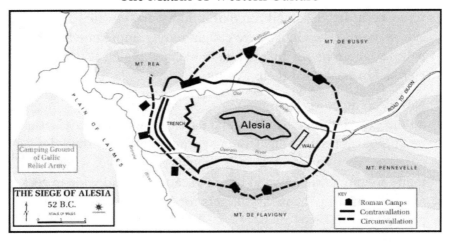

Caesar, describing himself in the third person, writes: *"Caesar thought that further additions should be made to these works, in order that the fortifications might be defensible by a small number of soldiers. Having, therefore, cut down the trunks of trees or very thick branches, and having stripped their tops of the bark, and sharpened them into a point, he drew a continued trench everywhere five feet deep. These stakes being sunk into this trench, and fastened firmly at the bottom, to prevent the possibility of their being torn up, had their branches only projecting from the ground. There were five rows in connection with, and intersecting each other; and whoever entered within them were likely to impale themselves on very sharp stakes."[81]*

The combined attack by the besieged army and the relieving army, led by a cousin of Vercingetorix, might have succeeded through sheer numbers, but Caesar managed to lead part of his forces to attack the relief army from the rear, which so demoralized the Gauls that they panicked and tried to withdraw, leaving the retreating army easy prey for the disciplined Roman soldiers. Caesar's return to Rome with one of his legions precipitated civil war and led to Caesar's appointment as perpetual dictator in 44 BC and the start of the Empire.

Pondering, executing and writing about military strategy, Caesar seems to turn war into a brutal art form.

Virgil, *The Aeneid*, 19 BC

Homeric Models

Virgil's epic of the founding of Rome owes much to Homer. Virgil boasted that he had managed to combine the *Iliad* and the *Odyssey* into a single book, but in reverse order: the first half of the *Aeneid* traces the travels of Aeneas and his men from Troy to Italy; the second half recounts the battles they had to fight to displace the area's inhabitants so that they could found the colony that would eventually become the Roman Empire.

Both Aeneas and Odysseus travel to the underworld to visit a parent. Aeneas' shield, adorned with scenes of Rome to come, is based on Achilles' shield in *The Iliad*. Like *The Odyssey*, the *Aeneid* begins *in medias res*, with Aeneas recounting his adventures to Dido, the Queen of Carthage. Like Homer, Virgil involves the gods heavily in the plot. Jupiter (head of the gods, counterpart to the Greek Zeus) favors the Trojan quest; Juno (his wife, counterpart to the Greek Hera) opposes it; Venus (the goddess of love, known in Greek mythology as Aphrodite) assists her son Aeneas just as Athena assisted Odysseus. Virgil's use of the historical present renders his epic more immediate than those of Homer.

The greatest obstacle Aeneas faces is his love affair with Dido, which occupies Book IV of *The Aeneid*. Aeneas tells his story of a seven-year voyage to Dido just as Odysseus recounted his tales to Nausicaa and her father. The challenge in this case lies not with some rival suitor, or the desire to return home to a long-suffering wife, but the call of duty. For Aeneas must make his way to the site of what will eventually become Rome, and this sacred obligation drives the narrative in Virgil's epic.

Aeneas' final challenge, the battle with Turnus, again takes shape in Homeric terms. "In his climactic moment—killing Turnus--Aeneas resembles, at one and the same moment, an Achilles avenging the death of a cherished comrade, a Hector defending his homeland successfully, and an Odysseus winning his rightful bride by killing her suitor, reclaiming his kingdom and laying the groundwork for its future."[82]

Augustan Patriotism

The *Aeneid* contains a number of prophecies of events that had already come to pass—nice work if you can get it—including references to Julius Caesar**Error! Bookmark not defined.Error! Bookmark not defined.** and to Virgil's patron Augustus.

From that noble blood will arise a Trojan Caesar,
His empire bound by the Ocean, his glory by the stars:
Julius, a name passed down from Iulus, his great forebear.

The theme of duty is announced in the opening lines of the poem:

Wars and a man I sing—an exile driven on by Fate,
He was the first to flee the coast of Troy,
Destined to reach Lavinian shores and Italian soil,
Yet many blows he took on land and sea from the gods above—
Thanks to cruel Juno's relentless rage—and many losses
He bore in battle too, before he could found a city,
Bring his gods to Latium, source of the Latin race,
But Alban lords and the high walls of Rome.[83]

Virgil "prophesies" the glories of the Roman Empire:

But you, Roman, remember, rule with all your power
The peoples of the earth—these will be your arts:
To put your stamp on the works and ways of peace,
To spare the defeated, break the proud in war.

"The *Aeneid* gave Romans a coherent myth and a literature to stand alongside the epics of Greece. The Romans felt they must be special people and Virgil confirmed this belief."[84]

Virgilian Simile

Perhaps determined to out-do Homer, Virgil creates dozens of extended metaphors. Where Homer prefers human metaphors, Virgil more often bases his figures of speech on animals or other aspects of nature. Virgil compares the climactic battle between Aeneas and Turnus to the encounter between two bulls. *"Charging like two hostile bulls fighting up on Sila's woods or Taburnus' ridges, ramping in mortal combat, both brows bent for attack and the herdsmen back away in fear and the whole herd stands by, hushed, afraid, and the heifers wait and wonder, who will lord it over the forest? Who will lead the herd?—while the bulls battle it out, horns butting, locking, goring each other, necks and shoulders roped in blood and the woods resound as they grunt and bellow out. So they charge, Trojan Aeneas and Turnus, son of Daunus, shields clang and the huge din makes the heavens ring."[85]*

Charged with transforming the Roman creation myth into literature, Virgil could hardly have done better than drawing on Homer as a point of departure.

Paul of Tarsus, *Epistle to the Romans,* 60 AD

Persecutor to Proselytizer

Paul of Tarsus, originally named Saul, grew up in the Jewish faith. Loyal to Jewish legal practices, Saul zealously opposed the new cult of Christian Jews. As we read in Acts 9:1, "Saul, still breathing threats and murder against the disciples of the Lord, went to the high priest and asked him for letters to the synagogues at Damascus, so that if he found any who belonged to the Way, men or women, he might bring them bound to Jerusalem." Then, the writer of Acts reports, Saul underwent a transfiguring experience on the road to Damascus when he reported hearing the voice of Jesus saying, "Saul, Saul, why do you persecute me?" Thereafter, as an ardent following of Christ, and taking the name of Paul, he traveled widely proclaiming the gospel. Unsurprisingly, this transformation did not sit well with Jews who now considered Paul a traitor to the faith. "Five times he received the punishment of thirty-nine lashes 'from Jews,' a punishment associated with synagogue discipline."[86]

Perhaps recalling the negative aspects of his new role as proselytizer Paul wrote, "Who will separate us from the love of Christ? Will hardship, or distress, or persecution or famine, or nakedness, or peril, or sword. ... No, in all these things we are more than conquerors through him who loved us. For I am convinced that neither death, nor life, nor angels, nor rulers, nor things present, nor things to come, nor powers, nor height, nor depth, nor anything else in all creation, will be able to separate us from the love of God in Christ Jesus our Lord." (Romans 8: 35-39)

Jews vs. Gentiles

Controversy arose over the question of whether Gentile (non-Jewish) Christians should be obliged to follow the same practices as Christians who had been brought up in the Jewish faith. Paul tried to find a diplomatic answer to the challenge of "how Gentiles can be added into God's people without disenfranchising God's 'original' people, the Jews."[87] Specifically, should Gentiles have to become circumcised and follow the Law of Moses, particularly the purity laws regarding food? Paul, seeking to remove any obstacles to the dissemination of the faith, argued that new Christians should not be bound by Jewish traditions. Others, including Peter, one of the original twelve disciples of Jesus, pursued a more moderate position.

"When Peter and Paul appeared before the gathered church in Antioch ... they could not agree concerning to what degree the Jewish food and purity regulations ought to be required of Gentile Christians during their common meals with those Jewish Christians who were still living and thinking ritually. ... On the one hand, Paul pleaded for the freedom of the Gentiles from all legal obligations. On the other hand, Peter ... decided that the Gentile Christians could by all means be expected to keep the so-called minimum Noahic commandments. Paul, however, considered this to be an offense against the 'truth of the gospel' and thus decided from then on to continue the mission to the Gentiles entrusted to him with his co-workers alone (and without these obligations)."[88]

Salvation by Faith

Paul's Letter to the Romans, written around 60 AD, addresses questions concerning Jesus' teachings and their implications for the newly-forming Christian communities. "The role that Romans has played in the history of Christianity manifests that it is the most important of the Pauline writings, if not of the entire New Testament. ... In fact, one can almost write the history of Christian theology by surveying the ways in which Romans has been interpreted."[89]

A recurring question revolved around the issue of salvation and whether it depended on carrying out works of the Law. "Paul's problem with 'works of the law' was that they excluded Gentiles from God's salvation in Christ. Jewish devotion to the law was wrapped up in the covenant that God made with Israel. But that covenant was made with *Israel* and not with the other peoples of the world."[90] Paul did not mince words: "For we hold that a person is justified by faith apart from works prescribed by the law." (Romans 3:28)

"Our 'works,' whether done in obedience to the law ... or to some other moral code, never can bring us into God's favor. Only faith, the humble acceptance of God's offer of salvation, can do so."[91] For Paul, salvation is by faith. "Therefore, since we are justified by faith, we have peace with God through our Lord Jesus Christ." (Romans 5:1) The letter to the Romans consistently proclaims "Paul's basic principle about God's gracious gift of salvation in Christ, independent of the works of the Law."[92]

One is impressed by Paul's willingness first to reverse the course of his career and then to resist compromise in preaching an originally Jewish religion to a larger Gentile audience.

Colosseum, 80 AD PLATE 4

Architectural

The Colosseum, the icon of imperial Rome, employed a number of architectural innovations that permitted the enclosure of far greater space than anything seen in Ancient Greece. The invention of the arch, in particular, overcame the limitations of the Greek post and lintel construction, permitting large-scale engineering projects such as aqueducts, bridges, public arenas, amphitheaters and stadiums. The principle of the arch, which directs the weight laterally and down, led naturally to the barrel vault, a series of arches placed one in front of the other, and the groin vault, two barrel vaults placed at right angles.

"Building work started under the emperor Vespasian in AD 72 with the opening ceremonies under his son Titus in 80. ... Its outer elevation comprised four stories, to a total of 157 feet. ... Inside, the arena ... could accommodate 87,000 spectators."[93]

Social

"In building the Colosseum Vespasian was dramatically making the point that the profits of Roman military success belonged, in part at least, to the common people of Rome. ... The Colosseum ... came to be seen as one of the most important arenas ... in which the emperor came face to face with his people—and to stand as a symbol of the encounter between autocrat and those he ruled. ... The Colosseum was very much more than a sports venue. It was a political theatre in which each stratum of Roman society played out its role. ... It was a vital part of Roman political life to be there, to be seen to be there and to watch the others."[94]

"When they arrived at the Colosseum, spectators would find that the entrance and exit routes for different classes of seating were planned ... in a complex pattern so that citizens of different status were kept rigidly separate."[95] A private tunnel allowed the Emperor to enter and exit without having to pass through the crowd. A series of tiers was reserved according to station in Rome's stratified society: senators; knights and nobles; wealthy citizens, poor citizens, other social groups (soldiers, foreign dignitaries, priests, etc.), the common poor, slaves, and women.

Gladiatorial

Cassio Dio describes the dedication of the Colosseum. *"There was a battle between cranes and also between four elephants;*

*animals both tame and wild were slain to the number of 9,000;
and women (not those of any prominence however) took part in
despatching them. As for the men, several fought in single combat and several groups contended together both in infantry and
naval battles. For Titus suddenly filled this same theatre with
water and brought in horses and bulls and some other domesti-
cated animals that had been taught to behave in the liquid element just as on land. He also brought in people on ships, who
engaged in a sea-fight there. ... There, too, on the first day there
was a gladiatorial exhibition and wild-beast hunt, the lake in
front of the images having first been covered with a platform of
wooden stands erected around it. On the second day there was a
horse-race, and on the third day a naval battle between 3,000
men, followed by an infantry battle."*[96]

"Gladiators were marginal outsiders in Roman society. ... There
is, however, plenty of evidence to suggest that gladiators were as
much admired and celebrated as they were abominated. ... It was
in fact a standing joke at Rome that women were liable to fall for
the heroes of the arena. ...Gladiators were not sexy and exciting
despite being beyond the social pale, but *because* they were."[97]
Members of the aristocracy would compete in producing the
most spectacular contests, to the point that the Senate had to limit
the amount spent to prevent members of the elite from bankrupt-
ing themselves. When Julius Caesar accumulated so many gladiators that the Senate feared the power of this "private army,"
they passed a law limiting individuals to owning no more than
640 gladiators.

"Whatever the death rate of gladiators in the Colosseum, it must
have been much worse for the beasts which took part in the
shows. ...Animals were not only brought to the Colosseum in order that they themselves should be killed. They were also used
to kill criminals and prisoners in the executions that took place in
the arena as part of the shows."[98] Yet despite popular tradition,

"the fact is that there are no genuine records of any Christians being put to death in the Colosseum."[99]

The Colosseum symbolizes the Roman Empire whose extent, by every measure, strikes us as colossal.

Ptolemy, *Almagest*, ca. 150 AD

Geocentrism

We tend to celebrate those capable of thinking "outside the box." Yet we need to reserve some admiration for Ptolemy, who thought so creatively "inside the box" that his calculations remained useful for more than a millennium. The box in question is, of course, the geocentric model of the solar system that Ptolemy inherited from his Greek counterparts. "Ptolemy came at the end of a long line of Greek thinkers who viewed the earth as the fixed and immovable center of the universe, around which the planets swung in concentric circles. To assert that the earth was at any place other than the center of the heavens was to deny humans their position of supremacy in the universe, to believe that human affairs were no more significant to the gods than those of other planets."[100]

Ptolemy's inheritance from the Greeks included another fundamental assumption, the sphericity of the heavens. Ptolemy wrote, "*If one assumes any motion whatever, except spherical, for the heavenly bodies, it necessarily follows that their distances, measured from the earth upwards, must vary, wherever and however one supposes the earth itself to be situated. Hence the sizes and mutual distances of the stars must appear to vary for the same observers during the course of each revolution, since at one time they must be at a greater distance, at another at a lesser. Yet we see that no such variation occurs.*"[101]

Retrograde Motion

Geocentrism and sphericity, despite their beauty as abstract concepts, suffered from a fatal flaw: they didn't always correspond with actual observations. In particular, the planets didn't move around the earth in simple circles but appeared occasionally—and perplexingly—to move backwards, retrograde motion. Our very word "planet" comes from the Greek for "wandering star," celestial bodies whose irregular movement across the heavens contrasted with the regular motion of the "fixed stars."

From the perspective of our heliocentric model of the solar system, with planets all tracing their various orbits around the sun, it is easy to see how this "retrograde motion" would arise. Since the earth completes its journey around the sun in a shorter time than the outer planets, as it "overtakes" them, so to speak, their motion viewed from the earth would seem temporarily to go "backwards."

Epicycles and Deferents

Lacking our perspective, Ptolemy had to invent a more complicated model to perpetuate geocentricity. According to this model, which managed to preserve the essential concept of circular motion, the planets moved circularly in "epicycles" which themselves moved circularly about the earth along an orbit called the "deferent." Ptolemy wrote, *"We can suppose that they have a concentric circle, but their uniform motion takes place not actually on that circle, but on another circle, which is carried by the first circle, and is known as the 'epicycle.'"*[102]

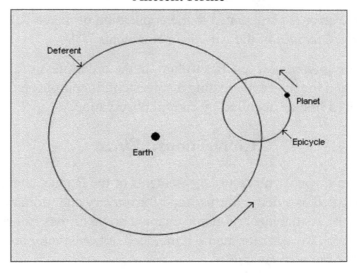

To modern eyes this model may seem ridiculously complicated, all to preserve the sacred notion of geocentricity. But the amazing thing is that using this model Ptolemy was able to compile tables of planetary motion whose accuracy sufficed for many centuries. "Given the physics of his day, Ptolemy's kinematic modeling works just as accurately at his level of precision as a heliocentric system would have done. ... At the opening of the seventeenth century there was still no observational way to distinguish between the two arrangements." Ptolemy's *Almagest* "became the fundamental astronomical text for over a millennium, and it served as the exemplar for Copernicus' *De revolutionibus* nearly fourteen centuries later."[103]

Ptolemy also wrote a geographical treatise whose validity was eventually put to the test by fifteenth-century explorations. "Ptolemy's diminution of the distance between Europe and Asia by some 50° longitude fortified Columbus's belief that he could easily reach the Orient by sailing westward across the Atlantic— perhaps even induced him to undertake his great voyage of discovery. Indeed, Columbus died in the conviction that the land he had first sighted was an outlying island of southeastern India;

and the error is perpetuated in the application of the name 'Indian' to the natives of the American continents."[104]

Ptolemy's *Almagest* testifies to faith in the orderliness of the universe and ingenuity in creating a consistent, if complicated, model to fit data acquired by careful observation.

Connections: *Virtus*

The word *virtus* embraces key elements of the Roman character. Personified as a deity, Virtus stood for bravery and military strength. As the ideal of manly character---*virtus* has its origins in the root word *vir*, or man—it included not only valor and courage but also civic duty.

Virtus in the sense of military strength underlies Caesar's *Commentaries*. The success of the Roman legions rested not only on their superior training but also on their ideal of valor. Civic duty guides Aeneas throughout his journeys in the first half of the *Aeneid*; valor and courage characterize his behavior in the battles of the second half. Paul of Tarsus invokes his birthright as a Roman citizen in demanding to be judged by Caesar, a stratagem allowing him to escape harsh treatment by the Jewish authorities. The spectacle of the Colosseum can scarcely be separated from the valor of the gladiators who fought there. Only Ptolemy seems to fall outside this descriptor, the cycles and epicycles of his *Almagest* perhaps better associated with the "music of the spheres" of his Greek forebears.

5th To 10th Centuries

Context

Barbarian Migrations

The old view of barbarians bent on destroying Rome has been replaced by a more balanced picture. "The barbarian tribes that pounded at the gates of the empire, before breaking them down and pouring through, were often, in reality, trading partners, allies, mercenaries and recruiting agents for the Roman state. By the time the western empire dissolved in the late fourth century, there were more Goth warriors than Roman legionaries in the service of the emperor."[105]

The expansion of the Roman Empire to the east and north inevitably resulted in clashes with barbarians, or non-Romans, migrating west and south. "The setting-up of customs posts and border patrols stopped this migration, leading to a build-up of population on the outside. This population pressure, rather than weakness at the centre, was most important in undermining Roman authority at the margins of the empire ... The number of barbarians fighting for the empire grew ever greater, power became diffused, and the discord between the various groups led not so much to the collapse of the empire, as to the irrelevance of central authority."[106]

Monasticism

Some followers of Jesus sought solitary worship, perhaps following Paul's injunction "Do not be conformed to this world, but be transformed by the renewing of your minds, so that you may discern what is the will of God." (Romans 12:2) In the 5th century Saint Simeon Stylites lived for thirty-seven years atop a pillar. Others gathered into small monastic communities. Toward the

51

end of the 5th century, St. Benedict of Nursia established organizing principles for western monasticism. "St. Benedict assured
his monastic community a regulated routine by setting down in
detail in his rule what the monks would do in the way of prayer,
work, and sleep during the twenty-four hours of the day. He en-
joined upon them strict observance of this rule, and swore them
to unquestioning obedience to their superior, the abbot."[107]

"The monastic day was filled with carefully prescribed activities:
communal prayer, devotional reading, and work—field work,
household work, or manuscript copying, according to need and
ability. ... Monks and nuns alike were pledged to the fundamental
obligations of poverty, chastity, and obedience. By relinquishing
all personal possessions, living a celibate life, and obeying the
abbot or abbess, Benedictines sought to resist the three great
worldly temptations of money, sex, and ambition."[108]

Clovis to Charlemagne

In the fifth century, Clovis, king of the Frankish tribes in the
former Roman province of Gaul, managed to consolidate warring
clans, though "his level of moral development appears to have
been no higher than that of his semicivilized neighbors. He was
as savage and treacherous as they were, although more cunning
and ambitious. He displayed his savagery by eliminating, by
means mostly foul, all who opposed him in his quest for power,
or whose lands he coveted, whether they were friends, relatives,
or enemies."[109] The story is told of the "looted vase of Soissons,
which had been smashed to pieces by a Frankish warrior who
refused to share the spoil. Clovis waited until the Champ de
Mars, the annual parade, of the following spring, where he chid-
ed the vase-breaker over the state of his equipment. As the warrior bent down to reach for a weapon, Clovis smashed his skull
with a battle-axe, saying '*Thus didst thou to the vase of Soissons.*'"[110]

Successors to Clovis, known as the Merovingian dynasty, dominated the region during the seventh and eighth centuries, an area further expanded in the early ninth century by Charlemagne. Were Charlemagne only a great warrior we would not celebrate him as one of the major figures of the Middle Ages. Charlemagne's reforms in education, language, administration and even music constitute a legacy known as the Carolingian renaissance. He recruited Alcuin, the most renowned scholar of his time, to improve the monastic schools. He adopted as a basis for education the classical divisions of the trivium (grammar; logical argument or dialectic; and rhetoric) and the quadrivium (arithmetic; geometry; astronomy; and mathematically-based music theory). He greatly increased support for scriptoria (centres for book-copying): most of the surviving works of classical Latin were copied and preserved by Carolingian scholars.

"One of the lasting legacies of the Carolingian renaissance was the script we still use today in printing. When Charlemagne became king, the script most commonly used by copyists was intentionally complicated, full of squiggles, curlicues, and enormous pen strokes, but in a few monastic scriptoria in Gaul they were already experimenting with a much more practical script. Its letters were uniform and properly aligned, and the overall effect was that they were much more legible. This script, which experts call the Carolingian minuscule, had an unprecedented success under Charlemagne and gradually replaced all previously used scripts across the immense territory of the empire."[111] The union of tribes depended on the force of Charlemagne's personality. After his death, the empire he had assembled gradually disintegrated.

St. Augustine, *The City of God*, ca. 420

Two Cities

"Augustine says that he was motivated to write the *City of God* by the sack of Rome by Alaric and his Gothic army in August 410 and subsequent pagan attempts to blame Christians for the event."[112] Blaming the fall of Rome on the Christians may strike us as totally irrational, but 14th-century Christians had no hesitation in blaming the Black Plague on the Jews, and 21st-century Americans all manner of ills on immigrants.

In writing *The City of God*, St. Augustine had two audiences. For non-Christians, Augustine refuted the charge that the Catholic Church should be blamed for the calamity. (Essentially, he blamed the Romans for foolishly entrusting their safety to pagan gods who could not protect them.) To Christians, Augustine argued that the followers of Jesus should be concerned with the mystical, heavenly City of Jerusalem (the New Jerusalem) rather than with Earthly politics. *"Yet there are no more than two kinds of human society, which we may justly call two cities, according to the language of our Scriptures. The one consists of those who wish to live after the flesh, the other of those who wish to live after the spirit. ... We know that if our earthly house of this tabernacle were dissolved, we have a building of God, a house not made with hands, eternal in the heavens. ... Accordingly, two cities have been formed by two loves: the earthly by the love of self, even to the contempt of God; the heavenly by the love of God, even to the contempt of self."*[113]

Neoplatonism

"Augustine saw the central task of a Christian scholar as confronting the question 'Where does evil come from?' If God was both good and all-powerful, then how did evil come into the world?" Augustine's question reflects the influence of Socrates and Plato. The idea that there is an abstract entity called 'evil' that is the opposite of an entity called 'good' had not occurred to other peoples at other times; it was a historical invention of post-classical Greece."[114]

Plato's Theory of Forms had considerable influence on Augustine's formulation of Christian theology. To begin with, it furnished a way of understanding God, the soul, and good and evil as immaterial but real. But where did human wickedness come from? "Augustine's answer lay in a doctrine that had become common currently among people of different faiths in the late Roman Empire—Original Sin."[115]

Original Sin

Regarding original sin, Augustine argued that man's pride and desire to trust his own authority made him sinful even before he committed the first sinful act. *"God, as it is written, made man upright, and consequently with a good will. (Eccles. 7:29) ... The good will, then, is the work of God; for God created him with it. But the first evil will, which preceded all man's evil acts, was rather a kind of falling away from the work of God to its own works than any positive work. And therefore the acts resulting were evil, not having God, but the will itself, for their end; so that the will or the man himself, so far as his will is bad, was as it were the evil tree bringing forth evil fruit.... And what is the origin of our evil will but pride? For "pride is the beginning of sin."*[116]

"The belief that humans carried some ineluctable stain, or damage, or corruption helped to explain the degree of suffering and uncertainty in a troubled period of history. ... The role of the true Christian was to fear God, to suffer and to await His judgment."[117] St. Augustine's gloomy perspective, which stands in marked contrast to the confidence of St. Paul ("We are more than conquerors"), shaped Christian thinking for centuries to come.

Augustine's theology attests to the human preference for dichotomy: good and evil; saved and condemned; pagan and Christian.

Gregory of Tours, *Ten Books of History*, 594

Good vs. Evil

If Herodotus found his calling as an historian in writing about "great and marvelous deeds," Gregory of Tours could be said to have discovered his historiographical role in distinguishing good from evil. For Gregory, the difference appeared as clearly as the white and black hats of early westerns. In contrast to Herodotus, writing more than two centuries after the events he described, Gregory, as bishop of Tours, was an active participant in the affairs of his time. "In place of the detached observer we should, therefore, probably see a man deeply involved in much of what he was recording, yet determined to distance himself in much of the record."[118]

Writing as both observer and participant placed Gregory in a delicate position. "Gregory not only had views on politics: he was involved in them. This is something that is not always apparent in his narrative. It is, nevertheless, a factor which needs to be kept in mind when reading what he has to say about his own times. As a player in a particularly brutal political world the bishop of Tours was well informed, but it was not always in his interest to state what he knew. ... As long as there could be doubt as to which party would come out on top Gregory seems to have hedged his bets."[119]

But Gregory had no doubts when it came to identifying good and evil. "For Gregory, the idea that history could simply be reduced to the opposition of good and evil was both the reason and justification for his writing; he felt the need to justify his work because it challenged traditional ideas on the writing of history. ... Gregory defined his subject-matter as people: those who behaved with a Christian social morality, and those who did not."[120]

Gregory also entertained no doubts about God's participation in the affairs of men. Gregory explains *"the present ills as the result of God's punitive intervention in history on account of the actions of contemporaries—the kings—against the churches. ... The previous generation of Merovingians had furnished the churches and monasteries with property; the present kings now destroy this property and lay it waste."*[121]

Roman Catholic vs. Arian

To earn Gregory's approval, it was not sufficient to be a Christian. One had to be the right kind of Christian, a Roman Catholic and not a heretic Arian. Many of the fiercest battles in the early Middle Ages took place between armies of orthodox Christians and heretical, non-Trinitarian Arians.

Gregory stated his position clearly in the prologue of his *Ten Books of History* (formerly known as *History of the Franks*). *"I would like to give a brief list of examples showing the happy outcome for the Christians who believed in the Trinity, and the disaster who befell the heretics who rejected it."*[122]

Clovis vs. Alaric

Baptism marked one's official acceptance into the Christian faith, although the sacrament might be postponed until quite late in life. Clovis, leader of the Franks, was the first of the barbarian leaders to adopt Christianity, becoming baptized as a Christian at the behest of his wife Clotilde. The conversion came about on purely practical grounds. "Losing a disastrous battle against the Alemanni he raised his eyes to heaven and invoked the god of his wife, shouting 'Jesus Christ, you who Clotilda maintains is the son of the Living God ... if you will give me victory over my enemies, then I will be baptized in your name.' In the next instant, the Alemanni turned and fled. Clovis accepted baptism, along with 3,000 of his men."[123]

Alaric II, leader of the Visigoths, was an Arian. For Gregory, the difference between the two was as clear as black and white. *"Clovis acknowledged the Trinity and, by his victory over the heretics, expanded his rule over all Gaul; Alaric rejected the Trinity and lost his kingdom, his people and eternal life. ... God is therefore shown to be an ever-present and active force in history."*[124] Gregory did not see Clovis himself as a particularly good man but as a representative of God. "Clovis' significance as the central figure of Book II lies not in his historical status as king of the Franks, but in his role as the instrument of God's will pitched against the enemies of orthodoxy."[125] In the ensuing battle, Clovis not only defeated the Visigoths but killed Alaric himself.

Living in tumultuous times, Gregory portrays all of human history, from the biblical era to his own, as a continuing conflict between good and evil.

5th To 10th Centuries

Beowulf, ca. 700

Kinship

Beowulf, probably written somewhere between the eighth and eleventh centuries, presents a picture of pagan values in the fifth and sixth centuries. "In the warrior society whose values the poem constantly invokes, the most important of human relationships was that which existed between the warrior—the thane—and his lord, a relationship based less on subordination of one man's will to another's than on mutual trust and respect. When a warrior vowed loyalty to his lord, he became not so much his servant as his voluntary companion, one who would take pride in defending him and fighting in his wars."[126] A moment's reflection will indicate the importance of a more or less constant state of warfare to keep the system working, and that pretty much describes the situation of the Germanic tribes.

A second important aspect of pagan values was the kinship code. "If one of his kinsmen had been slain, a man had a special duty of either killing the slayer or exacting from him the payment of *wergild* ('man-price'): each rank of society was evaluated at a definite price, which had to be paid to the dead man's kinsmen by the killer who wished to avoid their vengeance—even if the killing had been accidental."[127] Beowulf himself states that "*It is better for a man to avenge his friend than much mourn.*" The poem contains an example of the kinds of problems that might arise from such a value system, the sorrow of King Hrethel. "One of his sons had accidentally killed another: by the code of kinship Hrethel was forbidden to kill or to exact compensation from a kinsman, yet by the same code he was required to do one or the other in order to avenge the dead. Caught in this curious dilemma, Hrethel became so disconsolate that he could no longer face life."[128]

Youth and Age

The poem spans a full generation of human life, depicting the hero first as a young man then suddenly skipping across fifty years to show him as an old king. "This stark juxtaposition of beginning and end makes the poem seem like a diptych of the hero's rise and fall and suggests powerfully that even a long life like Beowulf's is a thing of fleeting brevity."[129] Parallel figures of speech unite the two sections. "The narrative is highly patterned. There is studied balance between the two parts of the poem, with the aged Hrothgar and the youthful Beowulf in the first part standing in poignant contrast with the aged Beowulf and the youthful Wiglaf in the closing episode. The contrast is underscored by the distribution of poetic formulae, with the epithets of the elderly which were applied to Hrothgar in the first part being used of the aged Beowulf in the second part, while young Beowulf's epithets fall to young Wiglaf. The pathos of inexorable ageing and decay is thus added to the hero's overthrow by time at the end of the poem."[130]

Like the forty-year period that occurs so frequently in the Bible, *Beowulf* keeps repeating a fifty-year span. "We are told that Hrothgar ruled Denmark for fifty years before Grendel attacked, while Grendel's mother ruled the monster-mere for fifty years before Beowulf attacked, and likewise Beowulf ruled Geatland for fifty years before the dragon attacked."[131] "At the end of the poem [the poet] leaves us with the impression that Beowulf's chief reward is pagan immortality: the memory in the minds of later men of a hero's heroic actions. The poem itself is, indeed, a noble expression of that immortality."[132]

Oral Tradition

The language of this epic of barbarian violence has a rough-hewn compactness that seems well-suited to its subject. We may call attention to alliteration (what the Germans call *Stabreim*, matching sounds at the start of a line, in contrast to *Endreim*, or similar sounds at the end of the line). We also note the presence of "kennings," or circumlocutions for commonplace objects, and compact adjectives formed by jamming nouns and verbs together.

- Alliteration: "Men pushed the well-braced ship from shore, warriors on a well-wished voyage."
- Kenning: "ring-giver" for "king"; "swan road" or "whale road" for "sea"
- Compact adjectives: "sea-skilled", "battle-brave", "blood-wet", "battle-hardened", "weary-hearted", "sword-wounded", "victory-blessed", "slaughter-bent"

"The *Beowulf*-poet's favoured form of artful alliteration appears to lie in the clustering of double alliteration, a pattern he repeats throughout the text to highlight a large number of key passages in the poem. ... Wordplay and localized sound-effects are the *Beowulf*-poet's stock-in-trade, and again emphasize the extent to which the poem is essential aural in nature, and deserves to be heard."[133]

The customs and value systems informing *Beowulf* witness the influence of Scandinavian traditions in the development of English literature.

The Book of Kells, ca. 800 PLATE 5

Gospel Books

The scriptoria of the early Christian monasteries played a key role in preserving Christian writings during a period of general illiteracy. The monks not only copied the words of scripture but decorated their work with illuminated art, sometimes in the form of elaborate capital letters at the beginning of a chapter, sometimes in the form of tiny figures filling unused spaces on the page. The Book of Kells also includes full-page illuminations for each of the evangelists. "The Gospels were the word of God, upon which doctrine was built, and they provided for believers the spiritual truth read publicly in the liturgy. The text's divine and authoritative nature provided the main reason for creating large, impressively decorated copies of it."[134]

Introducing Christianity to Ireland meant displacing Celtic pagan religion and introducing the Gospel message in a foreign language. Illustrations in the gospel books served the same purpose as stained glass windows in cathedrals: providing visual alternatives to a largely uncomprehended verbal message. "Pope Gregory the Great explained that the images provided 'a living reading of the Lord's story for those who cannot read.'"[135]

The Book of Kells, "is the most lavishly decorated of a series of gospel manuscripts produced between the seventh and ninth centuries, when Irish art and culture flourished at home and in centres of Irish missionary activity overseas. ... The great decorated pages, upon which the book's celebrity mainly rests, comprise symbols and portraits of the evangelists, including the gospels; portraits of Christ and of the Virgin and Child; and illustrations of the temptation and the arrest of Christ."[136]

Celtic Art and Christian Art

The artwork of the Book of Kells communicates the Christian message with a decidedly Celtic accent. The intricate geometric patterns of interlacing figures and the evocations of the goldsmith's art belong to an ancient pre-Christian tradition. The so-called insular style extends to the elaborate calligraphy, full of spirals, circles, and interlocking patterns.

Symbolic Message

"St. John, extravagantly haloed and seated on a throne, his scribble accoutrements to hand, is one of the most powerful images in the entire book."[137] The complicated symbolism of the portrait of St. John tells the story of the evangelist. "St John holds in his right hand a stylized version of a quill pen made from the tail feathers of a goose or swan. Scribes at the time also made some use of reeds. In his left hand, St John holds his gospel book, bound in red and purple. ... At the evangelist's right foot is an inkpot, probably made from a cow horn stuck into the earth."[138]

The picture of St. John appears to be held up by another personage whose hands, feet and a portion of the head can be seen at the margins of the portrait. "The figure has been identified as God embracing the cosmos and as Christ, triumphantly holding one of the nails of the crucifixion. ... The odd positioning of the John portrait—housed within the center of the hands, feet and head of another figure—might be understood as a reference to John's special status as the one who rested on the breast of Christ. The message is clear: The Lord can be partially apprehended through the Gospel of John."[139]

"The artist has exaggerated the size of the writing instrument, and the inkwell bears some resemblance to a chalice, drawing attention to the act of writing and of John's role as the one who 'from the Lord's breast drank in what he might give us to drink.'"[140] The unusual "doubling" effect extends to the gospel book itself, replicated in the volume in St. John's left hand.

The artwork associated with the great Gospel Book reveals an intriguing amalgamation of Celtic and Christian culture.

Plainsong, *Kyrie Orbis Factor*, 9th century

Charlemagne

The singing of chant, in one form or another, goes back to the earliest days of the Christian church. The actual repertoire of plainsong, however, probably dates from around the ninth century, when Charlemagne, as part of his campaign for regularization throughout his empire, eliminated the diversity of chant singing then in existence in favor of Roman chant, often called Gregorian chant even though neither the actual melodies nor an unambiguous notational system existed in the time of Pope Gregory.

Guido of Arezzo

Guido of Arezzo, who flourished in the early decades of the eleventh century, is credited with inventing modern staff notation to replace the earlier neumatic system in which marks placed over the syllables of the Latin text served to indicate pitch.[141] Guido's four-line staff established precise pitch relationships.

In modern notation:

The clef-sign at the top of the staff designates C on the top line. Counting down, we find the first pitch of the Kyrie to be A. When two notes are written together, the lower note sounds first;

thus, the first two pitches of the plainsong would be A and B ♭ .

Portions of the melody containing one pitch for each syllable of the text are said to "syllabic," as observed in the setting of "le-i-son." Portions of the melody containing several pitches for a single syllable are said to be "melismatic," as observed in the first syllable of "eleison."

While Guido's system furnished clear representations of pitch, it gave no indication of rhythm, aside from the dots calling for longer time values. Traditionally plainsong has been performed as evenly moving notes, although contemporary performers may have imposed rhythmic patterns of one sort or another. The absence of regular "beats," the unadorned melodic line, the narrow compass of the melody, and the use of modes different from modern major and minor scales all contribute to the "otherworldly" quality associated with plainsong.

Choir and Soloists

The earliest Christians met in house churches where they shared a meal, told stories about Jesus, and offered prayers. Over the years this simple pattern of worship developed into an elaborate ritual in which a priest celebrated the Eucharist before an audience of congregants. A multipartite liturgy included texts that varied with every celebration of the mass (the Proper) and texts that remained fixed (the Ordinary, comprising Kyrie, Gloria, Credo, Sanctus and Benedictus and Agnus Dei), each of which could be performed in plainsong.

The Kyrie, the shortest section of the Ordinary, consisted of a three-line prayer—*Lord, have mercy; Christ, have mercy; Lord, have mercy*—each line to be repeated three times (as indicated by the letters "*iij*" at the end of the line in our example). In performing the plainsong, a solo cantor would introduce the melody, followed by the rest of the choir for the repetitions.

65

From the earliest times of Christian worship, chant was performed without accompaniment—no instruments, no clapping, no dancing—in part to distinguish it from pagan rituals. In later centuries, composers would create more elaborate musical settings for celebrations of the mass, yet the repertoire of plainchant endured for hundreds of years as the basis of these settings, at first improvised and later written down.

Unadorned plainsong accompanied the Christian liturgy for hundreds of years, then served as the supporting foundation for the development of polyphony.

Connections: Dichotomy

A preference for dichotomy over continuity seems to be a fundamental trait of the human psyche. Human beings appear to favor categorization over continuum, particularly a division into two mutually exclusive groups or two opposites. Nowhere does this sense of black-and-white thinking emerge more clearly than in our repertoire of works from the 5th through 10th centuries. St. Augustine posited a dichotomy between the elect and the condemned, as manifested metaphorically in the two cities, one earthly the other heavenly. We observe a clear demarcation between the other-worldly performance of plainsong by a group of unaccompanied singers and the clapping, dancing, and instrumental accompaniment of pagan celebrations. Gregory of Tours' black-and-white vision of the world discerned a clear division between good vs. evil, Roman Catholic vs. Arian. The same dichotomy between good and evil describes the world of *Beowulf*, marked as well by kinship laws clearly separating friend and foe. The evangelical orientation of the *Book of Kells* belongs to a world clearly divided between Christian and pagan.

11th Century

Context

Feudalism

In a time of more or less continual armed conflict, personal safety ranked high on the list of priorities. Feudalism represents an organized attempt to meet this need. The lord of an estate granted land rights to a vassal, who in return promised military service to the lord, in the form of a specific number of knights. The vassal, in turn, could subdivide the parcel, called a fief, into sub-parcels and enter into contracts with sub-vassals, a process known as sub-infeudation. The result displayed a kind of pyramid structure at whose base lay the simple knight, as well as the serf who cultivated the land, and at whose summit stood the king, invested by God with the terrestrial expanse of his realm. Historian Norman Davies objects that "such models mislead by their artificial neatness and symmetry. In reality, feudal society was built on a confused mass of conflicting dependencies and loyalties, riddled with exceptions and exemptions, where the once-clear lines of service were fouled up by generations of contested privileges, disputed rights, and half-forgotten obligations. It was certainly hierarchical, but it was anything but neat and regular."[142]

Feudal practices "furnished the cement which prevented the complete dissolution of social life in the west and the advent of anarchy. ... When the vassal swore to be his lord's man during the feudal period, he assumed three major responsibilities. He swore to provide his lord military service, to furnish him counsel (court service), and to administer the fief which he received on this occasion. His military obligation required him to serve his lord as a knight forty days each year, and to supply additional knights in rough proportion to the size and value of his fief."[143] The knight is rightly regarded as the symbol of the feudal age.

Yet "for all the romantic images that today surround the medieval knight, he was, in essence, an armed thug. Mounted on a charger and clad in helmet and chain mail, he was the medieval equivalent of the modern tank. Fighting was what he had been trained for; it was the chief justification for his existence; and it was how he grew wealthy (through plundered goods, ransoms, and gifts from grateful nobles). ... Knights were violent men, primarily interested in defending and extending their own estates."[144]

Norman Conquest

In 1066 William of Normandy, exploiting what he perceived as a favorable imbalance of power between France and England, gathered his forces and crossed the British Channel, defeating Harold, Earl of Wessex, at the Battle of Hastings. Historians have depicted England as a country bound to be conquered by either Scandinavia or France. The Norman Conquest brought England into a thriving intellectual and artistic life; Scandinavian conquest would have cut England off from all this.

In the aftermath, William replaced the English ruling class with his own friends and clansmen, and ordered a formal census of the conquered country that has been preserved as the Domesday Book. The kingdom of England was thereupon "parceled out among the Norman knights and turned into a model feudal kingdom."[145] "The king and his nobility secured their conquest by erecting dozens of castles across the land. Because castles could not be built except by royal license and because private wars between vassals were banned, this flurry of castle building both pacified the countryside and strengthened royal power."[146]

Investiture Controversy

In the eleventh century bishops and abbots controlled significant amounts of land and wealth. The naming of these church officials therefore became more than a matter of ceremony and offered an opportunity to exercise power. Local kings saw no reason why the pope should control the investiture, especially when his seat of power remained geographically distant. The pope, needless to say, had a different view of the situation. Pope Gregory VII, having already promulgated doctrines regarding celibacy and papal infallibility, threatened to excommunicate any bishop who acknowledged the investing authority of the king.

The most celebrated incident in the ongoing controversy occurred in 1077 when the Holy Roman Emperor Henry IV asserted his right as a divinely appointed sovereign to lead the German church without papal interference. Pope Gregory promptly excommunicated him. Henry, finding himself in a hopeless situation, travelled to Canossa in the winter and, the story goes, stood bareheaded in the snow for three days before the pope agreed to see him, hear his confession, and effect a reconciliation.[147]

St. Anselm, *Proslogion*, ca. 1078

Scholasticism

St. Anselm, regarded as the "father of Scholasticism," played an active role in defending the realist position against that of the nominalists. The nominalists considered that universal ideas such as humanity, society, justice and goodness were merely words or names, serving no purpose beyond providing terms for intelligent discussion. "Their position was the reverse of the realists, who maintained that universal ideas were much more than mere words, that they were indeed subsistent entities and possessed true reality. ... For the realist, therefore, the general idea preceded the thing. The nominalist reversed this sequence. Men started with acts, he reasoned. After judging these acts as to their merit and reasonableness, he had invented the term justice in order to facilitate the process of evaluating behavior."[148] The very use of the term "realist" to refer to a belief in universal ideas indicates how thoroughly Platonist principles had informed the dialogue in medieval philosophy.

Ontological Argument

Anselm wrote: "*I began to wonder if perhaps it might be possible to find one single argument that for its proof required no other save itself, and that by itself would suffice to prove that God really exists, that He is the supreme good needing no other and is He whom all things have need of for their being and well-being, and also to prove whatever we believe about the Divine Being.*"[149]

The so-called "ontological argument" owes a good deal to Plato, who posited the existence of ideal forms, reflected or represented in everyday reality. St. Anselm argues that we cannot call something "good" if there were not some absolute standard of goodness, what Plato would have called the ideal form of The Good. (The same argument would apply to greatness or justice.) According to Anselm, the absolute Being, who incorporates Goodness, Justice and Greatness, is God.

In the *Proslogion* of 1078 Anselm writes: "*We believe that You are something than which nothing greater can be thought. ...It is one thing for an object to exist in the mind, and another thing to understand that an object actually exists. ... Even the Fool is forced to agree that something-than-which-nothing-greater-can-be-thought exists in the mind. ... And surely that-than-which-a-greater-cannot-be-thought cannot exist in the mind alone. For if it exists solely in the mind, it can be thought to exist in reality also, which is greater. If then that-than-which-a-greater-cannot-be-thought exists in the mind alone, this same that-than-which-a-greater-cannot-be thought is that-than-which-a-greater-can-be-thought. But this is obviously impossible. Therefore there is absolutely no doubt that something-than-which-a-greater-cannot-be-thought exists both in the mind and in reality.*"

Anselm "is setting out to establish that God exists, and begins by identifying to his wider audience (the observers of the disputation) that his middle term will be 'that than which a greater cannot be thought' (=X). He then begins the argument by identifying that God's existence is being called into question, and sets out to get his opponent, the 'fool,' to accept the middle term (X), and the major premise: X exists in the understanding (*in intellectu*) and in reality (*in re*). Once he has established the major premise, he argues for the minor premise: God is X. If God is not this, then something is greater than Him, which would mean the creature would be greater than the Creator, which is impossible."[150]

Divine Attributes

Anselm employs a similar series of arguments for describing the attributes of God. From the assumption "that God is whatever it is better to be than not to be," Anselm argues that God is omniscient, omnipotent, merciful, just, limitless, and eternal.

Are Anselm's premises true? "The idea that God is unsurpassably great seems to be part and parcel of Judeo-Christian theism, and to say that God is something than which nothing greater can be thought seems to be a succinct way of capturing what those in the Judeo-Christian tradition mean by 'God.'"[151]

The fractured syntax of "something-than-which-a-greater-cannot-be-thought" suggests the lengths to which the Scholastics were willing to go to erect a logical scaffolding for religious belief.

Bayeux Tapestry, ca. 1100 PLATE 6

The French Version

By 1066, feudal rules of allegiance between vassal and lord could affect the destiny of entire countries. When King Edward of England died at the beginning of 1066, several people laid claim to the throne, including Harold, Earl of Wessex, and William, Duke of Normandy. Just before his death the King had met with Harold. What really took place at the meeting? To the Normans it was simple: "Edward had not wavered for a moment in his choice of William and he was now sending Earl Harold on a formal embassy to Normandy to confirm to the worthy duke his happy status as the next king of England."[152]

Now Harold had sworn an oath of fealty to William, so when Harold had himself crowned king, William took this as an act of personal betrayal and an adequate excuse to invade England to seek redress. "The oath was a primary bond in the society in which these men lived. It bound the swearer both in sanctity and honour. To break such an oath was to incur the wrath of God and, which was no less certain, though possibly more immediate, the wrath of William."[153]

The English Version

Why did Harold go to Normandy if not to confirm William as the new king of England? Perhaps Harold wanted to go to Normandy to negotiate the release of his brother and nephew, who had been held hostage there for more than ten years. During the deathbed meeting with Harold, King Edward "was, in fact, advising Harold to stay away from Normandy; but that Harold nevertheless chose to make the journey at considerable risk to himself, in the hope of obtaining the release of his captive kinsmen."[154]

King Edward had, it is acknowledged, promised the throne to William, Duke of Normandy. But on his deathbed, he changed his mind and named Harold, Earl of Wessex his successor. "Under Norman law Edward's earlier choice of William would have been regarded as final and irrevocable. In England, the custom was different. ... A gift made by an Englishman at the point of death ... was regarded as valid and binding. ...In the absence of an agreed system of supranational law to determine which nation's law should apply, the dispute between two such proud and determined warriors as William and Harold could only be resolved by war."[155]

The Bayeux Conspiracy

The history of this conflict is portrayed in the Bayeux Tapestry, a long embroidered cloth 20 inches wide and two-thirds the length of a football field, which presents the narrative in what we might think of as cartoon form. The cloth, incorrectly called a tapestry, actually consists of wool yarn embroidered onto a linen backing using two kinds of stitches: a stem stitch for outlining shapes and creating the lettering, and couching, in which a piece of material is laid across the backing and stitched into place.

The victorious Normans dictated the content of the tapestry but the actual embroidery took place in England, which had the better craftsmen. One recent theory proposes that the English seam-stresses introduced a subversive subtext suggesting that the act of fealty sworn by Harold to William had been obtained under duress, and was therefore invalid. "It is a subversive account in which the Norman claim to the English throne, and much of the propaganda that the Normans were circulating is systematically contradicted."[156] "The tapestry tells us that the Norman claim to the throne was built upon a lie. It was the lie that near the end of his reign King Edward sent Harold to Normandy in order to confirm William's status as the next king. Harold had journeyed to the continent on his own account but foolishly he swore an oath in William's favour in order to extract himself from his prolonged and dangerous stay in Normandy."[157]

Regardless of which version we accept, the Norman Conquest had great consequences for western culture, replacing the Scandinavian influence in England with the Norman and transforming the English language as Anglo-Norman replaced Old English. "For hundreds of years the two languages existed side by side, French for the richer classes, English for those of middling status and the poor. ... Many living animals continue to be called by their old English names (sheep, cow, ox, deer) whereas once cooked and served up on the tables of the gentry they acquired names derived from the French (mutton, beef, veal, bacon, venison.)"[158] The Anglo-Saxon aristocracy disappeared, as William the Conqueror confiscated the lands of the English nobles who had fought with Harold and redistributed them to his Norman supporters.

Walter Benjamin's observation that "History is written by the victors" encounters complications in the apparent ambiguities embroidered into the Bayeux Tapestry.

Song of Roland, ca. 1100

Chanson de Geste

Tales of a hero's exploits, passing from one generation to the next, formed the basis of the 11th century *chansons de geste*, or songs of heroic deeds, performed by French travelling minstrels, accompanied by a medieval bowed fiddle. These songs depicted an unreal epic universe of colossal battles fought by warriors of extraordinary strength with magnificent horses and incomparable swords, all for the sake of valor and glory. We observe these features in the *Song of Roland*, a feudal epic of a masculine world "permanently geared to warfare."[159]

Historicity

We have cited several works that emerge from an oral tradition, including the works of Homer and *Beowulf*. In those cases, we have no way of distinguishing between historical fact and the poet's invention. Virtually the only information we have about the Trojan War, for example, comes from *The Iliad*. The *Song of Roland*, by contrast, provides a unique opportunity to observe the elaboration of a story over time since it is based on an actual incident about which we have independent information, a minor military skirmish called the Battle of Roncevaux Pass in 778. It may be enlightening to compare essential plot elements from the Song of Roland with what we learn in independent accounts.

Historicity of the *Song of Roland*	
Known fact	*Song of Roland*
Roland an army prefect	Roland depicted as the nephew of Charlemagne, the greatest warrior in the world
Defeat by a guerrilla army of Christian Basques	Defeat by 400,000 Muslim Saracens
Opportunistic ambush	Betrayal by Count Ganelon, Roland's stepfather
Charlemagne, age 38, rides north to attack the Saxons	Charlemagne, a snowy-bearded king 200 years old, returns to Spain to avenge the death of his knights

We note in particular how a small guerrilla army of Christian Basques has been transformed into a vast horde of Muslim infidels.

In the story, Roland has been appointed to lead the rear guard of Charlemagne's army. The critical moment of the battle occurs when Roland realizes the force has been ambushed. His companion Oliver urges Roland to sound his horn, named Oliphant, to summon Charlemagne. Roland, in a terrible error of judgment, claims such an act to be dishonorable. After most of his troops have been slaughtered, he finally reconsiders and blows the horn.

"The myth-making process itself militates against realism. Given that Roland must die, Christians are in the right, pagans in the wrong, Charles is Emperor, treachery must be punished, and so on, [the author] is constrained to make his story line conform to these inflexible parameters. On the other hand, he obviously feels free to elaborate the legend, to create new characters and situations, and to make legendary personages behave according to his poetic vision."[160]

Feudal Values

In the black-and-white morality of the Middle Ages, the highest virtue was loyalty and the direst evil betrayal. Roland epitomizes loyalty in his relationship with Charlemagne. "Roland's unswerving determination to play the role assigned to him and his exemplary death are Christlike and were intended to edify."[161] "Rash, arrogant, generous, outspoken to a fault, loyal, affectionate, and single-minded, he has all the qualities that endear a captain to his men and a romantic hero to his audience."[162] Ganelon personifies "treachery, a notion even more abhorrent in medieval society, which was structured on the basis of solemn vows of allegiance, than it is today."[163]

In contrast to the pagan world of *Beowulf*, the *Song of Roland* "is not merely Christian in subject; it is Christian to its very bones. ... And it is a Christianity as naive and uncomplicated as might be found at any time in the simplest village church."[164] For the author of this tale, "God has chosen Charlemagne and the Franks for a special task, that of establishing his rule throughout the world by means of armed conquest or conversion. ... The hero's suffering and death is an imitation of Christ, and his sacrifice constitutes a new kind of martyrdom."[165]

The *Song of Roland* offers an unusual insight into the process by which historical events could be translated into literature in the form of a *chanson de geste*.

Rise of Polyphony, *Alleluia Justus ut palma*, ca. 1100

Musica Enchiriadis

The medieval habit of embellishment, manifest in the scribal art of decorating illuminated manuscripts, extends to musical performance. "Beginning as an elaboration of plainchant, polyphony served almost exclusively as a means of increasing the splendor and solemnity of church services from the ninth century until well into the thirteenth."[166] When higher and lower voices sing the same melody they sound pitches separated by the interval of an octave. It required only a little imagination to think of doubling a plainsong melody at the interval of the fourth or fifth, the principal consonant intervals in the Middle Ages. This practice, called parallel organum, is described in the *Musica enchiriadis*, a treatise dating from the ninth century. The principal voice would sing the original plainchant while the so-called organal voice would sing at the interval of a fifth above it, matching the plainchant note for note.

Ad Organum Faciendum

Over time singers experimented with variations on strict parallel organum, and by around 1100 instructions for creating organum had been written down in a kind of recipe book called *Ad organum faciendum* (On Making Organum). We recall that a performance of plainsong included portions for a cantor or group of soloists and portions sung by the entire choir. As a rule, for example, a soloist would introduce the first line of the plainsong, partially to remind the other singers of the piece they were about to perform.

According to the rubric presented in *Ad organum faciendum*, the added polyphonic line, or organum, decorated those portions of the plainsong typically reserved for solo singers. As a rule, one note of organum would appear over each note of the original plainsong, but instead of being restricted to a single interval, the organal voice could make the interval of a unison, a fourth, a fifth, or an octave above the plainsong.

Alleluia Justus ut palma

In order to illustrate the procedure for making organum, the author of the *Ad organum faciendum* used the plainsong *Alleluia Justus ut palma*, named for the opening words of the text, "Alleluia. The righteous shall flourish like a palm tree and shall multiply like a cedar." In the first section of the organum, shown below, the organal voice follows the plainsong step by step except for a decorative melisma leading up to a unison on the final note. In the absence of any indications of rhythm we assume that the Alleluia was performed as a succession of even notes.

In this simple procedure, presumably the written version of an improvised practice, we see the roots of polyphony. "The invention of polyphony was undoubtedly the most significant event in the history of Western music. Once the concept had been accepted, organizing of the vertical (harmonic) dimension of music became a major preoccupation of both theorists and composers. … This would seem to be wholly justified, since it is precisely the systematic organization of vertical sounds that distinguishes Western music from all other musics, whether they be the products of primitive peoples or of highly sophisticated Oriental cultures. The distance between a work of the late twelfth century and one of the twentieth may seem immense. But the latter could not have been written if the development of the former had never taken place. And both stand in opposition to plainchant in their concern with the combination of simultaneous musical sounds."[167]

Being chosen as a textbook model assured immortality for *Alleluia Justus ut palma* as an exemplar of the embellishment of plainsong, a critical step in the development of polyphony.

Connections: Faith

The word faith describes two aspects of thought in the eleventh century that we would now separate into sacred and secular, a division that would not have seemed so apparent in the Middle Ages. Faith describes strong religious beliefs or a belief in the existence of God. Faith in the sense of fidelity describes allegiance to a duty or to a person, the foundation of feudalism.

St. Anselm devotes the *Proslogion* to prayerful expressions of faith as well as an ontological proof of God's existence. The Bayeux Tapestry explains the historic Battle of Hastings in terms of a betrayal of faith. From the perspective of the victorious Normans the conflict arose because Harold broke sacred bonds of fealty sworn to William the Conqueror. The Song of Roland glorifies the fidelity of Roland to Charlemagne and condemns the actions of the traitorous Ganelon. In this context, the development of polyphony may be seen as an act of faith, the improvised embellishment of sacred plainsong.

12th Century

Context

Crusades

During the twelfth century, the Christian church, approaching the apex of its power and influence, sponsored a series of Crusades, in an effort to recover the Holy Land from the Muslims. While unsuccessful in meeting their announced aim, the Crusades fostered important avenues of East-West trade. This trade brought not only new goods—spices, ivory, jade, diamonds, apples, oranges—but also new knowledge—algebra, optics, medical knowledge.

"The crusades fused three characteristic medieval impulses: piety, pugnacity, and greed. All three were essential. Without Christian idealism, the crusades would have been inconceivable, yet the dream of liberating Jerusalem from 'the infidel' and reopening it to Christian pilgrims was reinforced mightily by the lure of new lands and vast wealth. The crusaders were provided a superb opportunity to employ their knightly skills in God's service—and to make their fortunes in the bargain."[168]

"The conduct of the Crusaders was shocking—not only to modern sensibilities, but equally to contemporaries. ... They fleeced their subjects to fill their coffers. ... The cost in wasted lives and effort was incalculable. ... Murder and massacre in the service of the Gospel were commonplace. Seventy thousand civilians were said to have been butchered in cold blood in the initial sack of Jerusalem. ... In short, the Crusaders brought Christianity into disrepute."[169]

Universities

This same period saw the rise of European universities, perhaps the most important aspect of what has been called the renaissance of the 12th century. Prior to this time, intellectual life in Europe had been largely confined to the monasteries and mostly concerned with the study of liturgy and prayer. Now, independent centres of learning arose, supported by students (Bologna), the church (Paris), or the state (Oxford, Cambridge).

Celebrity professors lectured to students according to a curriculum based on the classic model of the trivium and the quadrivium. The trivium, the foundation of the medieval liberal arts education, comprised grammar, logical argument (dialectic) and rhetoric. Mastery of these subjects prepared students to undertake the quadrivium, consisting of arithmetic, geometry, astronomy and mathematically-based music theory. After finishing this basic program students could pursue advanced degrees in law, medicine or theology, the most prestigious and the most difficult discipline.

Mystics

While Crusaders sought to please God through militant activism, others sought union with God through withdrawal into monastic life. In contrast to intellectual proofs of God's existence, they sought direct experience of God's presence.

Hildegard von Bingen was a noted composer, musician, writer and philosopher who spent her life among the women attached to a Benedictine monastery in Germany. Though known for her theological wisdom, her influence "rested largely on a distinctly nonintellectual activity: mysticism. Always an element in Christian devotional life, mysticism became particularly important during the Central Middle Age, when the most celebrated Christian visionaries were women." While Hildegard had experienced visions since the age of three, she felt constrained to conceal this gift until a life-changing event persuaded her to breach her silence. *"And it came to pass ... when I was 42 years and 7 months old, that the heavens were opened and a blinding light of exceptional brilliance flowed through my entire brain. And so it kindled my whole heart and breast like a flame, not burning but warming ... and suddenly I understood the meaning of expositions of the books."* Hildegard's fame spread, and when consulted on theological matters, she answered "with wisdom, eloquence, and learning acquired in her monastic schooling *and* the power of direct revelation from God."[170]

Those who followed the path of mysticism were particularly attracted to the most mysterious aspects in the life of Jesus including his Transfiguration, which briefly revealed his heavenly glory, his Resurrection, and his appearances to his disciples and others after his death. Christian mystics adopted the practice of *lectio divina*, or prolonged meditation upon a brief passage of Scripture.

St. Sernin de Toulouse, ca. 1080-1120 PLATE 7

Pilgrims and Penance

Throughout the Middle Ages faithful Christians would make pilgrimages to sites associated with their beliefs. Jerusalem and Rome naturally ranked highest as desirable destinations but a pilgrimage to the Holy Land often raised insurmountable geographical obstacles. Many pilgrims chose instead to follow the Way of St. James, or Camino de Santiago, to the cathedral of Santiago de Compostela in northwest Spain, said to house the remains of St. James. Today one can comfortably complete the 800-kilometer journey on foot in about thirty days, spending the night in hostels all along the route. In the Middle Ages this pilgrimage presented a greater challenge. "It lasted several months and led them over hundreds of miles of toil and privation. They could never be sure of arriving at Santiago safely, let alone of ever seeing their homes again. It therefore comes as no surprise that the pilgrims also paid visits to other saints on the way, asking for their help and resting for a few days before continuing the journey to Santiago. For this reason, a large number of monasteries flourished along the route at this time."[171]

"Churches and monasteries en route were able to make considerable material gain from providing accommodation and facilities to worship. The wealth generated among the pilgrimage routes during the eleventh and twelfth centuries enabled religious communities to build vast new churches. Masons and sculptors were in constant demand and, understandably, frequented these routes and spread the new Romanesque style along the routes to Compostela from the 'Ile de France.'"[172] Why would anyone deliberately undertake such risks? The Church decreed that pilgrimages could serve as powerful instruments of penance for sins one had committed during one's life. The arduous trek to Santiago de Compostela was no sightseeing expedition but an act of preservation of one's immortal soul.

Romanesque Symmetry and Solidity

The largest of these "pilgrimage churches," St. Sernin de Toulouse, begun in 1080, displays the characteristics of Romanesque architecture. "The key architectural ingredient in Romanesque churches was the round arch—borrowed from Greco-Roman times—which appears in the portals, windows, arcades, and stone roofs of Romanesque buildings. The chief architectural achievement of the style was to replace flat wooden ceilings with roofs made of stone vaulting; this created buildings that were less susceptible to fire, more artistically unified, acoustically resonant, and massively built, since the immense downward and outward thrusts of these heavy roofs required huge pillars and thick supporting walls."[173]

Aisles, Ambulatories and Chapels

The influx of pilgrims brought much-needed income to the churches but also threatened to interfere with the churches' priestly functions. "Ways were sought of directing the pilgrims so that those coming in and out of the church did not cause disturbance detrimental to the liturgy of the monks in the choir."[174] Ambulatories were created that "led around the saint's tomb in the crypt, allowing the pilgrims to descend the stairs from one side aisle and return up via the other. In both these churches the ambulatory was extended to include a round or octagonal lady chapel behind an aisled approach."[175] In this way pilgrims could arrive at will, offer prayers and depart without affecting liturgical activities in the nave.

"At Toulouse one clearly can see how the builders provided additional space for curious pilgrims, worshipers, and liturgical processions alike. They increased the length of the nave, doubled the side aisles, extended the aisles around the eastern end to make an ambulatory, and attached a series of radiating chapels (for the display of relics) opening directly onto the ambulatory and the transept. In addition, upper galleries, or tribunes, over the inner aisle and opening onto the nave, accommodated overflow crowds on special occasions."[176]

The basilica of St. Sernin de Toulouse shows how a concern for what might nowadays be called the tourist trade could influence the very nature of ecclesiastical architecture.

Peter Abelard, *Sic et non*, 1121

Challenge of Aristotle

The rediscovery of Aristotle in the twelfth century represented a huge challenge to Islamic, Jewish and Christian religions. Aristotle posits a mechanistic God who is simply a prime mover, not an actor in human history. If true, this means that prayer is useless; providence and the grace of God do not exist. Aristotle's assumption that matter has always existed constitutes a denial of the Christian idea that God created the universe out of nothing. Aristotle's belief in a general, but not personal, immortality contradicts the Christian belief in the immortality of the soul.

Scholasticism and Dialectic

Philosophical debate in the twelfth century occurred not in the pages of scholarly journals but in university classrooms and campuses where students did not hesitate to take on their professors. "Very early on Abelard established his place as one of the most celebrated masters in Paris by challenging—and then defeating—his teachers and rivals in public disputation. In some cases, he literally drove these rivals out of business: he stole their students and set up his own schools (the first when he was only twenty-five) just down the road from them."[177]

The scholastic method consisted of separating ideas into individual units called *sententiae*, then juxtaposing apparently contradictory ideas. After that, the scholastic philosophers would endeavour to explain away the apparent contradiction by pointing out the ambiguous meanings of words or by applying the laws of logic to show that the apparent contradiction was only subjective with the reader.

Sic et Non

In *Sic et non* (Yes and No) from 1120, Abelard gathered thoughts from the church fathers and from the Bible for discussion and analysis. He assembled a series of 158 questions, each furnished with quotations that would support the answer "yes," and other quotations that would support the answer "no." In the prologue to the book, he outlines the methods by which one might harmonize these apparently inconsistent remarks.

"There are many seeming contradictions and even obscurities in the innumerable writings of the church fathers. Our respect for their authority should not stand in the way of an effort on our part to come at the truth. The obscurity and contradictions in ancient writings may be explained upon many grounds, and may be discussed without impugning the good faith and insight of the fathers. A writer may use different terms to mean the same thing, in order to avoid a monotonous repetition of the same word. Common, vague words may be employed in order that the common people may understand; and sometimes a writer sacrifices perfect accuracy in the interest of a clear general statement. Poetical, figurative language is often obscure and vague. ... In view of these considerations, I have ventured to bring together various dicta of the holy fathers, as they came to mind, and to formulate certain questions which were suggested by the seeming contradictions in the statements."[178]

Abelard did not actually employ the method himself but simply provided the materials for discussion. One example from the Prologue illustrates how the method might be applied to an apparent contradiction within the gospels. *"Again, let us explain simply why in Matthew and John it is written that the Lord was crucified at the third hour but in Mark at the sixth hour. There was a scribal error, and in Mark too the sixth hour was mentioned, but many read the Greek* epismo *as* gamma.*"*

Question 16, for example, takes up a basic question in the Aryan heresy: "The Son may be said to be begotten, not just born, of the Father ... or not."

Abelard then presents a collection of pertinent writings including the following:

- "Ambrose *On Faith*, to the Emperor Gratian: *These things must not be thought to be physically in God; the Son is incomprehensibly begotten; the Father begets without feeling, and yet he begets of himself and beyond understanding, so that true God begets true God.*
- "Jerome, on the definition of the catholic faith in the Nicene Creed: *The Savior himself says in the Gospel that he was born, always, from the substance of the Father (John 3:6) 'What is born of flesh is flesh, and what is born of spirit is spirit.'*
- "Augustine, *On the Trinity*, book five, chapter thirteen: *If the begetter is the beginning of that which he begets, the Father is the beginning of the Son, because he begets him.*"

Sic et non reflects Peter Abelard's utter confidence in the underlying logic and ultimate consistency of Christian doctrine.

Chrétien De Troyes, Lancelot, The Knight of the Cart, 1168

Courtly Romance

Eleanor of Aquitaine enjoyed the unique position of being both Queen of France and Queen of England with two successive husbands. Her court at Aquitaine is associated with the development of courtly love and, with it, the courtly romance. According to the rubrics of courtly love, the knight would pledge his allegiance not to a noble lord but to a high-born lady like Eleanor. His acts of valor would be performed on her behalf, his exploits and quests carried out to gain her favour. Historians disagree about whether these liaisons were sexual or platonic, or whether courtly love was simply a literary fiction, but Eleanor's invention gave birth to some remarkable works of literature, the chivalric romances.

Ambivalent Treatment of Women

We notice a peculiarly ambiguous treatment of women in the chivalric romance. On the one hand, as we read in *Lancelot*, knights were obliged to protect innocent women. "As *Lancelot* appears to be telling us, the service of Woman, Love, and the Heart constitutes a proper—perhaps even the proper—venue of authentic knightly prowess."[179]

Which customs were, in those days,
That a knight finding a lady
Or a girl, alone and unguarded
Should sooner cut his own throat
Than do her the slightest harm

But if the lady is protected by an escort and the knight defeats him, she becomes no more than a piece of chattel.

... But when a knight
Was her escort, that knight could be challenged—
And should he be beaten in battle,
Conquered by force of arms,
The winner, without any shadow
Of disgrace, could do as he liked
With the woman.

At one point in the story, a knight who has won a young girl by this means becomes indignant when asked to release her.

Deeply upset, the young
Knight swore he'd never
Surrender what he'd won, declaring,
"Let God deprive me of all
Life's pleasures, if I let her go!
It was I who won her, and I'll
Keep her: she belongs to me!"

Submissive Author, Submissive Knight

Lancelot, the Knight of the Cart was written by Chrétien de Troyes toward the end of the 12th century according to specific instructions given by Eleanor's daughter. "Chrétien describes his obedient service to the countess with the same language he later uses for Lancelot's submission to the queen."[180]

Because my lady of Champagne
Wants me to start a new
Romance, I'll gladly begin one,
For I'm completely her servant
In whatever she wants me to do.[181]

Lancelot performs heroic deeds, the same as any other chivalric hero, but the distinctive character of Chrétien's Lancelot, as specified by his royal patron, lies in the knight's complete submission before the lady. Lancelot faces heroic hazards in the form of the Perilous Bed, the Fiery Lance, the amorous maiden, the Sword Bridge, and a duel with the queen's abductor. These adventures provide exciting reading. But the distinctive element of Lancelot lies in its subtitle, "the knight of the cart." In medieval times, the cart contained only convicts. For a knight to ride in a cart would be the deepest humiliation.

Any knight who's ridden in a cart
Has lost his honor forever.

Yet this is what the lady requires Lancelot to do. "The principal characters in Chrétien's other romances are motivated above all by the desire to avoid being shamed. For the male roles, this entails a determination never to act in a cowardly fashion on the battlefield, whether in war or in the mock warfare of the tournament. But Lancelot willingly abases himself in the tournament of Nouauz by going badly at the behest of Guinevere, who uses the command as an identity test. As a result, he misses his blows in the joust, avoids engagements, and attracts the mockery of the crowd.[182] For two days Lancelot suffers humiliation before the queen, rejoicing in Lancelot's complete submissiveness, orders him to fight his best.

Then Lancelot turned his horse,
Heading straight for a singularly
Elegant knight and striking
So hard that he hurled him to the ground
At least a hundred feet
Away. Wielding sword
And spear alike, he fought
So well that whoever was not
Engaged in combat was delighted
To watch him, and even many
In the middle of the battle were dazzled,
Thrilled to see how he tumbled
Knights to the ground, and their horses
Falling with them.

One marvels at Eleanor of Aquitaine's intellect in inventing a parallel universe to feudalism in the form of the courtly romance and her force of will in persuading Chrétien to bring it to literary life.

Leonin, *Viderunt omnes*, 12th century

Ars Antiqua

The *ars antiqua* is a retrospective term, like "acoustical guitar" or "natural turf," invented in order to differentiate it from its 14-century successor, the *ars nova*. Paradoxically, we look at music of the *ars antiqua* in terms of its rhythmic innovations. Until the time of Leonin, polyphony—two or more lines of independent melody sounding simultaneously—occurred through improvisation. "A composer of music in modern society differs greatly from his medieval counterpart, and the farther back one goes the more this is true. Indeed, it can be fairly said that prior to the twelfth century there were no composers of polyphony, only performer-creators, so closely united was composition to performance. ... Only in the twelfth century, when a system of notation was developed that made it possible to isolate and manipulate in graphic form the two essential elements of music—pitch and rhythm—was it possible to create a work *a priori*, outside the realm of performance."[183]

We know about Leonin's work from the accounts of an anonymous student, writing a hundred years later. Leonin "is credited by the theorist Anonymus 4 with perhaps the single greatest achievement in the development of early polyphony, the creation of the so-called *Magnus liber*. This collection is believed to constitute the matrix in which polyphony was transformed from performance practice into 'composition' in the modern sense of the word."[184]

Rhythmic Modes

This transformation from improvisation to composition required the invention of a rhythmic practice whereby two or more independent lines could be coordinated. "What is most important for the history of western music, the works of Leoninus were conceived and notated in varying degrees according to a rudimentary system of musical meter and rhythm, the rhythmic modes. While it would be rash to claim that Leoninus 'invented' meter and rhythm—such musical elements are as primordial as music itself—nevertheless it is in his *Magnus liber organi* that can discern for the first time a conscious and thoroughgoing attempt to notate as well as generate meter and rhythm."[185]

The rhythmic modes, derived from metrical principles of Greek prosody, consisted of a set of six patterns:

Pattern	Name	Modern notation
1. Long-short	Trochee	♩ ♪
2. Short-long	Iamb	♪ ♩
3. Long-short-short	Dactyl	♩. ♪ ♩
4. Short-short-long	Anapest	♪ ♩ ♩.
5. Long-long	Spondee	♩. ♩.
6. Short-short-short	Tribrach	♪♪♪

Theorists described six rhythmic modes but in practice only modes 1, 3 and 5 were commonly used.

Organum and Discant

We recall that plainsong could be either syllabic (one note to a syllable) or melismatic (more than one note to a syllable). Thus, in the opening of the *Viderunt omnes* chant, the first syllable of "omnes" is melismatic.

Leonin's organum duplum, or two-part organum, on this chant displays two different styles. He writes florid organum when the original plainsong is syllabic. The tenor sustains the pitches of the plainsong while the duplum sings florid organum above it. But when the plainsong becomes melismatic—as in the first syllable of "omnes"--performance in florid organum would take too long, so discant style is used. In this case, the tenor moves in the even notes of mode 5 while the duplum performs in mode 1, with occasional used of mode 6.

"In essence, the Notre Dame School's unique contribution consisted of replacing the even, unmeasured flow of earlier polyphony (and plainchant) with recurrent patterns of long and short notes. The different patterns of these notes are known as *rhythmic modes*, and they are identified by what we now call *modal notation*. ... The introduction of rhythm and meter may be credited to Leonin, but the complete system of rhythmic modes and modal notation took longer to develop."[186]

The logical organization of rhythmic patterns in the form of rhythmic modes proved to be an essential step in the development of polyphony, that emblematic characteristic of western music.

Connections: Rediscovery

Rediscovery—finding again something that had been lost, ignored or forgotten—can be associated with each of the elements in our repertoire of the twelfth century. The Romanesque cathedral rediscovered and re-applied the round arch associated with Greco-Roman architecture. Scholasticism emerged from the rediscovery of Aristotle which posed a challenge to theologians in the late Middle Ages. Peter Abelard brought to light writings from the earliest church fathers to the present as potential material for resolving theological questions. Chrétien de Troyes worked on French translations of the Roman poet Ovid, and one scholar has drawn connections between Chrétien's tale of the submissive knight, *Lancelot, the Knight of the Cart,* and Ovid's *Servitium amoris* (the slave of love). The rhythmic modes, Leonin's great contribution to the development of polyphony, derive from principles of Greek prosody. Whether one wants to consider these links as examples of rediscovery, or whether they might better be described as revival, the connections between twelfth century culture and that of the distant past seem inescapable.

13th Century

Context

Agricultural Improvements

The prosperity of thirteenth-century Europe rested in large measure on improvements to agricultural practices that permitted greater yields from the same amount of land. The single most important contribution to agriculture came with the adoption of the heavy plow capable of cutting through rich soil and equipped with a metal blade designed to withstand hard use.

Norman Davies cites five developments that were necessary before the iron plow could come into its own. "First was the breeding of heavy farm-horses—an offshoot of the Carolingian charger. Second was the horse-collar ... which enabled the draft animal to haul maximum loads without being throttled. Third was the horseshoe, adopted ca. 900. Fourth was the cultivation of oats, the workhorse's staple food. Most important of all was the introduction of the three-field system of crop rotation. The change from the two-field to the three-field plan greatly improved crop yields while increasing the peasant family's productivity by at least 50 percent."[187]

Order of St. Francis

St. Francis of Assisi, one of the most beloved figures of the Middle Ages, experienced a vision that led him to renounce his heritage of wealth and embrace a life of poverty. Pope Innocent III, perhaps seeking to defuse increasing criticism of the church's affluence, authorized the Order of Franciscans in 1210 as a mendicant order devoted to preaching the word among common people. Rejecting the need for learned traditions, the Franciscans centered their teaching on personal experience, Christian love, and simple stories.

"Francis and his followers [wandered the countryside] preaching, serving, and living in self-conscious imitation of Christ. ... The Franciscan ideal was based above all on the imitation of Christ. Fundamental to this ideal was the notion of poverty, both individual and corporate. The Franciscans subsisted by working in return for their food and other necessities."[188] "The extraordinary fame of St. Francis was both evidence of the desire for simple spirituality and an inspiration for those who sought a different kind of Christianity. ... He had no desire to challenge the authority of the Church; instead he founded an order of monks who, rather than shutting themselves away from the world, would work among the people."[189]

Albigensian Crusade

Our modern embrace of multiculturalism and tolerance of diversity may hinder us from understanding how strongly the medieval church insisted on orthodoxy and how brutally it could punish heresy. While we may appreciate the urgency with which early Christians addressed troubling doctrinal issues, we may still be perplexed that the church, at the apex of its power in the thirteenth century, should have found it necessary to suppress local variations to the faith. The fate of the Cathars, a sect in the south of France, reminds us of the dangers of totalitarianism in whatever form.

The Cathars, rejecting the material wealth and power of the church, sought to return to the simplicity of the early followers of Jesus. "Their morality stressed a rigorous rejection of all material things—of physical appetites, wealth, worldly vanities, and sexual intercourse—in the hope of one day escaping from the prison of the body and ascending to the realm of pure spirit."[190] "Catharism possessed a number of features which both the common people and aristocracy found appealing. Since the clergy was to have no wealth, the nobility could hope to deprive the church of what property it held. What attracted commoners was the use of the vernacular in a relatively simple liturgical service in which all could participate."[191]

The pope called on the Cathars to renounce this heterodoxy then launched the Albigensian Crusade, a war not against infidel Moslems but against European Christians, which in the space of twenty years eliminated the threat by killing every one of its adherents. An unfortunate side effect of the pope's campaign was the appointment of inquisitors, "endowed with sweeping powers. As they traveled through southern Europe looking for heretics, they employed torture, secret testimony, conviction on slight evidence, denial of legal counsel to the accused, and other practices that far exceeded the carefully defined limits of medieval canon law. To the inquisitors and those who supported them, this excess was absolutely necessary; they exercised a kind of martial law, required by the urgency of the war against heresy."[192] Such weapons, once invoked, proved difficult to surrender in years to come.

Notre Dame Cathedral, 1163-ca. 1270 PLATE 8

Height

The Late Middle Ages witnessed an ecclesiastical building boom. "Between the eleventh and the thirteenth centuries, Europe as a whole experienced a surge of prosperity that was directly reflected in an unprecedented population explosion. ... A feeling of confidence in the future, both material and spiritual, was one of the factors that gave rise to the Gothic era."[193] France, in particular, witnessed the construction of majestic structures whose spires pointed optimistically toward heaven. "From the earliest part of the Gothic era, it was practically inconceivable to build a cathedral that was less than a hundred yards long. This desire for great size was expressed in the building's vertical measure as well. Indeed, a veritable race seemed to define the terms of the relations between cities wanting to proclaim their vitality and economic prosperity through the height of their cathedrals."[194]

Such aspiration required new methods of construction, for the builders of the Gothic cathedrals were exploring new architectural territory. The ogive, or ribbed arch, replaced the heavy barrel vault associated with Romanesque architecture. "It was the ogive alone—later aided by the flying buttress—that enabled men to build more flexibly, more imaginatively, and on a scale unprecedented in European life."[195]

Light

Ever-higher walls introduced a new problem: the cathedral may have been impressively tall but its interior was depressingly dark. Introducing windows required relieving the weight-bearing function of the exterior walls through the addition of so-called flying buttresses. Soon a new competition arose to see how much stone could be replaced by glass without leading to a collapse of the structure. "One way of looking at Gothic architecture is to say that it was characterized by a reduction in the surface area of the masonry walls constituting the building. Bays and windows became larger, and stained glass was used plentifully in the spaces once occupied by walls. The cathedral was gradually transformed from a book of stone into a book of glass."[196]

The construction of Notre Dame had been well advanced when the Second Master demanded a major revision to introduce more light. "From the beginning, the natural illumination of Notre Dame had been deemed inadequate, and as the first third of the thirteenth century came to a close, newer buildings began to make this flaw seem especially troubling. The large windows of more recent structures as well as the less saturated colors of their stained glass, some of which was even executed in grisaille, made for much brighter interiors. The darkness of Notre Dame now became intolerable, for it made the great church seem positively archaic by comparison with the newer buildings. If it was to retain its preeminent architectural status, a way would have to be found to rectify this deficiency. Rebuilding from scratch was out of the question, so a decision was made to enlarge the clerestory windows."[197] "This necessitated a rebuilding of the vaults of the tribune and the addition of even stronger, more extended buttresses against the outer walls."[198]

Financial Foundation

One should not imagine that the medieval cathedral sprang into existence through the voluntary efforts of an army of craftsmen donating their services as an act of Christian piety. A project needing nearly a century to complete rested on a foundation of secure finances. "The cathedral building-site required a vast and specialized workforce as well as a multitude of suppliers to provide the stone, wood, and iron workshops with ample quality materials. While the building sites depended unquestionably on the rhythm of the seasons, they operated primarily according to the rhythm of money. When there was a lack of it, the building site stood still for some time—a week, entire months, or even years."[199]

The Church was not above exploiting its role as gatekeeper to heaven in order to finance cathedral construction, in the process drawing on funds on which the disadvantaged faithful depended. "Declaring that one wanted to bequeath one's land and one's wealth (or even part of it) to contribute to the work on the cathedral meant that one was assured of being remembered in masses and prayers (which was so important for the salvation of the soul) that would be said in this place. The poor and the most destitute were thus the true losers in the great wave of offerings and various kinds of gifts that were now being diverted from strictly charitable purposes to the bishop's church, the church of the whole city."[200]

In contrast to the static symmetry of the Parthenon, the Gothic cathedral fairly bursts from its foundations in heavenward aspiration.

Fibonacci, *Liber abaci*, 1202

Zero

Leonardo of Pisa, better known as Fibonacci, has been described as "the greatest mathematician of the Middle Ages."[201] This description reflects a European bias since Fibonacci's most important accomplishment lay in bringing to the West mathematical procedures already well established in the East. His *Liber abaci* introduced three elements of arithmetic that we now take for granted but without which modern mathematics could never have developed. The first is the Hindu-Arabic system using a single symbol to represent each of the numbers from 1 to 9. Thus, the symbol "8" offers a far more convenient representation than the equivalent Roman numeral VIII. The second is the idea of place value, that the "8" in "81" represents ten times the value of "8" by itself. The third is the concept of zero, which did not exist in Roman notation and which is absolutely necessary to distinguish, say, "8" from "80" or "800." These procedures allowed for multiplication and division in the manner taught to schoolchildren nowadays but which remained impossible otherwise. (Multiplication using Roman numerals required cumbersome repeated addition.)

Rabbits

We most commonly associate the name of Fibonacci with a sequence of numbers that emerge from a problem posed in the *Liber abaci*: "*A certain man had one pair of rabbits together in a certain enclosed place, and one wishes to know how many are created from the pair in one year when it is the nature of them in a single month to bear another pair, and in the second month those born to bear also. ...* Leonardo wanted the reader to assume that once a pair of rabbits becomes fertile, they continue to produce offspring every month."[202]

The so-called Fibonacci sequence appears when we begin counting the rabbits month by month

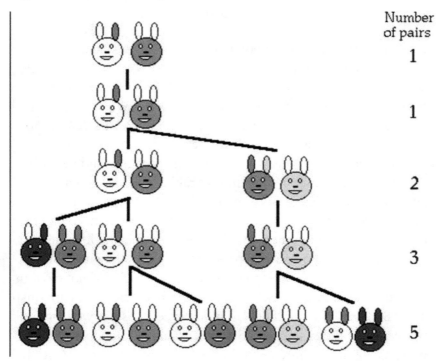

	Number of pairs
	1
	1
	2
	3
	5

We observe that each succeeding term in the sequence results from adding together the two preceding terms. Thus, the next term in the sequence would be 3 + 5 or 8.

Φ (Phi)

The so-called "golden ratio," or Φ (Phi), exists between two numbers if their ratio is the same as the ratio of their sum to the larger of the two numbers. Expressed algebraically, Φ =
$$\frac{a}{b} = \frac{a+b}{a}$$
If we let a = 1 and solve the resulting equation, Φ comes out to be 1.6180339 ... (an indefinitely repeating decimal). A great deal of nonsense has been written about Φ. The "golden ratio" does not lie at the heart of the pyramids nor of the Parthenon. Picture frames whose dimensions display the golden ratio are not necessarily more pleasing than any other, and "discovering" the golden ratio in works of art usually involves a shameful amount of fudging, based on the "false notion that the Golden Ratio provides a universal canon of ideal beauty."[203] But Φ does have a strong connection with the Fibonacci sequence, because the ratio between successive elements in the sequence becomes closer and closer to Φ as the numbers become greater. For example, 233 divided by 144—numbers that appear later in the Fibonacci sequence—gives a value of 1.6180555, accurate to four decimal places.

The Fibonacci sequence, and thus Φ, also turn up unexpectedly in other mathematical problems. "A child is trying to climb a staircase. The maximum number of steps he can climb at a time is two; that is, he can climb either one step or two steps at a time. If there are n steps in total, in how many different ways, C_n, can he climb the staircase? If there is only one step ($n = 1$), clearly there is only one way to climb it, $C_1 = 1$. If there are two steps, the child can either climb the two steps at once or take them one step at a time; thus, there are two ways, $C_2 = 2$. If there are three steps, there are three ways of climbing: $1 + 1 + 1$, $1 + 2$, or $2 + 1$; therefore $C_3 = 3$. If there are four steps, the number of ways to climb them increases to $C_4 = 5$: $1 + 1 + 1 + 1$, $1 + 2 + 1$, $1 + 1 + 2$, $2 + 1 + 1$, $2 + 2$. For five steps, there are eight ways. ... We find that the number of possibilities, 1, 2, 3, 5, 8, ..., form a Fibo-nacci sequence."[204]

Fibonacci, by organizing and transmitting principles originally associated with commercial computation, provided a basis for the advancement of mathematical number theory.

Gottfried Von Strassburg, *Tristan*, 1210

Unconventional Courtly Love

The story of Tristan and Isolde has its source in Celtic legend. Tristan has been sent to Ireland by his uncle, King Mark of Cornwall, to escort his bride Isolde. During the voyage, Tristan and Isolde accidentally drink a love potion, intended for Isolde and Mark, and fall madly in love. Isolde has every reason to hate Tristan, who killed her uncle Morold. (Never mind that Morold was a nasty piece of work who collected annual tribute from Cornwall in the form of thirty young men to become his slaves.) And Tristan has every reason to respect his oath of fealty to King Mark. He manages to resist the love potion for the duration of the voyage, but upon their arrival in Cornwall the pair become lovers.

Like Chrétien de Troyes, Gottfried von Strassburg seems to en-joy playing with the conventions of the courtly love story. "It may seem strange to a modern reader that in one of the world's great love stories the hero and heroine do not fall in love until halfway through the poem and are permanently separated three-quarters of the way through the poem. Furthermore, the first half of the poem is devoted not to the early history of the lovers but to a description of the life of Tristan alone, preceded by the story of the life and death of his parents."[205] Moreover Tristan, far from being nobly born, is a bastard whose father is dead and whose mother dies in childbirth. In the course of the poem Tristan does indeed kill two giants and a dragon, but he succeeds more through resourcefulness and trickery than through traditional knightly skills.

Synthesis of Opposites

The issues and values clearly belong to the 13th century, but the conflicts and contradictions feel quite modern as Gottfried explores a sequence of opposites. The first is the opposition between joy and sorrow. Tristan's very name, derived from *triste*, the French word for sorrow, reflects the sorrowful circumstances of his birth, as his mother died upon learning of his father's death in battle. When Tristan and Isolde drink the love potion, Gottfried writes, *"The two were one both in joy and in sorrow"*: joy in ecstatic love, sorrow because love and honour are presented as two ideals which Tristan and Isolde are unable to reconcile. The absence of a Christian framework is remarkable for the 13th century. Gottfried's courtly romance adopts an original, almost existential viewpoint: people have to live in a world of misfortune and disappointment without relief in the form of divine intervention.

A second opposition appears between honour and adultery. Though the courtly romance appears to be an exaltation of adulterous love, Tristan and Isolde employ one ruse after another to preserve the appearance of honour with the tacit acceptance of King Mark. Finally, acting reluctantly on the testimony of his courtiers, King Mark puts the queen on trial: an ordeal by red-hot iron. The lovers stage an elaborate charade in which Tristan, disguised as a pilgrim, assists Isolde's disembarkation from a boat and then faints in her lap. At the trial, Isolde avoids death by swearing to the king *"That no man in the world had carnal knowledge of me or lay in my arms or beside me but you, always excepting the poor pilgrim whom, with your own eyes, you saw lying in my arms."*

A third opposition lies in the derivation of the words "potion" and "poison" from the same Latin root. The potion becomes a symbol of fatal passion embodying both the noble and the evil. The love potion leads Tristan to abandon his duty to King Mark and leads Isolde to order Brangäne's death. We note that Tristan is twice wounded by poisoned weapons: on the first occasion, he is healed by Isolde's mother; on the second occasion, he dies because Isolde cannot come in time to heal him. In Gottfried's *Tristan*, we see a dramatic treatment of the conflict between the rules of feudal loyalty and courtly love.

Irony

Tristan seems almost modern in its use of irony. The hero, suffering from a grievous wound, disguises himself as "Tantris" and seeks the assistance of Isolde who, in healing him has healed her worst enemy. Tristan persuades King Mark to seek a bride but then, sent to Cornwall to escort Mark's bride, he becomes a cuckolder.

And then there is that love potion. "The potion has been brewed by the Queen, who, of course, intends it for Mark and Isolde on their wedding night, so that they will be united in love. The fact that the potion is now drunk by Tristan and Isolde is the crowning irony of fate, which reverses all previous trends."[206]

Gottfried von Strassburg reworked an ancient Celtic tale into an ironic critique of the value systems underlying feudal society and chivalric literature.

Perotin, *Sederunt principes*, 13th century

Organum Quadruplum

The same anonymous student responsible for giving us what little information we have on Leonin, described Perotin as "*Mag-*

nus (the Great) and *optimus discantor* (best composer of discant)."[207] Perotin has been celebrated as the first composer to
write four-part polyphony (organum quadruplum), an accomplishment that more than one scholar has been moved to compare
with the construction of the cathedral with which Perotin's music
is associated. "Not only was Perotinus the first to write for four
voices, he was the first to realize a wholly new sound ideal for
sacred vocal polyphony, one perhaps not out of harmony with
the vast, but carefully regulated space of the virtually completed
cathedral."[208] "Never before had musical structures attained
such astonishing dimensions. It would seem that, as the nave of
Notre Dame neared completion, the cathedral's unprecedented
size and magnificence stirred Perotin to fill the vast space with
music of equal splendor. For his successful achievement of this
goal he well deserves to be remembered as Perotin the Great."[209]

Modular Construction

Sederunt principes, Perotin's most celebrated work, takes as its
point of departure the plainsong setting of two verses from Psalm
118: "The princes sat, and spoke against me: they have persecuted me unjustly. Do thou help me, Lord my God: Save me for
thy mercy's sake." How did Perotin turn this brief monophonic
melody into organum quadruplum whose duration in performance exceeds twelve minutes? "Perotinus undertook a radically new approach to musical organization. In his great quadrupla
the expansive and wide-ranging melismas of earlier composers
are replaced by shorter, often symmetrical phrases which, because all voices begin and end together, create blocks or modules
of sound, and these in turn are balanced, shaped, and interposed
to produce a brilliantly original form of musical architecture."[210]
Occasionally all of the upper voices move in the same rhythm.

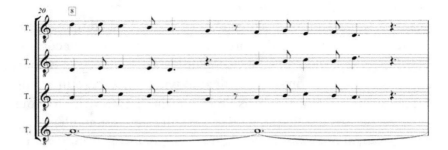

Voice Exchange

Perotin occasionally repeats a passage, redistributing the pitches among the vocal lines, a procedure known as voice exchange. In the following examples, the upper voice remains the same while the two intermediate voices exchange parts.

Followed shortly thereafter by

Such procedures indicate a marked degree of planning on the part of the composer. This is no longer improvised music. "At least some sections must have been composed with fore-knowledge of what all the voices would do, and the exchange of melodies among three voices means that no voice can be omitted without destroying the musical design. We may safely assume, therefore, that Perotin conceived *Sederunt* as a four-voice orga-num and that he planned in advance the complex interrelation-ships of its different voices. ... We shall probably not be far wrong in regarding voice exchange as the basic device from which the Notre Dame composers evolved ways of organizing and integrating the simultaneous melodies of polyphony."[211] "The importance of Perotinus in the history of Western music can hardly be overemphasized. In many ways, he is the first modern composer."[212]

Perotin's majestic organum quadruplum pointed the way from written-down improvisation to structured composition.

Thomas Aquinas, *Summa Theologica*, 1274

Faith and Reason

One of the greatest thinkers to attempt a synthesis of classical and Christian thought was St. Thomas Aquinas. His *Summa*

Theologica of 1274 endeavored to integrate Aristotelian science with Christian revelation, for St. Thomas believed that there is not one truth in science and another in faith, but a single truth that encompasses both. "Since both order in the universe and reason in the human mind were deliberate creations of God, it was a legitimate enterprise, indeed a Christian duty, to use the gift of reason to explore the meaning of God's creation."[213]

"Like Abelard, Aquinas assembled every possible argument, pro and con, on every subject that he discussed, but unlike Abelard he drew conclusions and defended them with cogent arguments. Few philosophers before or since have been so generous in presenting and exploring opinions contrary to their own, and none has been so systematic and exhaustive."[214]

Format of the *Summa*

"Thomas's *Summa Theologica* is one of the great works of Christian thought. … Its three parts consist of no fewer than 2668 articles, or mini-disputations. Each of these mini-disputations follows a standard form: (1) posing the question to be examined (e.g. "Was it fitting for the Word to be incarnated?"), (2) giving a series of arguments against the answer that Thomas intends to support (usually three or four, sometimes more), (3) citing an authoritative text (most often from the Bible) as the proof or principle of the position to be taken (called the *sed contra*), (4) arguing for his own position in what is called the body of the article (*corpus*), and finally (5) answering the objections one by one."[215]

Quinque Viae

Part 1, Question 2 contains the celebrated *Quinque viae*, or five proofs of the existence of God.

Format	**Example** (considerably abridged; Aquinas'

	words in italics)
Question (general topic)	Concerning God
Article (question)	Whether God exists
Videtur ("it seems that"= wrong answers)	*It is implied in the name God that there is a certain infinite goodness: if then God existed, no evil would be found. But evil is found in the world; therefore, it is objected that God does not exist.*
Sed contra ("but on the contrary" = alternative answer)	*But as against this note what is said of the person of God (Exod. III., 14) I am that I am. Conclusion. There must be found in the nature of things one first immovable Being, a primary cause, necessarily existing, not created; existing the most widely, good, even the best possible; the first ruler through the intellect, and the ultimate end of all things, which is God.*
Responsio (response = arguments for correct view)	God's existence can be proved in five ways. The First Way: The argument from motion: whatever is in motion must be put in motion by another. But a thing cannot be both mover and moved. *Therefore, it is necessary to go back to some first mover, which is itself moved by nothing—and this all men know as God.*
	The Second Way: The argument from causes: there can be no effect without a cause. *We find in our experience that there is a chain of causes. ... But if the chain were to go back infinitely, there would be no first cause, and thus no ultimate effect, nor middle causes, which is admittedly false. Hence, we must presuppose some first efficient cause—which all call God.*

	The Third Way: The Argument from Possibility and Necessity: we find in nature things that are possible to be or not to be, i.e., contingent beings. But not all things can be contingent, or else there would be nothing to bring them into being. *Hence there must be presupposed something necessarily existing through its own nature, not having a cause elsewhere but being itself the cause of the necessary existence of other things—which all call God.* The Fourth Way: The Argument from Degree: We find a greater or lesser degree of goodness, truth, nobility or the like. But there must exist something that is the truest, the best, the most noble, etc. *Therefore, there exists something that is the cause of the existence of all things and of the goodness and of every perfection whatsoever—and this we call God.* The Fifth Way: The Argument from Design: We see natural bodies that operate according to a plan. *Therefore, there is something intelligent by which all natural things are arranged in accordance with a plan—and this we call God.*
Refutation of arguments in *videtur*	As Augustine remarks, "since God is the supreme good he would permit no evil in his works unless he were so omnipotent and good that he could produce good even out of evil."[216]

The *Summa Theologica* reflects St. Thomas Aquinas' perfect faith that he possessed the rational weapons to defend Christian truth in its encounter with Aristotle, the greatest pre-Christian intellect.

Connections: Consolidation

Nowadays we commonly use the word consolidation in such phrases as "consolidation of assets" or "consolidation of power," both apt descriptions for the policies of the church in the 13th century. The word also signifies making firm or secure or joining together into one whole. The latter phrase could describe the practice of Perotin in planning a polyphonic structure in four voices, the earliest example of pre-conceived composition as opposed to notated improvisation. Leonardo of Pisa, better known as Fibonacci, compiled a synthesis of all arithmetical knowledge in his *Liber abaci*, a consolidation of mathematical thought to his time. Gottfried von Strassburg's *Tristan* represents a consolidation in the sense of a synthesis of opposites—joy and sorrow; honor and adultery—into one whole, the courtly romance. Consolidation in the senses both of balancing opposing forces and of making firm or secure describes the construction of Notre Dame Cathedral. The later addition of flying buttresses as stabilizing elements brings the synthesis out in the open. Finally, the *Summa Theologica* of St. Thomas Aquinas represents a monumental consolidation of classical and Christian truth.

14th Century

Context

Natural Disasters

A physical chill settled on the 14th century at its very start: the so-called Little Ice Age. The advance of polar and alpine glaciers lasted until about 1700. The resulting shorter growing season meant disaster, for population increases in the previous century had already reached a delicate balance with agricultural techniques.[217] People ended up slaughtering their plow animals and eating their sowing seed just to remain alive, even to the point of abandoning their children to fend for themselves, a plight that may have given rise to the tale of Hansel and Gretel. "In the autumn of 1314, extraordinary rains began to fall, rains that were the prelude to several years of very cold and wet winters. ... Famine came, and it lasted for seven hard years, from 1315 to 1322. ... By the time it ended, the Great Famine—the worst famine in European history—had carried away at least 10 percent of the population."[218]

The worst was yet to come. "The 'Black Death' of 1347-50 stopped Europe's petty troubles in their tracks. ... It was fueled by a devastating brew of three related diseases—bubonic plague, septicemic plague, and pneumonic or pulmonary plague. The first two variants were carried by fleas hosted by the black rat; the third, airborne variant was especially fast and lethal. ... Crowded tenements and poor sanitation, especially in the towns, provided excellent encouragement for the rats. The result was mass mortality."[219] No one suspected rats and fleas as being the actual carriers and the concept of contagion remained unknown. The Black Death returned several more times in the course of the century, infecting those born since the previous outbreak and lacking immunity. It has been estimated that the Black Death wiped out a third of the population of Europe.

Babylonian Captivity and Great Schism

The fourteenth century represents a period of some embarrassment for the Roman Catholic Church. In 1305 Clement V, a Frenchman named to be pope, declined to serve in Rome and moved the papal court to Avignon. Seven popes, all French, lived and ruled in Avignon over 67 years, an era sometimes referred to as the Babylonian Captivity, after the prolonged exile of the Jewish people in Babylon.

The situation did not improve when Gregory XI moved the papal court back to Rome. After Gregory's death in 1378 the cardinals resolved to elect an Italian pope, Urban VI. They soon regretted their decision and, without removing Urban, elected a new pope, Clement VII, who moved the papal court back to Avignon. This impasse continued even after the death of the two rival popes, as Boniface IX became pope in Rome while Benedict XIII became pope in Avignon. In 1409 the College of Cardinals, despairing of the situation, elected yet another pope, Alexander V. The Great Schism did not end until the Council of Constance replaced all three popes by Martin V in 1414.

Hundred Years' War (1337-1453)

The Hundred Years' War between England and France was a series of battles seeking to resolve the contradiction of a state occupying both sides of the English Channel. Where the French invaded England in the 11th century, the English now invaded and devastated France. William the Conqueror held the throne of England as vassal to the French king (a source of discontent for the English); the English king at times held more land in France than did the French king (a source of discontent for the French).

Norman Davies describes the Hundred Years' War as "a historians' label ... for a long period of troubles. ... Outbreaks of temporary peace punctuated the normal predominance of fighting. And war involved the unbridled license of the soldiery. Medieval military logistics and technology did not facilitate the rapid settlement of disputes. Armies were tiny, the theatres of operations vast. A defeated enemy could easily retire and recoup. Action was directed at local castles and strong-points. Sieges were more common than set battles. The spoils of war were more desired than mere victory."[220]

Judith Bennett notes that war now began to affect ordinary people in unfortunate new ways. "Because infantrymen and archers were more important, peasant boys and men were trained, mustered, and marched off to war. Because armies fought for longer periods over broader areas, forced requisition of food and livestock emptied peasant larders and barns. Because armies were more expensive to feed and maintain, tax burdens grew heavier, year by year. Because military tacticians began to favor strategic devastation, armies deliberately burned fields, razed villages, and ravaged towns. And because gangs of unpaid soldiers terrorized villages and towns during intermittent truces, peace could be as dangerous as war."[221]

Giotto, *Entrance of Christ into Jerusalem*, 1306
PLATE 9

Arena Chapel

In contrast to the usual procedure, in which an artist is engaged to decorate an existing building, Enrico Scrovegni called upon Giotto himself to design the building that would house his frescoes. "The design of the original Arena Chapel was one which reversed the normal order of things by subordinating architecture to decoration. ... Within this creative process, Giotto the painter dominated Giotto the architect, designing a building in which murals, stained glass and architecture were fully integrated."[222]

The frescoes, which cover the walls and ceiling of the chapel, present a series of scenes tracing the life of Christ, the story of Mary, and the Last Judgment. The pictorial decoration has been described as "a carefully conceived, ingeniously accomplished, and perfectly unified scheme in which the design, placement, and function of virtually every element, very often even the most seemingly trivial or marginal, stems from a plan that embraces the entire pictorial program."[223]

Realism of Space

The perfection of perspective as an artistic practice required several centuries but we find early applications of the technique in Giotto's *Entrance of Christ into Jerusalem*, especially in the towers at the right of the scene. Yet for the most part Giotto relies on other techniques to achieve the illusion of three dimensions such as forced perspective (the palm gatherers in the background are smaller than the foreground figures) and overlapping bodies whose combined volume gives a sense of depth. Giotto presents solid figures with the suggestion of anatomical detail beneath their garments. The garments themselves have form and weight, a tactile quality associated with Giotto's art. The two-dimensional halos in the painting represent a holdover from medieval thinking, somewhat incongruous in a painting employing geometrical perspective.

In contrast to the static formal solemnity of the procession, Giotto fills the right-hand side of the painting with comic elements. "The *Entry into Jerusalem* becomes an eruptive celebration that seems to encircle Christ with followers packed behind, children above, crowds ahead, and a cloak underfoot. In the course of this outpouring, Giotto introduces the odd-looking figure of a momentarily blinded child bending over—not in a reverent bow,

but in an effort to free his head and arm, which are caught outside in with his clothes inside out. Even his neighbors seem
comically deformed by their mildly clownish actions. Behind
him, a seemingly limbless mannequin of a man pulls at the sail-
like sleeve of his deflating garment, and below him a turtle-
headed youth hyperextends himself across virtually half the foreground—and on one knee."[224] Giotto's choice of a vantage
point—the viewer's eye level falls in the lower half of the painting—seems to give the spectator a place in the scene. Giotto has
simplified the crowd scene by dividing it into three blocks of
figures, with Christ bridging the gulf between the apostles on the
left and the upward slope of the welcoming crowd on the right.

Realism of Time

Giotto's approach to time represents an innovation in art. To
begin with, the scenes in the Arena Chapel are clearly set in a
contemporary time-frame. "The entire story, and the separate
scenes in detail, are represented in a concrete period, the time in
which Giotto lived. ... Much of the architecture is Gothic, thirteenth or fourteenth century, with sharply pointed arches, porti-
coes, and wooden beams, enhanced by curtains, household
goods, and objects of common use, which bring the narration into the concrete reality of a specific time and an urban space well
known to the faithful who entered the chapel."[225]

In addition, Giotto offers not a static tableau but a scene of bus-
tling activity caught in a particular moment in which "the gently
comic, helter-skelter antics of humankind" convey a strong sense
of movement.[226]   The boys precariously mounted on tree
branches and the central figure rescuing some object from the
donkey's next step contribute to the immediacy of the moment.

By making the image seem to escape into three dimensions and
endowing his figures with the illusion of movement Giotto
makes a radical departure from the static design of medieval art.

William of Ockham, *Sum of Logic*, 1323

Franciscan Poverty

Francis of Assisi was authorized by Pope Innocent III in 1210 to lead a mendicant order dedicated to preaching the word and caring for the poor. "The Franciscans, as a preaching order devoted to teaching about Christianity in part by example, had attempted from their inception to model the first-century activities of Jesus and the Apostles as they imagined them, and so upheld a very serious ideal of communal living and of mendicant poverty. As individuals, they owned no property—no land, no animals, no machinery, no tools, no mechanisms of conveyance, no slaves, nor even food and clothing."[227]

Francis himself could be fairly described as apolitical but later members of the Franciscan order found it increasingly difficult to reconcile the simplicity of Christ's life with the ostentatious acquisition of wealth on the part of the Christian church. William of Ockham, a member of the Franciscan order, became embroiled in controversy when asked to resolve the question known as apostolic poverty. The pope argued that Adam and Eve owned property in the Garden of Eden. William argued that the whole concept made no sense: Adam and Eve had the right to use anything they found in the garden but this did not constitute a property right since it could never have been the basis for a legal claim. Somewhat imprudently, William went on to argue that papal affluence stood in such obvious contradiction to the Christian principle of apostolic poverty that the Pope could be considered a heretic. Not surprisingly, the Pope not only rejected the argument but excommunicated William.

Occam's Razor

Albert Einstein is reported to have said, "Everything should be made as simple as possible, but not simpler." The remark echoes a famous phrase attributed to William of Ockham, *Non sunt multiplicanda entia sine necessitate* ("Entities must not be multiplied beyond necessity.") In other words, given a choice of explanations, prefer the least complicated. This phrase could be aptly applied two centuries later when Copernicus put forward a heliocentric model of the solar system. While his model may not have conformed to the biblical account preferred by the Church, it was undeniably simpler than the Ptolemaic system of cycles and epicycles.

"Occam's Razor is frequently expressed in the statement 'Beings are not to be multiplied beyond necessity.' Ockham himself never puts it that way but often says equivalent things: 'Plurality is not to be posited without necessity;' 'what can happen through fewer principles happens in vain through more;' 'when a proposition is verified of things, more things are superfluous if fewer suffice,' and so on."[228] For theological reasons, Ockham allowed exceptions such as the doctrine of the Trinity, which might otherwise fail the test of simplicity.

William of Ockham did not invent the principle of parsimony. Aristotle wrote that "God and nature do nothing that is pointless." In other words, God avoids wasted effort. This can be considered to be a "metaphysical razor" since it makes claims about the nature of reality. By contrast, Occam's Razor simply provides a guideline for deciding between opposing hypotheses. "Ockham's razor is a methodological principle, not a metaphysical one."[229]

Nominalism

We recall Plato's belief that if different things possessed the same attribute, there must be an abstract Form just as real as the things themselves. Aristotle, by contrast, insisted "that there could not be two worlds, one of Forms, where the source of intelligibility resides, perfect and unchanging, and another where the effects of intelligibility rage, waxing and waning. … For Aristotle, individuals, not general forms, are metaphysically primary."[230]

Given his preference for simplicity, it should come as no surprise that William of Ockham would have sided with the nominalists, who denied the existence of universals, in opposition to the realists, who defended the Platonic model of ideal forms. "Aristotle, and Ockham in his turn, were what we call *empiricists*, people who privilege the role of sensory experience above all else in the production of what is properly called 'knowledge.' Aristotle and most medieval philosophers were thus *direct realists*, believing that we sense, usually directly and unproblematically, the external world around us. … Ockham followed Aristotle in this direct realist view."[231]

William of Ockham's career illustrates what could happen in the Middle Ages when a refusal to compromise before the power of the papacy might lead to excommunication and mortal danger.

Machaut, *Ma fin est mon commencement*, ca. 1360

Ars Nova

What is new about the "new art" of the *ars nova*? In contrast to the relentless triple meter of music composed in the so-called *ars antiqua*, the new music of the fourteenth century permitted duple as well as triple meter. Composers of the *ars nova* exploited this new-found rhythmic freedom to create works of considerable complexity and variety.

Where earlier medieval music accepted only the fourth, fifth and octave as consonances, music of the *ars nova* increasingly treated the interval of the third as a consonance, producing vertical combinations that sound more modern to our ears than music of the *ars antiqua*. Finally, in addition to sacred works based on plainsong, composers of the fourteenth century produced secular music with no reference to the plainsong repertoire.

Self-Referential Rondeau

Guillaume de Machaut's fondness for recondite riddles can be plainly seen—if not actually heard—in his most celebrated rondeau, *Ma fin est mon commencement*. The verse structure of the rondeau calls for a two-line refrain (labelled A B) interspersed with other verses.

Ma fin est mon commence-ment	A	My end is my beginning
Et mon commencement ma fin	B	And my beginning my end.
Et teneure vraiement	a	And the tenor [is sung] in the normal way
Ma fin est mon commence-ment	A	My end is my begin-ning,
Mes tiers chans trois fois seulement	a	My third voice [sings] three times only
Se retrograde et einsi fin	b	Turns back on itself and thus ends.
Ma fin est mon commence-ment	A	My end is my beginning
Et mon commencement ma fin.	B	And my beginning my end.
		[Trans. Virginia Newes]

The chanson associated with the rondeau text consists of two musical sections, indicated by A and B, either in capitals (for the refrain) or small letters (for the verses). Each line of the French text ends on one of two rhymes: "ent" for A and "in" for B.

"The text of 'Ma fin est mon commencement,' unusually for Machaut's puzzle pieces, hides a musical process (rather than a woman's name)."[232] The rondeau "follows the pattern of a riddle: Who am I? Who says *I* in the poem, who pronounces 'my end,' 'my beginning,' 'my third voice'? The poem itself does. Its structure resembling what it is about, the poem poses as a poetico-musical art."[233]

Puzzle Notation

The notation of the rondeau presents a puzzle for the performer. "The textual content of the song itself instructs the singers on how to put the music together. Without reading the poem closely and studying visual clues such as the upside-down text (found in all of the manuscript copies), it would be impossible to sing the song. ... It tells us that the cantus part starts at its end, not its beginning, and that the tenor part can be produced by reading the *cantus* part in its normal way that is, from beginning to end. ... The third voice, the contratenor, is arrived at by reading it forwards, to produce the A section of the contratenor part, and backwards, to produce the B section: taking into account the standard rondeau form (ABaAabAB), the contratenor indeed turns back on itself three times as the poem indicates. ... The text of the cantus part is written upside down to tell the singer to read the music from left to right, since the melody itself is read only backwards and not upside down like the text."[234]

Like the musical puzzles in Machaut's sacred works, the game here is directed at the performer, challenged to extract a three-voice composition from two musical lines. "Perhaps the most remarkable feature of the rondeau is that despite all of these complicated musical relationships and the unusual method of arriving at all of the parts, in performance it unfolds just as a rondeau should, using the same harmonic language, syntax and formal structure projected by Machaut's other rondeaux."[235] Even the most attentive listener will not be able to hear the concealed retrograde relationship. "For the listener, the process remains obscure; it is only the reader who can apprehend the subtleties and intricacies of the song's construction."[236] The score that follows is a modern solution to the puzzle notation.

14th Century

Ma fin est mon commencement

Ver.0.0.3

Guillaume de Machaut
Transcribed by n. nakamura, 2004

Machaut displays his creative gifts, as well as his predilection for puzzles, in both the text and the music of this witty rondeau.

Chaucer, *The Canterbury Tales*, 1380-1390

Unorthodox Pilgrimage

Pilgrims occupied a special place in medieval society. "Set apart from their fellows by a distinctive garb, they served as visible reminders of the essentially ascetic, otherworldly thrust of the Christian religion."[237] Pilgrims dressed unostentatiously, bore identifying symbols, like the shell logo carried by modern travelers along the Camino de Santiago, and were expected to conduct themselves in a reverential manner throughout. "To underscore their spiritual orientation, pilgrims were supposed to make their wills before they left and to give up their worldly wealth. In the eyes of the law they were considered dead: they did not have to pay taxes or tolls nor honor their feudal obligations since, as pilgrims, they owed allegiance only to God and to the saints. They were also expected to pray, to fast, and to give alms to the needy."[238]

The picture presented in *The Canterbury Tales* departs considerably from this model. "Chaucer's pilgrims are not dressed as they should be nor doing what they should be doing: they are wearing bright garments like the Wife of Bath's scarlet hose rather than traditional pilgrims' tunics; they are eating and drinking heartily rather than fasting; they are on horseback rather than barefoot; they are engaging in a storytelling contest rather than praying."[239]

The Wife of Bath, in particular, treats the pilgrimage as a kind of medieval singles cruise rather than a religious event. "On the Canterbury pilgrimage the Wife of Bath may be as intent on finding her sixth husband as on responding to spiritual impulses; other Chaucer pilgrims are drinking heavily, and all are telling and listening to stories, many of which are bawdy. ... Paradoxically then, the underlying idea of a straightforward journey focused exclusively on a spiritual goal—the "way" to salvation—

was undercut by the temptation to make the journey's pleasures— "wandering by the way"—a major priority."[240]

Self-Referential Narrative

The work as a whole consists of twenty-four stories set within a framing tale: from the outset the author has created a level between story and audience. Next, the characters on the pilgrimage comment on each other's stories, functioning as an active audience so that we, as readers, become an audience two levels removed from the story-teller. Chaucer avoids authorial didacticism or moralizing by presenting multiple perspectives.

But what makes *The Canterbury Tales* stand out as an example of literary self-awareness is the way Chaucer portrays his characters through their stories: each tale tells a tale about its teller. The Wife of Bath's Tale includes a queen whom a knight must obey to save his life, an old woman who demands his complete obedience, and the knight's subjection in surrendering a critical choice to his wife's judgment. The Wife of Bath's indomitability comes across in her story, which constitutes a defence of female sovereignty: according to the story, what women most desire is mastery over their partners.

Carnivalesque Inversion

Chaucer's pilgrimage often resembles a carnival. "In the Late Middle Ages carnival activities, though they culminated on Mardi Gras, could last as long as three months and could invoke a wide range of activities. …The carnivalesque is closely linked to the deeply rooted human attempt to create a zone of freedom beyond the strictures imposed by the reigning orthodoxies and power structures, be they secular or religious."[241]

The Wife of Bath appears as a particularly carnivalesque figure. "Her celebratory attitude toward her own sexuality, her willingness to associate herself with the earthy and the physical, her delight in seizing the clerical prerogative of assigning meaning to authoritative texts, her pride in having mastered her first three husbands—all reflect carnival values. We have seen that role reversals and overturnings, specifically of the weak over the strong, were an important part of the festival atmosphere."[242]

Carnival celebrations featured inversions of the social hierarchy such as a fool decked out in bishop's attire and preaching to the crowd. The Wife of Bath thoroughly inverts the traditional subservience of wife to husband. Her tale ends happily when the man accepts what she sees as his proper place:

To their lives' end they lived in perfect joy;
And may Christ Jesus send us husbands who
Are meek and young, and spirited in bed;
And send us grace to outlive those we wed;
And I pray Jesus to cut short the lives
Of those who won't be governed by their wives;
And as for all old and ill-tempered skinflints,
May heaven rain upon them pestilence!

Chaucer invested the oldest form of literature, the telling of tales, with striking novelty by multiplying the levels of speaker, listener, and literary frame.

Connections: Self-awareness

One can only speculate on how the artists of the fourteenth century developed an awareness of their own personality or individuality. Did the succession of catastrophes throughout the century foster a sense of irony in the form of gallows humor? Did the weakening hold of religion allow people to imagine themselves as independent actors and not simply agents of God? Whatever the cause, the works in our repertoire display a self-awareness that forms a strong contrast with the works of previous centuries.

Giotto's *Entrance of Christ into Jerusalem* communicates a consciousness of the spectator not apparent in, for example, the artwork of the Book of Kells. William of Ockham's *Sum of Logic* is a self-referential work of reasoning about reasoning. Machaut's puzzle motet *Ma fin est mon commencement* has a self-referential text portraying a rondeau seemingly aware of itself. Chaucer's *Canterbury Tales* present multiple levels of self-awareness as pilgrims comment on each other's stories and serve as an audience within the framing narrative to which we are the audience.

15th Century

Context

Age of Discovery

The so-called Age of Discovery resulted in a remapping of the world. Christopher Columbus sought unsuccessfully to find a sea route to India, but his misunderstanding of geography led him to call the inhabitants of the Americas "Indians." Columbus committed a double error: he thought the globe considerably smaller than it actually is and that the ocean extended without interruption from Europe to Asia. If the American continents had not existed, the world would have been a lot smaller in diameter. Given the actual size of the globe, if the American continents had not existed, the distance from Europe to Asia would have been too great for his supplies of food and water. Happily, his two errors cancelled each other out.

A few years after Columbus' historic voyage, Vasco da Gama commanded the first ships to sail directly from Europe to India, rounding the southern tip of Africa and opening a direct sea route to Asia. His explorations contributed to Portugal's success as a colonizing power, with outposts in East Africa supporting trade routes to the Far East.

Ferdinand Magellan was the first person to cross the Pacific Ocean, sailing west from Europe to Asia. He is credited with the first circumnavigation of the earth, although the actual voyage was completed by a fellow navigator after Magellan's death in the Philippines. The voyage established the need for an International Date Line when sailors returning in 1522 found their calendars a day behind.

Purgatory and Spanish Inquisition

In addition to the long-established states of heaven and hell, the Middle Ages saw the invention of an intermediate state called purgatory, a painful period often associated with fire. "Although not fully elaborated until the Council of Florence (1438-1445), teachings about purgatory had long influenced the practices of ordinary Christians. Christians undertook a variety of good works to free their own souls and the souls of loved ones from the purifying tortures of purgatory: pilgrimages, appeals to saints, masses for the dead, veneration of relics, charitable bequests, and the purchase of indulgences. Increasingly, salvation seemed a goal that could be achieved through almost mechanistic means. Piety and inner spirituality mattered, of course, but so too did a myriad of pious deeds."[243]

The late fifteenth century also saw the beginning of the Spanish Inquisition. In contrast to the 13th-century inquisition launched by the church against the Cathars, the Spanish Inquisition was begun by Ferdinand and Isabella, sponsors of Columbus' expeditions. While initially intended to test the validity of voluntary Jewish and Moslem conversions to Christianity, the Inquisition eventually obtained conversions through persecution and torture.

Royal Revenue, Royal Power

New military technology in the fifteenth century changed not only the nature of warfare but also the balance of power between the king and the landed aristocrats. Under the feudal system, based on the knight as a fighting unit, the king had to rely on the assistance of sovereign lords in order to wage war. The longbow, developed in the British Isles in the thirteenth century, threatened the knight's dominance since "a skillful archer could kill a knight at two hundred yards. ... To counter these new weapons, the knight kept putting on more armor [which] almost immobilized him. … Against another development, the knight was even more helpless, and that was artillery. This had reached a level of efficiency early in the fifteenth century that doomed the castle. And when the walls of his castle came tumbling down, little remained of the means by which the landed aristocracy had acquired his dominant position. It had come time for him to bow to the superior power of his king and retire to his château or manor house."[244]

The rise of the medieval town, whose trade could be taxed under royal edict, also contributed to the power of the king, who could now raise his own army instead of relying on the feudal levy. "With his greatly increased revenues, the king was also able to maintain a loyal and expanding bureaucracy with which to extend the machinery of royal administration throughout his realm. ... The change in the art of war and the rise of towns helped the king destroy the political autonomy of the landed aristocracy."[245]

Robert Campin, *Merode Altarpiece*, ca. 1425-1438
PLATE 10

Renaissance Realism

We observe in Campin's triptych an advance in the technique of linear perspective. All the parallel lines converge toward a fixed point corresponding to the observer's point of view, a technique which calls attention to the presence of an observer. Notice the ceiling beams and the angle of the bench on which Mary leans, a convergence repeated in miniature in the window shutter. The systematic foreshortening of objects proportional to their distance helps to create the illusion of three dimensions. In this case the convergence of lines has been carried to such an extreme that the book, the candle and the vase look ready to slide right off the table.

We notice many elements of realism in this encounter between the Virgin and an angel in a middle-class Flemish kitchen, the first such portrayal of the Annunciation scene. We note in particular the realistic use of light and shadow. The donors of the commission wait at the gate in the left panel; the cityscape can be seen through the window in the right panel. Mary occupies herself not with cooking or housework—the scene takes place in a kitchen, after all—but with the pious reading of what we assume to be the Bible.

Medieval Symbolism

Religious symbolism fills the domestic scene:

- The tiny figure of Christ, holding a cross, flies down to Mary on the left side of the picture, representing her impregnation by God
- The play of light on the folds of Mary's dress creates a star
- The lilies and water basin symbolize Mary's chastity and purity
- The scroll and book represent the Old and New Testaments: Mary and Christ child are seen as the fulfillment of prophecy
- Unexplained mysteries include the extinguished candle; the four lions in the bench; the missing candle in the candleholder on the hearth.

Joseph's Mousetrap

What on earth is Joseph doing in an Annunciation scene, evidently fashioning a mousetrap? Art historian Meyer Schapiro explains: "This detail of the mousetrap is more than a whimsical invention of the artist, suggested by Joseph's occupation. It has also a theological meaning that was present to the minds of Christians in the Middle Ages, and could be related by them to the sense of the main image of the triptych. St. Augustine, considering the redemption of man by Christ's sacrifice, employs the metaphor of the mousetrap to explain the necessity of the incarnation. The human flesh of Christ is bait for the devil who, in seizing it, brings about his own ruin. The devil exulted when Christ died, but by this very death of Christ the devil was vanquished, as if he had swallowed the bait in the mousetrap. He rejoiced in Christ's death, like a bailiff of death. What he rejoiced in was then his own undoing. The cross of the Lord was the devil's mousetrap; the bait by which he was caught was the Lord's death."

Schapiro goes on to explain the sexual significance of the mousetrap. "In popular magic and folklore, the mouse is a creature of most concentrated erotic and diabolic meaning. It is the womb, the unchaste female, the prostitute, the devil; it is believed to arise by spontaneous generation from excrement or whirlwind; its liver grows and wanes with the moon; it is important for human pregnancy; it is a love instrument; its feces are anaphrodisiac; the white mouse is also the incarnation of the souls of unborn children. ... This conception of the mouse as evil and erotic is shared by the folk and by learned men. In the Renaissance, scholars like Erasmus and Alciati write of the mouse as the image of the lascivious and the destructive. To see the mousetrap of Joseph as an instrument of a latent sexual meaning in this context of chastity and a mysterious fecundation is therefore hardly arbitrary. What is most interesting is how the different layers of meaning sustain each other: the domestic world furnishes the objects for the poetic and theological symbols of Mary's purity and the miraculous presence of God; the religious-social conception of the family provides the ascetic figure and occupation of Joseph; the theologian's metaphor of redemption, the mousetrap, is, at the same time, a rich condensation of symbols of the diabolical and the erotic and their repression; the trap is both a female object and the means of destroying sexual temptation."[246]

The triptych format of the *Merode Altarpiece* turns a solitary encounter between Mary and the angel into a communal event, with Joseph protectively fashioning a mousetrap on one side and concerned neighbors looking in on the other.

Villon, Ballade des dames du temps jadis, 1461

Poète Maudit

Thief, whore-mongerer, murderer, and the greatest poet of his time, François Villon took on the role of a "poet accursed," an outlaw from fifteenth-century Parisian society, celebrating low life rather than courtly love. We see in his work a record of his own troubled vagabond life. In fact, most of the information we have on Villon comes from court files. "Villon was a marginal figure, a poet from the city streets. He wrote about the bliss and calamities of love and sex, about money trouble, drinking, life on the road, and learning to get by. His raw honesty and gritty urban realism has made him a perennial favorite with avant-garde poets."[247] Villon's work abounds with references that would be familiar to fifteenth-century denizens of the Left Bank. "Writing primarily for a small circle of acquaintances, Villon enjoyed making private jokes that only his immediate audience would be able to understand and appreciate."[248]

Aware that his chosen lifestyle might preclude the enjoyment of old age, Villon joked in his poems about ending up on the gallows.

Je suis Françoys, dont il me poise, Né de Paris, emprès Pontoise, Et de la corde d'une toise Sçaura mon col que mon cul poise. (Today we would write "pèse"	France's I am; my lookout's glum. From Paris (near Pontoise) I come And soon my neck, depending from A rope, will learn the weight of my bum.

in place of "poise." The word "toise" refers to a measure of length roughly six and a half feet.)	

Medieval Testament

Villon's longest work adopts the medieval form of the mock testament, a parody of legal dispositions "presented as the last will and testament of a poor, lovelorn scholar named François Villon"[249] in which the poet distributes fictitious bequests to parents, comrades, women, tavern-keepers, court officials and executioners. His *Ballade des dames du temps jadis* (Ballade of Yesterday's Belles) appears as one chapter within the testament.

Ubi Sunt

The *Ballade des dames du temps jadis*, "drawing on historical, mythological, literary, and religious sources, sets forth a series of names, each evoking a story (often of a tragic nature) that enriches and dramatizes the *ubi sunt* theme."[250] The phrase "ubi sunt" (from the Latin for "where are they who came before us") appears in many medieval poems on human mortality. Villon uses the phrase to refer to the transience of feminine beauty as well as intimating his own mortality. "Typical of the genre, Villon recites a litany of queens, loves, and heroes who, for all their glory and renown, are gone, leaving nothing but the sound of their famous names."[251]

The first stanza features women from antiquity, including Echo, the nymph who drew Zeus' amorous attentions. Hera, Zeus' wife, took revenge by turning her into an "echo" and condemning her only to be able to repeat the last syllable of words. The second stanza belongs to contemporary women including Heloise, the well-educated fifteen-year-old whose affair with her tutor, Peter Abelard, led to his castration, and a queen who had punishable relations with her professors and then, to avoid public disclosure of her deeds, arranged to have her lovers thrown into the Seine from the window of her bedroom. Her lover Buridan, warned of the fate that awaited him, was saved by his students who placed a barge full of hay beneath the window. They then threw a large rock into the river to imitate the sound of a body hitting the water. The third stanza evokes historical or semi-legendary women including Joan of Arc who, toward the end of the Hundred Years' War, roused the French armies to expel the English. The English captured her, pronounced her a witch, and burned her alive at the stake in 1431. The underlying tone of violence reflects the attitude of a poet who did not find life easy.

Villon's elegiac ballade on fleeting fame seems consistent with a life devoted to the pleasures of the present moment.

Ockeghem, *Missa prolationum*, mid-15th century

Prolation

In the *Missa prolationum* "Ockeghem set himself technical hurdles of the utmost complexity."[252] An appreciation of Ockeghem's remarkable achievement requires understanding certain musical procedures governing rhythm and pitch. The 14th-century *ars nova* liberated musical rhythm by permitting the division of main beats into two parts, what we now call duple meter, instead of being restricted to division into three parts. A collection of writings by the theorist Philippe de Vitry in 1322 established four possible divisions of main beats and secondary beats into triple or duple time.

Term	Modern notation	Beats in a measure
Perfect time, major prolation	9/8	♪♪♪ ♪♪♪ ♪♪♪
Perfect time, minor prolation	3/4	♪♪ ♪♪ ♪♪
Imperfect time, major prolation	6/8	♪♪♪ ♪♪♪
Imperfect time, minor prolation	2/4	♪♪ ♪♪

The prolation essentially determined whether the longest note value should be divided into three parts or two parts. In major prolation, the equivalent of the modern whole note would be divided into the equivalent of three half notes. In minor prolation, the modern whole note would be divided into the equivalent of two half notes. The *ars antiqua* allowed only major prolation; the *ars nova* in addition permitted minor prolation.

Progressive Canons

Medieval composers generally built their polyphonic masses on the foundation of a pre-existing plainsong melody, called the *cantus firmus*. "In some respects, the most intellectually impressive examples of artifice and complexity are those works in which composers deprived themselves of the traditional building block of the cantus firmus and depended entirely on their own imagination. One example of this type, Johannes Ockeghem's *Missa prolationum*, has been called 'perhaps the most extraordinary contrapuntal achievement of the fifteenth century."[253]

In a canon, one voice exactly imitates another, either at the unison, as in "Row, Row, Row Your Boat," or at some other interval. In the *Missa prolationum,* "the interval between the voices of the successive canons grows steadily from the unison in Kyrie I through the octave at the 'Osanna' of the Sanctus, after which it contracts to the fourth in the 'Benedictus' and Angus Dei I and finishes at the fifth in Agnus Dei II and III."[254] Now comes the tricky bit. Each movement consists of two double canons, and each of the four voices moves in a different prolation, or time signature!

Sanctus

The pattern of progressive canons may be seen in the three sections of the *Sanctus* movement:

Sanctus, sanctus, sanctus: canons at the 6th
Pleni sunt caeli: canons at the 7th
Osanna in excelsis: canons at the octave.

The juxtaposition of prolations may be observed in the "Osanna" section:

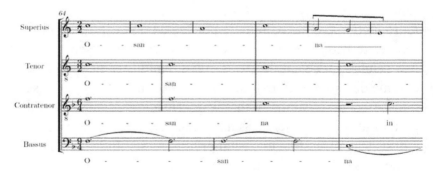

The upper voice, or Superius, sings at a canon of the octave from the second voice, or Tenor. The third voice, or Contratenor, sings at a canon of the octave from the lowest voice, or Bassus. But because of the different prolations, each voice moves at a different speed.

"The *Missa prolationum* may well be the most extraordinary contrapuntal achievement of the 15th century; using all four of Philippe de Vitry's prolations simultaneously, it presents a series of canons whose interval of imitation expands from the unison progressively through to the octave in accordance with a complex combination of verbal instructions, rests and mensural signs. Surprisingly, the result is a graceful, euphonious composition that gives the listener no hint of the intricate technical problems it embodies."[255] "In overcoming the immense conceptual problems posed by the technical demands he placed on himself ... Ockeghem displayed compositional virtuosity of the highest order and managed at the same time to write superb music."[256]

Ockeghem's virtuoso celebration of the new rhythmic freedom of the fifteenth century goes so far as to present four different prolations, or time signatures, all at the same time.

Leonardo da Vinci (died 1519), *Notebooks*

Scientific Method

As a painter Leonardo da Vinci seems almost ubiquitous. Thousands throng to see *Mona Lisa* every year in Paris; millions see reproductions of the painting emblazoned on everything from scarves to fridge magnets. Leonardo's *Last Supper* enjoys no less celebrity. Leonardo the scientist remains something of an enigma despite recent exhibits devoted to his notebooks. Essentially, Leonardo wanted it that way. He adopted mirror writing partly out of convenience as a left-hander, partly to render his entries less accessible to casual prying eyes. "In Milan, he designed his studio so that the platform holding his work could be lowered through the floor to the story below, using a system of pulleys and counterweights, to hide it from inquisitive eyes whenever he was not working."[257] He announced plans to organize and publish the material in his notebooks but never carried out the plan. As a consequence, Leonardo's scientific investigations—which extended to optics, acoustics, fluid dynamics, geology, botany, mechanics, aerodynamics, and human anatomy—never entered the mainstream of western thought. When we examine the notebooks now we see inventions, discoveries and patterns of thought that might have changed the history of science and technology had they only come to light during his lifetime.

The modern scientific method of examining data for patterns and then proposing and testing hypotheses finds a forerunner in Leonardo. "Leonardo's view of natural phenomena is based partly on traditional Aristotelian and medieval ideas and partly on his independent and meticulous observations of nature. The result is a unique science of living forms and their continual movements, changes, and transformations—a science that is radically different from that of Galileo, Descartes, and Newton."[258] Leonardo wrote, *"First I shall test by experiment before I proceed farther, because my intention is to consult experience first and then with reasoning show why such experience is bound to operate in such a way. And this is the true rule by which those who analyze the effects of nature must proceed: and although nature begins with the cause and ends with the experience, we must follow the opposite course, namely, begin with the experience, and by means of it investigate the cause."*[259]

"One hundred years before Galileo and Bacon, he single-handedly developed a new empirical approach to science, involving the systematic observation of nature, logical reasoning, and some mathematical formulations—the main characteristics of what is known today as the scientific method."[260]

Dream of Human Flight

Dreams of human flight can be traced as far back as the story of Icarus in Greek mythology, but Leonardo was the first to translate the dreams into working models based on a detailed study of the flight of birds. "His 'science of flight' involved numerous disciplines—from fluid dynamics to human anatomy, mechanics, the anatomy of bir ds, and mechanical engineering. ... Unfortunately, the limitations of these materials—wooden struts, leather joints and thongs, and skin of strong cloth—make it evident why Leonardo could not create a viable model of his flying machines, even though they were based on sound aerodynamic principles."[261] Eventually he abandoned that avenue but developed plans for a glider and a parachute which modern experiments have demonstrated to be practicable.

Anticipation of Later Discoveries

Recent research into Leonardo's notebooks have uncovered a multitude of discoveries historically attributed to later scientists in the mainstream. Studying the growth of trees "[Leonardo] discovered not only that this process generates the annual growth rings in the cross sections of a tree's branches and trunks, and that the approximate age of a cut tree can be determined by counting those rings, but also—remarkably—that the width of a growth ring is an indication of the climate during the corresponding year. *'The rings on the cut branches of trees show the number of their years,'* Leonardo recorded ... *'and the greater or smaller width of these rings show which years were wetter and which drier.'*"[262] The process was finally "rediscovered" in 1937.

Leonardo's notebooks contain sketches clearly demonstrating the parabolic nature of ballistic trajectories and remarks revealing an understanding of what would later become known as Newton's Third Law of Motion. "If he had shared his discoveries and discussed them with intellectuals of his time, his influence on the subsequent development of Western science might well have been as profound as his impact on the history of art."[263]

Leonardo da Vinci, too involved with present investigations to trouble with future publication, deprived western science of a timely appreciation of his work.

Connections: Janus

Janus, the Roman god of beginnings and endings, is generally depicted as a figure with two faces, looking both to the past and to the future. The fifteenth-century works from our repertoire similarly face in two directions, backward toward the Middle Ages and forward toward the Renaissance.

Robert Campin's *Merode Altarpiece* displays Renaissance realism in setting the Annunciation in a bourgeois kitchen but the painting is also replete with medieval symbolism with an entire panel devoted to the symbolism of the mousetrap. François Villon adopts the medieval testament as a receptacle for modern subversive subject matter. The *Ballade des dames du temps jadis*, in particular, looks back to women of antiquity and forward, or at least sideways, to women of Villon's own time. Ockeghem's *Missa prolationum*, filled with medieval canons and rhythmic games, adopts Renaissance smoothness of melodic lines, imitation, and innovative canons at the intervals of the 2nd, 3rd, 6th and 7th. Leonardo da Vinci, in the notebooks whose very existence emerged only after his death, shows himself to be an Aristotelian polymath while anticipating scientific and technical discoveries often by centuries.

16th Century

Context

Protestant Reformation

According to Roman Catholic theology, works of mercy, charity, prayer and penance could serve to obtain an "indulgence," or relief from time spent in Purgatory after death as punishment for sins. In the early 16th century the church hit upon the idea of selling indulgences to pay for the reconstruction of St. Peter's Basilica in Rome. This corruption of the faith proved to be the last straw for a German monk named Martin Luther, who expressed his discontent in a letter of protest to the archbishop in 1517. According to legend, Luther posted a copy of the letter, containing 95 theses, to the church door.

Luther articulated a number of tenets intended to reform what he saw as abuses in the church:

- Every man is his own priest and can communicate directly with God
- Believers can read and interpret the Bible according to their own consciences
- Christ, not the Pope, is the sole head of the church
- Salvation is by faith alone, not by actions such as prayer, almsgiving or sacraments

Luther's translation of the Bible into German made scripture accessible to ordinary people. His German Mass provided the new Protestant religion with a basic liturgy and his composition and arrangement of hymns provided music for the new church, with "A Mighty Fortress Is Our God" being the best-known example.

Luther never intended to provoke a revolution, but if he hoped to change the church through gentle persuasion he was disillusioned when the Council of Trent confirmed the essential role of the pope, the ordained clergy, and the sacraments. The wars of religion that burned throughout the 16th century made it clear that Luther had provoked a paradigm shift. In Germany, the Peasants' Revolt in 1524 looked upon the Lutheran Reformation as justification for a revolt against authority in general, a result that appalled Luther. The Peace of Augsburg included the celebrated phrase *cujus region, ejus religio,* which meant that each prince had the right to decide between Catholicism and Lutheranism within his domain, but permitted no individual freedom of religion.

"Luther was no progressive. Instead he saw the excesses of the Church in Rome as a despicable modern trend and wanted a return to the simple piety of the past—the early Christian church was his ideal. ... The task of humans is not to discern a better way but to suffer and live in fear of God. ... Intimations of salvation came not through buying indulgences, or making gifts, or even performing good works or obeying church law, but through faith and faith alone."[264] In practical terms, Protestants stood for the rejection of the authority of the Pope and the supernatural powers of the clergy (in general, members of the Protestant clergy took the title of ministers rather than priests); the substitution of vernacular language for Latin in worship; the reduction in the number of sacraments from seven to two or three and the redefinition of the sacraments as symbolic acts; the denial of transubstantiation and the repudiation of the worship of saints, the veneration of the Virgin Mary and the use of icons and relics.

Counter-Reformation

The Council of Trent, far from modifying church dogma to meet Luther's objections, maintained a strongly conservative stance. "It confirmed that Church alone could interpret the Scriptures, and that religious truth derived from Catholic tradition as well as from the Bible. It upheld traditional views of original sin, justification, and merit, and rejected the various Protestant alternatives to transubstantiation during the Eucharist."[265] It stressed the importance of the seven sacraments and the essential role of the ordained priesthood. And it confirmed prevailing practices such as "the cult of relics, the invocation of saintly intercessors, and the devotion, above all, to Mary"[266]

Scientific Revolution

Early in the sixteenth century Copernicus, on the basis of his own experiments and data provided by fellow astronomer Tycho Brahe, reached the unavoidable conclusion that the Sun, not the Earth, was the center of the solar system. Aware of the opposition that this idea would encounter, he postponed publishing it for nearly thirty years until 1543.

It remained for Johannes Kepler to perfect the Copernican model by proposing, and offering detailed calculations to support, the idea of elliptical instead of circular orbits. "But it was the Florentine, Galileo Galilei, one of the first to avail himself of the newly-invented telescope, who really brought Copernicus to the wider public."[267]

Michelangelo, Sistine Chapel Ceiling, 1511 PLATE 11

Julius II, Warrior Pope

Pope Julius II was accustomed to exercising power and getting his own way. "Donning armor, personally leading his troops"—and reciting Virgil to spur them on—" recapturing Bologna from the upstart Bentivogli family, driving the 'barbarian' French from Italy, Julius expanded the Papal States to their farthest limits ever and consolidated papal power for the church's political and economic survival."[268] In 1505 Julius ordered the destruction of the basilica of St. Peter's and its replacement by a new, gigantic church. "The proportions, geometry, and classical references of New St. Peter's were understood by contemporaries as potent symbols of church renewal and papal power."[269]

"Michelangelo never wanted to paint the Sistine Chapel ceiling. He was daunted by the difficulty of the task and made it clear from the start that he resented the commission, which had been imposed upon him by the imperious and demanding 'warrior pope', Julius II."[270] It started off far worse. The initial project was to be an enormous tomb. Then came a three-times life-size sculpture of the pope. Michelangelo demurred.

In the early spring of 1508, Michelangelo was summoned again to Rome. "Once more, the pope urged him to undertake the painting of the Sistine Chapel ceiling. Once more the artist resisted. But in the end, he had no alternative but to swallow his disappointment about the tomb [to which he had already committed considerable effort and expense] and do the pope's bidding."[271] Michelangelo "was about 33 years old when he began. Although in the early stages he employed some assistants, he soon went about painting the immense surface practically single-handed."[272]

Dignity of Man

Michelangelo's overall plan for the chapel included scenes from the time before Moses on the ceiling and two cycles of frescoes on the walls, one depicting the era under Moses, the other the era under the grace of Christ. The nine central narratives from Genesis were subdivided into three groups: stories of the Creation, Adam and Eve, and Noah.

"The ceiling's central triad of images begins with *The Creation of Adam,* a majestic depiction of the moment when God imparts life and a soul to the first of men. It is among the most dynamic and startlingly original of all Michelangelo's inventions. Like many famous pictures, it can all too easily be taken for granted. The overwhelming familiarity of the composition, its beguiling power and simplicity, can obscure its true qualities. Only on close, careful inspection does the work disclose its range of meanings and subtleties of expression."[273]

Michelangelo, of course, was not the first artist to represent this archetypal scene from Genesis, but he made it distinctively his own. "In early Christian depictions of the creation of man, God had usually been truncated to a mere hand gesturing from a strategically placed cloud. He had developed into the familiar figure of an old man with a beard by the middle of the fifteenth century, but there was no precedent for showing him 'in the act of flying through the air,' let alone dressed in clinging draperies that reveal his legs from the thigh down. The fingertip act of creation was also Michelangelo's own invention."[274] "The misery of man, sinful and fallen, was not a neglected theme in Renaissance thought, but his dignity, especially as created 'in the image and likeness' of God and as 'more wondrously' restored by Christ, emerged in the era with new prominence."[275]

Christ, the Second Adam

"The scene also implies Christ's redemptive Incarnation, for Christ was commonly referred to as the second Adam." As St. Paul writes in 1 Corinthians 15:22, "For as in Adam all die, so in Christ all will be made alive." Later in the same Epistle we read, "The first man was of the dust of the earth; the second man is of heaven." "Thus, the woman under God's left arm, from whose loins the green drapery originates, was probably intended to be Eve, preordained from the beginning and standard prefiguration of the Virgin, the vessel of Incarnation. If so, the robust child held by the two fingers of God's left hand—as a celebrant priest would hold the Host—most probably prefigures the sacrificial Christ."[276]

The originality of Michelangelo's treatment of traditional themes reflects the humanistic spirit of direct access to God's message. The artist exhibited a "strong and inalienable belief in his own right to read and interpret the Bible." It is this independence of mind, "just as much as his brilliance of imagination and abilities with a paintbrush—that makes the paintings of the Sistine chapel ceiling so powerful and unique."[277]

Michelangelo used the framework of Genesis both to prefigure the coming of Christ and to assert the dignity of man created, after all, "in God's image."

Erasmus, In Praise of Folly, 1511

"Prince of Humanists"

Recovering and studying texts from the past constitutes one of the pillars of Renaissance humanism. For Desiderio Erasmus "the project of re-reading the past became connected with the need for spiritual reform across all Christendom. For too long had Scripture been the property of the Church. For too long had theologians been allowed to barnacle the words of the old and New Testaments with their own complex interpretations and exegeses. It was time to recover God's message in its purity—and to contemplate that message, as if for the first time, in a state of spiritual innocence and nakedness."[278]

Erasmus wrote: *"I wish that every woman might read the Gospel and the Epistles of St. Paul. Would that these were translated into every language ... and understood not only by Scots and Irishmen but by Turks and Saracens. Would that the farmer might sing snatches of Scripture at his plow, that the weaver might hum phrases of Scripture to the tune of his shuttle."*[279] To promote this idealistic goal Erasmus published a Greek translation of the New Testament, then used it to improve the traditional Latin translation found in the Vulgate.

Mockery of Orthodoxy

Erasmus' most celebrated work, *The Praise of Folly*, written in 1509 and published in 1511, attacks hypocrisy of every stripe. Though a committed Christian, Erasmus does not hesitate to pillory Christian practices. "Not just pious ceremonies like the cult of saints, the office prayers, and pilgrimages, but also the spiritual way of the mystics and pious rapture, and the *bonae literae* are called into question. ... But behind all of this mockery lies a steady faith in the Creator who seeks to redeem humans through the folly of the cross—not excepting even Erasmus, who dares sport with the biblical personifications of Wisdom and Folly."[280]

Disparity between Christ and Christianity

Like the Franciscans, Erasmus was troubled by the obvious disparity between the life of Christ and the institution of the Christian church. He criticized the enforcement of unquestioning orthodoxy: *"They force everyone to a recantation that differs but a hair's breadth from the least of their explicit or implicit determinations."* He mocked the contrast between the simplicity of Jesus' life and the opulence of the clerics': *"scarce any kind of men live more voluptuously or with less trouble ... whereas if there be anything burdensome, they prudently lay that on other men's shoulders."*

Erasmus ridiculed the tendency of theologians to become mired in intrinsically unresolvable questions. *"They explicate the most hidden mysteries according to their own fancy—as how the world was first made; how original sin is derived to posterity; in what manner, how much room, and how long time Christ lay in the Virgin's womb; how accidents subsist in the Eucharist without their subject. ... At these, they prick up—as whether there was any instant of time in the generation of the Second Person; whether there be more than one filiation in Christ; whether it be a possible proposition that God the Father hates the Son; or whether it was possible that Christ could have taken upon himself the likeness of a woman; ... and what Peter had consecrated if he had administered the Sacrament at the time the body of Christ hung upon the cross; or whether at the same time he might be said to be man; whether after the Resurrection there will be any eating and drinking, since we are so much afraid of hunger and thirst in this world. ...To speak briefly, all Christian religion seems to have a kind of alliance with folly and in no respect to have any accord with wisdom."[281]* And yet, for all his critical barbs, Erasmus remained loyal to the church. Erasmus "was the principal practitioner of Christian humanism. ... He did more than anyone else to marry the new humanism with the Catholic tradition."[282]

Erasmus saw no reason why his devotion to Christianity should prevent him from ridiculing the hypocrisy of the Christian church.

Machiavelli, *The Prince*, 1513

Florence and the Medicis

Machiavelli's *The Prince*, written in 1513 but not published until 1532 after Machiavelli's death, might be described in modern terms as an extended interoffice memo. Machiavelli, a civil servant, shares thoughts with his employer, Lorenzo Medici, on how to gain and maintain power. The Medici family, which exercised power in Italy for four hundred years, produced three popes and numerous rulers of Florence. Although Florence was technically a democracy, the Medici family, which rose to power as bankers to the pope, effectively ran civic affairs through a patronage network. The Medici family commissioned Machiavelli to write a history of the city. Lorenzo the Magnificent, in addition to exercising control over the political life of the city, distinguished himself as a great patron of the arts, giving support to Leonardo da Vinci among others.

Mercenaries and the Fall of Rome

In Florence, "the militia decayed as an institution because hired mercenary troops were more effective. New technology, including artillery and firearms, demanded professional expertise. ... Regardless of their expertise and availability, Machiavelli emphasized the unreliability of mercenary forces, because these soldiers had little reason to risk their lives in battles when their own homes and lands were not at stake."[283]

Machiavelli illustrates his arguments with examples drawn from history, and offers a clear explanation of the fall of the Roman Empire. *"Experience has shown that only princes and armed republics achieve success, and that mercenaries bring nothing but loss. ... If we consider what was the start of the downfall of the Roman Empire, it will be found that it was simply when the Goths started to be hired as mercenaries. ... Mercenary commanders are either skilled in warfare or they are not: if they are, you cannot trust them, because they are anxious to advance their own greatness, either by coercing you, their employer, or by coercing others against your own wishes. If, however, the commander is lacking in prowess, in the normal way he brings about your ruin."*[284]

Realpolitik

Machiavelli's analysis of what we would now call *Realpolitik* may strike us as distressingly modern. As we read some of the more celebrated excerpts from his work we are likely to think of illustrations from contemporary politics. "Machiavelli made a significant break with the idealism of earlier writers by offering a body of political theory that he said should be measured not by its adherence to abstract standards of truth and moral goodness, but by the beneficial material effects it would bring. ... [*The Prince*] was the first to argue explicitly that good government requires the skillful use of cruelty and deception to continually take what belongs to others."[285]

Lessons for The Prince

- *If a prince wants to maintain his rule, he must be prepared not to be virtuous.*
- *It is far better to be feared than loved if you cannot be both.*
- *One must know how to color one's actions and to be a*

> *great liar and deceiver.*
> - *A prince, therefore need not have all the good qualities I mentioned above, but he should certainly appear to have them.*
> - *Princes should delegate to others the enactment of unpopular measures and keep in their own hands the means of winning favors.*
> - *Strive assiduously to escape the hatred of the most powerful classes.*
> - *An able prince should cunningly foster some opposition to himself so that by overcoming it he can enhance his own stature.*

"Machiavelli argued that politicians should not look to principles or rationality to guide them, but should learn to understand the situations that continually arose, and try to make them work to their advantage. ... Before Machiavelli it had been assumed by philosophers and political thinkers that abstract rational consideration and analysis would reveal the right way in which a city should be governed, or a war undertaken, or one's life planned out. But Machiavelli, through real experience, and living at the end of his city's glittering century, knew this to be a foolhardy illusion."[286]

Machiavelli could not have been the first to observe the workings of power politics but he was the first to put his observations into writing so inflammatory that it was published only after his death.

Luther, *95 Theses*, 1517

Leo X and Johannes Tetzel

"In 1517, everything that Luther was beginning to discover about righteousness and faith collided with the Roman church's system as it found most blatant expression in his Saxon neighborhood through the activities of one Johannes Tetzel. ... A gifted preacher and a superior salesperson, he used his moonlighting role as an inquisitor to intimidate opponents even as he peddled instruments that he claimed offered sinners spiritual release. Proceeds from his sales went to Pope Leo X in Rome, Archbishop Albrecht in Mainz, and Tetzel himself."[287] "In the autumn of 1517, still thinking he could work within the official church system, Luther somewhat ingenuously appealed to his own bishop and to Archbishop Albrecht to take their responsibilities seriously. The scandalous indulgence system, he charged, was dangerous to the exploited Saxon people."[288]

According to legend, Luther posted a copy of the letter, containing 95 theses, to the church door. Among the points in Luther's "Disputation on the Power and Efficacy of Indulgences" we find:

28. It is certain that when the penny jingles into the money-box, gain and avarice can be increased, but the result of the intercession of the Church is in the power of God alone.

50. Christians are to be taught that if the pope knew the actions of the pardon-preachers, he would rather that St. Peter's church should go to ashes, than that it should be built up with the skin, flesh and bones of his sheep.

86. Why does not the pope, whose wealth is today greater than the riches of the richest, build just this one church of St. Peter with his own money, rather than with the money of poor believers?

"Here I Stand. I Can Do No Other"

Luther continued to write pamphlets denouncing the pope's abuse of power, daring even to question the doctrine of papal infallibility. Gutenberg's recently-invented printing press allowed the wide dissemination of Luther's incendiary ideas. "While Lu-

ther's *Ninety-five Theses* burst on to the European scene like
wildfire, they were, frankly, not all that original or inflammatory.
In fact, Leo X (so the story goes) dismissed Luther's theses as
the ranting of another 'drunk man.'"[289] But Luther's continuing
criticism of the church eventually presented a threat that could
not be ignored.

The pope demanded that Luther recant all of his writings. Luther
refused in memorable words: "Unless I am convinced by the testimony of the Scriptures or by clear reason ... I am bound by the
Scriptures I have quoted and my conscience is captive to the
Word of God. I cannot and I will not retract anything, since it is
neither safe nor right to go against conscience.' Some reports
having him adding, 'Here I stand. I can do no other.'"[290]

Luther on Romans

We can imagine that Martin Luther identified with Paul of Tarsus as a Christian apologist whose very life was threatened by
established authority. Paul, raised as a Jew, encountered conflict
with both the Jewish establishment and the new Christian communities. Luther, an Augustine monk within the Roman Catholic Church, encountered opposition and eventually excommunication for his divergent beliefs. "Luther tended to read Romans
as an ancient parallel to his own experience. Paul was cast in the
role of the reforming Luther, and the Jews took the place of a
legalistic Roman Catholicism."[291]

Luther explains his definition of faith in his Introduction to St.
Paul's Letter to the Romans, in which he maintains that while
faith will naturally lead to doing good works, salvation comes
from the faith, not from the works. *"Faith is not that human illusion and dream that some people think it is. When they hear and
talk a lot about faith and yet see that no moral improvement and
no good works result from it, they fall into error and say, 'Faith
is not enough. You must do works if you want to be virtuous and*

get to heaven.' ... It is impossible that faith ever stop doing good. Faith doesn't ask whether good works are to be done, but, before it is asked, it has done them."[292]

Rebuffed in his efforts to reform the Church from within, Luther accepted the unsought challenge of leading a new religion by providing it with a vernacular Bible, music for worship and a theological framework.

Castiglione, The Book of the Courtier, 1528

The Book of the Courtier represents a compendium of Renaissance thought, with the many-sided courtier viewed as the successor to the medieval knight. The book purports to be a series of conversations carried on by a company of nobles over a series of evenings. The hostess has proposed as a topic of conversation the qualities that constitute the perfect courtier, and her guests put forth a seemingly impossible list of requirements.

Perfezione

Castiglione writes, *"The first and true profession of the courtier must be that of arms. ... Let him also stand out from the rest as enterprising, bold, and loyal to whomever he serves. ... I would have him demonstrate strength and lightness and suppleness and be good at all the physical exercises befitting a warrior. ... I should wish our courtier to be an accomplished and versatile horseman. ... It is also fitting that the courtier should know how to swim, jump, run and cast the stone. ... I should like our courtier to be more than an average scholar. ... He should have a knowledge of Greek as well as Latin. He should be very well acquainted with the poets, and no less with the orators and historians, and also skilled at writing both verse and prose.... I am not satisfied with our courtier unless he is also a musician and unless as well as understanding and being able to read music he can play several instruments."*[293]

Sprezzatura

Castiglione created a new term, *sprezzatura*, in reference to the attitude of nonchalance with which the courtier's artfulness should be carried off. "What he describes under that term is an art that hides art, the cultivated ability to display artful artlessness, to perform any act or gesture with an insouciant or careless mastery that delivers either or both of two messages: 'look how artfully I appear to be natural'; 'Look how naturally I appear to be artful.' ... It is the ability to show that one is not showing all the effort one obviously put into learning how to show that one is not showing effort."[294]

Castiglione advises the courtier to *"Practice in all things a certain nonchalance which conceals all artistry and makes whatever one says or does seem uncontrived and effortless. ... He should let it seem as if he himself thinks nothing of his accomplishments. ...He should always be well briefed and prepared for everything he has to do or say, though giving the impression that it is off the cuff."*

An additional aspect of sprezzatura is "a form of defensive irony: the ability to disguise what one really desires, feels, thinks, and means or intends behind a mask of 'apparent reticence and nonchalance.'" This nonchalance is "a guarantee that the ambition and aggressiveness the courtier pretends to mask is really there, and available for his prince's use. ...The performance of sprezzatura is thus a figuration of power. ... Sprezzatura is to be worn as a velvet glove that exhibits the contours of the handiness it conceals."[295]

Virtù

While remaining constantly attuned to the prince's every desire and whim, the ideal courtier must also be the embodiment of virtue, employing powers of gentle persuasion to guide the prince back to the moral straight-and-narrow when he shows signs of being overly influenced by Machiavelli. "The Courtier should not bend further than the bounds of morality will allow. ... Even at the risk of being dismissed, he must not let obedience to his prince make him betray his moral self. .... [The Courtier] "must try to veer the prince away from immoral action and induce him to be virtuous. ... The solution lies in the courtier's beautiful and graceful attributes. These make him so attractive that the prince will desire his company and may heed his advice."[296]

The consequence of these conflicting goals puts the courtier in a constant state of performance anxiety. "Not only because the courtier is always performing before an audience composed of performers like himself, and not only because he knows they are performing, and knows they know he is performing. There is also anxiety about the performer's own practice of dissimulation—about his need to keep the performance of naturalness from being spoiled by unwanted leakages of the less ideal nature he is expected to suppress/transcend."[297]

Castiglione's depiction of the perfect courtier—expected to excel in every field without apparent effort and to lead his ruler into virtue while appearing to be completely compliant—may seem like a perfect nightmare.

Copernicus, On the Revolutions of the Heavenly Spheres, 1543

Copernicus' Simplification

Our long-standing acceptance of a heliocentric model of the solar system makes it difficult for us to appreciate the remarkable act of courage and creativity that produced it. After all, our eyes tell us daily that the sun, like the moon, revolves around the earth and that the planets do the same, albeit with occasional "retrograde motion." The geocentric model enjoyed both centuries of acceptance and the imprimatur of the church. "Prior to the publication of Copernicus's book, the Judeo-Christian world believed that a perfectly still earth rested in the center of God's universe, and that all heavenly bodies—the sun, the other planets, the moon, and even the distant stars—revolved around it. This conviction was based on the teachings of Aristotle and the writings of Claudius Ptolemy. The Church had long embraced the paradigm because it conformed to scripture and placed humans at the center of God's firmament. Copernicus's revolutionary work not only presented an entirely different cosmology, but once accepted, it required a titanic shift in mind-set and belief. No longer the center of God's creation, the earth became just one of the other planets. By extension, the primary position of God's highest creation, humankind, was also diminished."[298]

Copernicus acknowledged the novelty of his idea. *"The great majority of authors of course agree that the earth stands still in the center of the universe, and consider it inconceivable and ridiculous to suppose the opposite. But if the matter is carefully weighed it will be seen that the question is not yet settled and therefore by no means to be regarded lightly."* But he offered what we would now term a relativistic argument to the effect that if a ship is moving quietly on the water, passengers might think *"that the boat with all on board is standing still."*[299] Others before Copernicus had doubted the geocentric model. "Yet, no one until Copernicus attempted to develop a comprehensive and complete *system* to supplant Ptolemy's. This was the key—Copernicus provided all of the data and mathematics that any other serious student of the heavens would need to conduct inquiries using his heliocentric model of the universe."[300]

Galileo's Proof

Even if Copernicus tells us that we must not trust our eyes, we would welcome some visual confirmation of a model obliging us to jettison the Ptolemaic model that has served us well for fifteen hundred years. Happily, Galileo succeeded in furnishing this confirmation. "In Ptolemy's universe, Venus should never be observed as a full disc; ... but if it orbited the Sun, then it should display a full range of phases, just like the moon. ... Galileo's observations showed that Venus did display the complete range of phases from crescent to full and back again and, hence, the traditional Ptolemaic view was false."[301]

Kepler's Improvement

While Copernicus rejected Ptolemy's geocentric model of the solar system he remained faithful to the notion of circular orbits that had informed astronomical thought since before the time of Pythagoras despite occasional computational anomalies. "Kepler was troubled by certain discrepancies in the orbits of the planets. ... Though there was only an eight-degree inconsistency with perfect circular orbits, those eight degrees could not be ignored. There had to be some way to explain it. By 1605, after incredible effort, Kepler devised the idea that carved his very important place in the history of science—an ellipse. *With reasoning I derived from the physical principles agreeing with experience, there is no figure left for the orbit for the planet except a perfect ellipse.*"[302]

Johannes Kepler, like Copernicus able to visualize a new reality, found that replacing the circles with ellipses made the discrepancies disappear. "Copernicus, and all astronomers, had believed that the only possible shape for an orbit was a perfect circle or sphere, since God the creator would build only with a perfect shape. For the deeply religious Kepler to break from this belief was remarkable."[303]

Copernicus' geocentric model of the solar system, while satisfying the requirements of Occam's Razor, had to overcome both longstanding tradition and papal authority.

Lassus, *De Profundis*, 1584

Renaissance Ideal

In contrast to medieval music, which set an underlying text without attempting to express its meaning in music, Renaissance music placed a high value on somehow capturing the sense of a text in musical terms. Gioseffo Zarlino, a contemporary theorist, explained the ideal in *The Harmonic Institutions* (1558). *"Harmony and rhythm should follow the dictates of speech: that is the rule. For it is necessary that in a given text, be it an oration or a narrative or an imitation (which are sometimes found in speeches), that if the material is lighthearted or mournful, full of gravity or entirely without it, honest or lascivious, the harmony and rhythm should reflect it. . ..Thus it would not be fitting to set a lighthearted text to a mournful harmony and a grave rhythm; and conversely it would not be appropriate to have a text that is mournful and lachrymose set to a lighthearted harmony and lively rhythms. For a sad text should be set to a sad harmony and somber rhythms. Everything should be done in proper relationship."*[304]

Musica Reservata

Zarlino offers general instructions for composing music whose overall effect suits the overall effect of the underlying text. But some composers pursued the ideal of expressiveness to the level of individual musical details, a technique known as *musica reservata.* "There is probably no single, simple definition of *musica reservata.* But we can generally understand the term as referring to late-sixteenth-century music that expressed the meaning, emotion, and imagery of the text with an intensity (at least to contemporary ears) unknown to previous generations; it was, moreover, music intended for an elite, cultivated audience."[305] Lassus, also known as Orlando de Lasso, stands out among Renaissance composers for his skill in musical expressiveness. "Lasso's passionate commitment to the idea that music should heighten, enhance, and even embody textual meaning elicited a boldness and directness that sets him apart. ... The degree to which his music is informed and controlled by the words can scarcely be exaggerated. Almost every page reveals particular compositional decisions made to heighten, illustrate, or embody a literary meaning."[306]

Word-Painting in *De Profundis*

A close examination of *De Profundis,* from Lassus' Penitential Psalms, shows how the composer succeeds in creating musical ideas appropriate to details of the psalm text. Each of the ten sections of the text includes the plainsong melody of Psalm 130 within a texture ranging from three to six vocal lines.

Latin	English	Music
De profundis clamavi ad te, Domine; Domine, exaudi vocem meam.	From the depths, I have cried out to you, O Lord; Lord, hear my voice.	Leap of a large interval for "clamavi," crying from the depths
Fiant aures tuæ in-tendentes in vocem depreca-tionis meæ.	Let your ears be at-tentive to the voice of my supplication.	"Being attentive" is "echoing"—two voices sing the plainsong melody in a canon at the 5th
Si iniquitates ob-servaveris, Domine, Domine, quis sus-tinebit?	If you, Lord, were to mark iniquities, who, O Lord, shall stand?	To express "mark-ing iniquities," two voices sing the plainsong in *inversion*.
Quia apud te propi-tiatio est; et propter legem tuam sustinui te, Domine.	For with you is for-giveness; and be-cause of your law, I stood by you, Lord.	To express "I stood by you" the outer voices sing in nearly the same rhythms
Sustinuit anima mea in verbo ejus: Speravit anima mea in Domino.	My soul has stood by his word. My soul has hoped in the Lord.	The second sylla-ble of "sustinuit" is *sustained* for three beats
A custodia matutina usque ad noctem, speret Israël in Domino.	From the morning watch, even until night, let Israel hope in the Lord.	
Quia apud Domi-num misericordia, et copiosa apud eum redemptio.	For with the Lord there is mercy, and with him is plente-ous redemption.	"With the Lord"—two outer voices sing mostly "with" each other rhyth-mically

Et ipse redimet Israël ex omnibus iniquitatibus ejus.	And he will redeem Israel from all his iniquities.	Very low tessitura for the verse about "iniquities"
Gloria patria et filio, et spiritui sancto.	Glory be to the Father, and to the Son, and to the Holy Spirit.	
Sicut erat in principio et nunc et semper et in saecula saeculorum, Amen.	As it was in the beginning, is now and ever shall be, world without end, Amen.	One half chorus imitates the other for "as it was in the beginning"

"If one characteristic feature should be emphasized more than any other, it is his deriving inspiration chiefly from the words he set, allowing them to generate most of the musical details in his works. More than any of the other great composers of the late sixteenth century except the virtuoso madrigalists, Lasso believed that the words were to be masters of the music."[307]

Lassus epitomized the new Renaissance relationship between words and music in which music not only set words but was shaped by words.

Shakespeare, *Hamlet*, ca. 1600

Transcending Tradition

Contemporary audiences would have sought, and found, in *Hamlet* characteristic elements of the Elizabethan revenge play:

- A secret murder (usually a good king killed by a bad one)
- A visit by the ghost of the murder victim to a kinsman to seek revenge
- Period of intrigue by and against the avenger
- Madness, either real or feigned, by the avenger
- Violent ending including death of the avenger

At the beginning of the play Hamlet grieves the death of his father, the King of Denmark, the usurpation of the throne by his father's brother Claudius, and the quick marriage of Claudius to Hamlet's widowed mother Gertrude. The ghost of Hamlet's father discloses that he has been murdered by Claudius, and calls upon his son to seek revenge. Although Shakespeare wrote the play in the 16th century, the action seems to take place in the 11th century. We recall the medieval code by which the death of a kinsman must be avenged. The play continues with a period of intrigue between Hamlet and Claudius. Hamlet pretends to be mad in order to gain information, and Ophelia really goes mad. By the end of the play nearly all the main characters have suffered violent deaths, by Elizabethan standards a very satisfactory body count. But in place of the cardboard figures found in contemporary revenge plays Shakespeare creates three-dimensional characters that bring a genuine sense of personality to the stage.

Christian vs. Classical Values

If the Renaissance can be characterized as "an uneasy alliance of classical and Christian elements, then no single issue was more perfectly calculated to expose the inner tensions of the age than revenge. ... The classical heroic tradition, especially as embodied in the classical epics, viewed revenge as a noble activity. ... Christianity arose in conscious opposition to classical values. ... Jesus is in every respect the antithesis of the classical hero."[308]

Hamlet finds himself torn between two conflicting sets of values. "From the very beginning, the ghost places the prince in a double bind, a situation in which, no matter what he does, he will be forced to violate some legitimate principle."[309] The most famous soliloquy of the play, "To be or not to be," represents Hamlet wrestling with this very issue, the choice between suffering the ills of the world and taking resolute action against them. Hamlet faces the moral question of whether or not he should take private revenge. As for Horatio's statement that "Something is rotten in the state of Denmark," it can be argued that the ghost embodies that rot.

"Who's There?"

Shakespeare poses the play's central question of identity in the opening line, "Who's there?" The key issue that Hamlet must decide is whether the ghost is really his father, Old Hamlet, or an evil spirit. Hamlet resolves to talk with the ghost in hope of determining its identity:

Be thou a spirit of health or goblin damn'd,
Bring with thee airs from heaven or blasts from hell,
Be thy intents wicked or charitable,
Thou com'st in such a questionable shape
That I will speak to thee. (Hamlet, I/4, 41-44)

Hamlet's devotion to his father prevents him from considering another possibility: that the ghost is really his father and *also* an evil spirit. Hamlet cannot make up his mind.

The spirit I have seen
May be a devil; and the devil hath power
T'assume a pleasing shape; yea, and perhaps
Out of my weakness and my melancholy,
As he is very potent with such spirits,
Abuses to damn me. (Hamlet, II/2, 627-632)

Our natural sympathies lie with the victim of a murder but what was Old Hamlet really like? Young Hamlet tends to idealize his father, who in fact seems to have been a hard, unforgiving warrior king. The view of Old Hamlet as an egocentric misogynist from whom Gertrude was quite relieved to escape supports the interpretation of his ghost as malevolent. "Gertrude and Claudius certainly are one of the happiest marriages in Shakespeare until the Ghost sets young Hamlet upon his very hesitant quest for revenge."[310]

So what should Hamlet do in response to the ghost's insistence on revenge? Hamlet undertakes to test the authenticity of the ghost's claim by staging a play, referred to as "The Mousetrap," which will recreate the murder of the former king and allow Hamlet to decide the nature of the ghost. When Claudius interrupts the play, and leaves the room, Hamlet becomes convinced of his culpability and plans to kill him. Hamlet's repeated suspicions of the ghost's nature help to account for his hesitation in carrying out its orders. The seemingly innocuous question, "Who's there?", that opens the play proves to be the key to understanding it.

In *Hamlet* Shakespeare looked behind the conventions of the revenge play to explore the clash of classical and Christian values in the Renaissance, where purgatorial spirits could represent either tradition.

Connections: Humanism

Humanism embraces the revival of classical letters; a way of life centered on human interests, values, and dignity; and a reliance on reason instead of religion. If the last two aspects of this definition sound particularly modern in comparison with descriptions we have offered up to this point, it should come as no surprise that the sixteenth century has often been chosen by historians to mark the beginning of the modern age.

Michelangelo's *Creation of Adam* notably asserts not simply the majesty of God but also the dignity of man. Erasmus, called the "Prince of Humanism," prepared a Greek translation of the New Testament and then used it to improve the existing Latin translation. Machiavelli's *The Prince* achieves much of its modernity by centering on human interests and values. Luther, in defending his reformist positions, continually asserts the primary importance of Scripture and the right of each individual to read and interpret it. Castiglione's *The Book of the Courtier* focuses entirely on criteria for producing the ideal Renaissance man. The Copernican Revolution, as communicated in the works of Copernicus himself as well as Galileo and Kepler, relies firmly on human reason in place of religious authority. The music of Lassus differs from that of his predecessors in its insistence that music should serve the text. Finally, Shakespeare's *Hamlet* focuses on human personality and interiority.

17th Century

Context

Le Roi Soleil

Louis XIV, the Sun King, not only emblazoned the sun motif throughout his residence but turned his daily routines into a drama, beginning with "the rising of the sun," in which the king got up, assisted by several personal attendants, and ending with "the setting of the sun," in which these same attendants helped the king get ready for bed. Just as the planets revolved around the sun, so France and the court revolved around this sovereign, whose reign spanned more than 72 years.

To prevent any of the nobles from establishing an independent power base, the king moved the center of government from Paris to Versailles, capable of housing ten thousand courtiers and their attendants, and required the nobles to reside there. The court of Versailles became a focal point for drama, music and opera as well as a hub of diplomacy. "The spectacular royal balls, ballets, concerts, plays and hunts, the fêtes and the fireworks in the Grand Parc, all served to cement the subservience of his leading subjects, and to create a sense of national community. ... But his greatest talent was for publicity. Versailles was the symbol of an ideal which far outshone the facts of French reality. For Frenchmen and foreign visitors alike, the splendours of its ceremonies undoubtedly created the illusion that the *Roi Soleil* stood at the centre of a system of perfect authority."[311]

The king's minister of finance Colbert helped to extend absolute central control to the financial realm. Under Colbert tax collection became more efficient, notably through the elimination of aristocratic exemptions. Colbert oversaw the enforcement of a mercantilist policy which aimed for a positive balance of trade by encouraging exports and discouraging imports through the use of protective tariffs, government subsidies and monopolies. Ideally, raw materials would be transported on French ships from French colonies in the New World to be used for French manufacturing and sold to other markets for the benefit of French trade.

English Civil War

To whom should the king answer? Louis XIV would have answered only to himself, or, if feeling generous, to God. But England had a tradition that even the king should be subject to the rule of law. Increasingly, Parliament believed that the king should be the servant of the people, not a welcome idea to rulers who still espoused the divine right of kings. The English Civil War occupied the entire second half of the seventeenth century before finally resolving the question on the side of parliament.

"The most surprising element of the civil war, to modern minds at least, is that it was fought in order to preserve, or to reinstate, ancient traditions. ... Both sides in the civil war explicitly appealed to ancient tradition for justification of their cause. Royalists believed that any challenge to the monarchy destroyed an ancient concept of divine order, while parliamentarians wanted the restoration of their ancient rights established under English common law, which the king and his predecessors had degraded."[312]

Settlement of the Americas

The initial encounter between European civilization and existing tribes and kingdoms in North and South America ended badly for the latter. Even before the start of deliberate aggression, the introduction of European diseases among peoples with no prior exposure to them proved devastating. "A Spanish expedition into Texas in 1528 introduced typhus; influenza was brought to the Gulf coast in 1559, smallpox to Florida in 1564, to Carolina in 1615 and Maryland in 1616, and plague to Virginia in 1607 and Maryland and Massachusetts in 1616. Native Americans had no resistance to any of these Eurasian pathogens, and though the numbers were unrecorded, they certainly perished in tens, and probably hundreds, of thousands."[313]

In South America, Spanish conquistadors unhesitatingly decimated indigenous people in pursuit of natural resources, especially gold and silver. In North America, the desire for land overcame any consideration for those already residing on it. And the requirements for raising first sugar, and then tobacco and cotton led first to the enslavement of natives and then the importation of slaves from Africa.

"Perhaps all we can learn is that one human civilization, finding itself with a military advantage over another, is quite capable, even if its members believe themselves to be civilized beyond all others, of inflicting unspeakable brutality with the aim of destroying that other civilization. And we know that this is true because it happened."[314]

Monteverdi, *Orfeo*, 1607

Florentine Cameratas

The humanistic goal of recreating classic art forms encountered an apparently insuperable obstacle when it came to music. Plato and Aristotle wrote eloquently about both the power of music and the necessity of restraining its effects. Yet in the absence of actual musical examples, how was one to proceed? Poets, musicians and other intellectuals gathered in Cameratas (or "learned societies") in Florence and elsewhere in Italy to grapple with the problem. "The Camerata enterprise attested to a profound nostalgia for the golden age of Greek culture and a passionate desire, as the Renaissance came to its close, to rekindle the lost ancient unity of word and musical tone hinted at in ancient texts. The

Greeks viewed poetry and music as interwoven arts that found their most notable expression in the tragedies performed in fifth-century Athens at the Theater of Dionysus. ... Members of the Cameratas in Florence believed that the musical style of declamation, which had been such an important feature of performance in the ancient theater, had to be resurrected."[315]

Recitative and Realism

The difference between dramatic time and musical time posed another challenge. A review of the music we have already examined shows how even a brief poetic text can occupy an appreciable amount of time when set to music. "The idea of a play sung from beginning to end created devilish problems for the early experimenters. Musical form usually depends on repetition for comprehensibility. In other words, melodic material has to be repeated for an audience to recognize the motifs, and the repetition can create pleasure for listeners. Drama, on the other hand, requires a sequence of ongoing events moving towards a crisis and resolution. How could a drama, which is inherently forward moving and evolving, be continuously linked with music, which demands some form of repetition to generate comprehensibility as well as pleasure?"[316] The solution came with the invention of recitative, a style of singing whose rhythms and melodic inflections imitate those of declamatory speech. With narrative recitative to advance the action of the drama, a composer might then insert arias, choruses, or instrumental interludes, based on more formal musical structures, at moments of particular emotional intensity.

But would audiences accept the idea of continuously sung drama? The earliest operas focused on the myth of Orpheus, whose singing was said to be able to enchant even savage beasts. "There can be no doubt that all authors deliberately sought to justify singing of songs—*cantar recitando*—by choosing for protagonists such musical figures around whom other singers gather quite naturally."[317] "They could argue that their operas did not violate verisimilitude, since Orpheus was a notable *singer*. What could be more lifelike than a lead character who is famous as a singer, doing onstage what he does best?"[318]

Music Serves the Text

According to the legend of Orpheus and Eurydice, before their wedding Eurydice is bitten by a snake and dies. "Desperate, Orpheus decides to attempt an impossible task, to descend to the underworld to rescue his beloved."[319] In Monteverdi's opera *Orfeo*, Orpheus summons all of his musical powers in an effort to persuade Charon to ferry him across the river Styx. "Orfeo's solo, 'Possente spirto,' is a sequence of four strophic variations followed by two contrasting recitative or arioso passages. The slow instrumental bass line remains the same while Orfeo sings his four strophes with increasingly virtuosic ornamentation. The verses of his plea are punctuated by elaborate instrumental interludes."[320]

Monteverdi's musical accompaniment draws on the symbolic associations of various instruments. "After my dear wife was deprived of life, my heart is no longer with me" is accompanied by trombones, traditionally associated with the underworld. "To her have I turned my way through the dark air, not toward the Inferno, for everywhere is paradise that has such beauty," is accompanied by a harp. "The harp, an instrument long symbolic of heaven, was suggested by Orfeo's references to 'paradiso' and contrasts its 'celestial' harmonies with the infernal gloom on stage."[321] The vocal line becomes more and more virtuosic as Orpheus pursues his plea, reaching its peak at "Orfeo son io" (I am Orpheus).

Finally, Charon falls asleep and Orpheus is able to steal his boat and cross the river.

In *Orfeo* Monteverdi almost single-handedly translated opera from an academic exercise into an enduring art form.

Descartes, *Discourse on the Method*, 1637

Deductive Reasoning

Imbued with our own way of thinking about the world, we may have difficulty imagining that people did not always think the way we do. The work of René Descartes, often described as the "father of modern philosophy," helped to shape our modern world-view by presenting a radical alternative to existing perspectives. "Because the Reformation and Counter-Reformation were tearing holes in the certainties of religious belief, the scientific revolution could begin, by allowing the light of secular reason to shine through the gashes; and once people started to see by that light it became inextinguishable."[322]

Descartes' celebrated assertion *cogito ergo sum* ("I am thinking, therefore I must exist") represents the distillation of systematic doubt. Having questioned everything he could imagine, Descartes found that he could not doubt his own existence, because otherwise who could be having his thoughts? Enraptured with deductive reasoning, Descartes wrote: *"The long chains of simple and easy reasonings by means of which geometers are accustomed to reach the conclusions of their most difficult demonstrations led me to imagine that all things, to the knowledge of which man is competent, are mutually connected in the same way, and that there is nothing so far removed from us as to be beyond our reach, or so hidden that we cannot discover it, provided only we abstain from accepting the false for the true, and always preserve in our thoughts the order necessary for the deduction of one truth from another."[323]* One could scarcely ask for a better articulation of Enlightenment optimism.

Problem-Solving

Descartes displayed an unbounded confidence in the capacity of human reason. "The essence of Cartesianism is distilled in the belief that with technology, humans can solve not just any technological problem but any problem at all."[324] In his *Discourse on the Method* Descartes proposed an analytical procedure for solving mathematical problems:

"1. To never take anything to be true that I do not know evidently to be such.

2. To divine each difficulty that I examine into as many parts as is possible and that is required to best resolve it.

3. To conduct my thoughts in order by commencing with the most simple objects and easiest to know, to ascend little by little as by degrees to knowledge of the most complicated; and to assume an order even between those that do not precede one another naturally.

4. To make enumerations so complete, and reviews so general, that I am assured to have omitted nothing."[325]

Analytical Geometry

The *Discourse on the Method* concludes with an essay on *La géometrie* in which Descartes explains the principles of analytical geometry combining the methods of geometry and algebra. We are familiar with the notion of a grid: many cities are laid out on a latticework of streets and avenues, allowing a given intersection to be easily identified. For Descartes, a point on a geometrical plane can be given an address in terms of its position along two axes: the horizontal and the vertical.

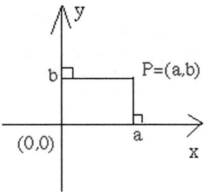

In this case, point P has an address of (a, b): "a" units along the horizontal, or x-axis, and "b" units along the vertical or y-axis. We can represent not only individual points but entire curves. In principle, every curve corresponds to an equation that uniquely describes the points of that curve. For example, $x^2 + y^2 = r^2$ is the equation of a circle with its centre at the origin and radius r.

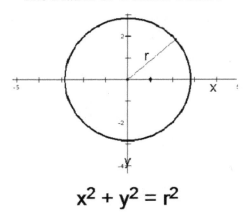

$$x^2 + y^2 = r^2$$

Our contemporary faith in science and technology finds its source in the work of Descartes. "The seventeenth-century rise of Modern Science, the eighteenth-century Enlightenment, the nine-teenth-century Industrial Revolution, your twentieth-century per-sonal computer, and the twenty-first-century deciphering of the brain—all Cartesian. The modern world is Cartesian to the core—this world of high technology, mathematical physics, cal-culators and robots, molecular biology and genetic engineering—a world in which deductive reason guides and controls not only our science, technology, and practical action, but most of our moral decisions as well."[326]

Descartes' rationalism, the source of modern scientific thinking, swept away superstition, and along with it myth, mysticism, intu-ition and spirituality.

Velásquez, *Las Meninas*, 1656 PLATE 12

Artist-Courtier

If you were an artist serving in the court of Philip IV of Spain and desirous of elevating your position, how might you employ your talents in pursuit of that end? You might endear yourself to the king by producing numerous portraits of his daughter, the

Infanta Margaret Theresa. But if you had the gifts of Diego Velásquez you might choose as the setting for a portrait your own
studio, filled with copies of the works of Rubens. "Rubens, who
had been knighted by Philip IV in 1631, was inevitably for Velásquez the model of the modern artist-courtier, and the pictures
within the picture in *Las Meninas* provided another bit of ammu-
nition in his own struggle for social as well as artistic recognition. ... Velásquez pictured the scene in a room ... hung with
paintings after Rubens ... that represent the status of painting as a
liberal art."[327]

Fictive Mirror, Fictive Portrait

The king, sensitive to his aging, had forbidden Velásquez to
paint his portrait, so the artist, wishing to depict himself as worthy to stand beside royalty, conceived of an enormous painting of
the royal couple but angled it out of the spectator's view. The
royal family actually witnessed the artist at work producing the
painting we know as *Las Meninas*. According to Antonio Palo-
mino, a contemporary writer, "This painting was highly es-
teemed by His Majesty, and while it was being executed he went
frequently to see it being painted. So did our lady Doña Mariana
of Austria and the Infantas and ladies, who came down often,
considering this a delightful treat and entertainment."[328] One can
thus imagine a scene very much like the one presented in the
painting.

An otherwise scrupulously accurate rendering of the artist's studio includes one important invention: a mirror against the far
wall showing the royal couple as they pose for the large, invisible portrait. The artist not only appears in the painting but completely controls the situation since only he can see the portrait.
Las Meninas, therefore, is not a painting about a king but a painting about painting and, by extension, the noble status of the artist. "The impossible and prohibited royal portrait did not exist in
reality, as it had never really been painted. ... The mirror was the

only architectural or decorative element in the room that did not actually exist. ... Velásquez invented the looking glass in *Las Meninas* in order to introduce the king and queen discreetly into his composition. It is the one inaccuracy in his portrayal of the chamber. Fictive mirror, fictive royal portrait."[329]

Suspended Moment

The execution of a portrait requires the immobility of the subject, often repeated over a succession of sittings. In this sense, the artist takes control of time. Since the advent of photography, we have become accustomed to seeing action frozen to preserve a particular instant. A spectator in the seventeenth century would have found the treatment of time in *Las Meninas* somewhat shocking. One of the ladies in waiting reaches out to the Infanta; the courtier at the rear door is captured in mid-step, while the artist himself holds his brush poised over his palette. "Everything in the painting is slippery, every action is suspended: it is *about* to happen or it has *just* happened. ... In *Las Meninas* time seems to be frozen, as if it had been stopped in a precious moment that gives the event a rare quality."[330]

Finally, the artist's glance fixes us, the spectators, in position— he controls us, too. Standing in the same position as the royal couple, we assist in fulfilling "Velásquez's aim to create a work that would symbolize the nobility of the art of painting."[331] Art dares depict what words dare not speak: compare the size of the artist in Velásquez's painting with that of the king.

Molière, *Le Misanthrope*, 1666

Rules of Drama

Molière inherited a number of rules from antiquity, honoring the belief that the ancient Greek writers had already achieved the absolute of beauty in literature. From Aristotle came the rules of the three unities of place, time and action, which Molière observes by setting the drama in a single place (Célimène's salon), allowing the action to unfold in real time, and confining the action to one central story (Alceste's pursuit of Célimène). From the Roman lyric poet Horace came the edict that the object of drama is "to please and to educate."

Then there were the rules of French classic drama: *Les bienséances* (nothing should be presented that offends good taste, even if they are historical events); and *La vraisemblance* (actions should be believable—no soliloquies, no machines, no magic, no *deus ex machina* to rescue a hopelessly complicated plot with a last-minute wave of the wand).

Finally, there were rules governing the language of the drama. The text had to be written in *alexandrins*—twelve-syllable lines of classic tragedy and comedy, with a caesura in the middle and set in rhymed couplets.

Je veux qu'on soit sincère,// et qu'en homme d'honneur On ne lâche aucun mot //qui ne parte du cœur.
I would have people be sincere, and that, like men of honour, no word be spoken that comes not from the heart.

Rules of Society

Within these restraints Molière created *Le Misanthrope,* a comedy that mocked the hypocrisy of French court society: the irony that Alceste, obsessed with honesty, should pursue Célimène, a notorious liar; the exaggeration of Alceste's one-man revolt against society, and his impossible standards for his beloved, who must join him in a reclusive existence; the buffoonery of the pompous, litigious poetaster Oronte, who demands Alceste's honest opinion of his work, then takes offense when he receives it.

"Game playing and play-acting with love are central and inter-acting parts of this piece of theater. Themes of falseness and sincerity are clearly being dealt with here, although we must be alert to the need for a cautious assignment of values of morality to certain characters or attitudes they represent. In a simple ex-ample, it is obvious that some social good can be served by de-liberate insincerity which flatters a person harmlessly."[332]

Breaking the Rules

Malicious gossip and character assassination must be contained within certain limits. "The one rule of the game of love and self-love, which is understood by all except Alceste, is that the ego is permitted a certain self-indulgence but not to the point where it disrupts the opportunities of other people to enjoy the same pleasure."[333]

Célimène, a more skilled player than Alceste, also ends up break-ing the rules. "Célimène is proceeding to her own downfall when her comments on Alceste, Oronte, and the foppish noble-men Acaste and Clitandre, her suitors, are brought to confront her in letters at the end of the play. She will overstep the rules of the game, just as Alceste has done. ... In the cases of Alceste and Célimène people are wounded too much to pardon. Real harm to positions of social power cannot be allowed."[334]

At first hoping to change her flirtatious nature by the force of his own virtue, Alceste finally insists that Célimène renounce socie-ty and join him in solitude, a proposal that the twenty-year-old girl indignantly rejects.

Moi, renoncer au monde avant que de vieillir, Et dans votre desert aller m'ensevelir!	Me, renounce the world be-fore growing old, And go bury myself in the wilderness with you!

A conventional romantic comedy would find some way to reconcile Alceste and Célimène but Molière insists on breaking that rule, too. "Over the end of the dark comedy hangs an aura of tragedy betokened by the separation and futility of two extraordinary lives."[335]

Molière's subversive comedy, meticulously observing external rules of drama, pillories the hypocrisy of a rule-bound social order and even thwarts one's expectations of a comedic happy ending.

Newton, *Principia Mathematica*, 1687

Laws of Motion

The English poet Alexander Pope famously wrote, "Nature and nature's laws lay hid in night; God said 'Let Newton be' and all was light." Newton's accomplishments, particularly in the fields of physics and mathematics, elevated science to a new level in the public mind and led to efforts in every field of study to discover universal laws.

Newton's Laws of Motion now seem so commonplace that they tend to be regarded as self-evident. In the language of the *Principia Mathematica* they read:

Law I: *"Every body continues in its state of rest, or of uniform motion in a right line, unless it is compelled to change that state by forces impressed upon it."* (A projectile would continue indefinitely in its path but for the force of gravity.)

Law II: *"The change of motion is proportional to the motive force impressed; and is made in the direction of the right line in which that force is impressed."* (In modern language, force is proportional to acceleration)

Law III: *"To every action there is always opposed an equal reaction: or, the mutual actions of two bodies upon each other are*

always equal, and directed to contrary parts."[336] (Perhaps the
clearest example of this principle comes in the form of the recoil
from the firing of a cannon or rifle.) "The first two laws are deductions from the historical experiments of Galileo, but the principle expressed in the third law is one Newton himself introduced."[337]

Universal Gravitation

The climactic point in the *Principia Mathematica* comes with
Newton's formulation of the law of universal gravitation. *"That
there is a power of gravity pertaining to all bodies, proportional
to the several quantities of matter which they contain. That all
the planets gravitate one towards another, we have proved before; as well as that the force of gravity towards every one of
them, considered apart, is inversely as the square of the distance
of places from the centre of the planet. And thence it follows,
that the gravity tending towards all the planets is proportional to
the matter which they contain.*"[338]

The familiar story of Newton discovering gravity after being
struck in the head by an apple overlooks three critical elements
in his formulation: 1. In contrast to Aristotle, who maintained
that the apple had a natural inclination to seeking its proper
place, Newton said instead that the apple was obeying an outside
force, the force of gravity; 2. In contrast to previous beliefs that
terrestrial forces were distinct from celestial phenomena, Newton
insisted that a single gravitational force described all phenomena;
3. In contrast to the idea of the earth pulling everything toward
it, Newton proposed that the mass of the apple also exerted a
gravitational force upon the earth.

"Newton's *Principia* tried to explain all the motions of the heavens according to the law of universal gravitation. [Before New-
ton] gravity came to be regarded as an attribute of any large material body, and was spoken of as the tendency by which various

celestial bodies tend to unite and come together. Newton's master stroke lay in generalizing this to a law of universal gravitation, wherein every particle of matter, however small, attracts every other particle. In its modern form, the principle states: *Any two material particles attract each other with a force varying directly with the product of their masses and inversely with the square of the distance between them.*[339] In symbolic form, $F = GMm/d^2$, where F represents force, M and m the masses of the particles in question, d the distance between them, and G a universal constant.

Calculus

Newton wrote in 1676, "If I have seen further, it is by standing on the shoulders of giants."[340] Standing on the shoulders of giants like Copernicus, Galileo, Kepler and Descartes, Newton was able to see far enough to create the calculus, one of the great achievements of western culture. (The need for calculus was widely recognized, and the German mathematician Leibniz formulated essentially the same ideas at about the same time as Newton.)

Why was calculus necessary? Calculus allows one to determine the instantaneous speed of objects moving at varying speeds, such as the planets. Calculus in general deals with rates of change, and since change forms an essential part of disciplines ranging from chemistry and physics to economics, sociology, business and medicine, it becomes apparent why the invention of calculus had such a substantial influence.

Standing on the shoulders of giants enabled Newton to see how local regularities fit into larger universal principles, an attitude that presaged the current search in physics for a "Theory of Everything."

Hobbes, *Leviathan*, 1651

Natural Law

Both Hobbes and Locke began their political treatises by speculating on the condition of humans in the so-called "state of nature," an imaginary situation without any government whatever, but the two men took radically different positions on what the state of nature might be like. Writing in the spirit of Newton, Hobbes proposed some twenty laws of nature, which begin:

First Law: every man ought to endeavor peace, as far as he has hope of obtaining it; and when he cannot obtain it, that he may seek and use all helps and advantages of war.

Second Law: a man may be willing, when others are so too... to lay down this right to all things; and be contented with so much liberty against other men as he would allow other men against himself.

Third Law: Injustice, therefore, is failure to perform in a covenant; all else is just.

"The best strategy to obtain security is to master as many others as one can; but because this is true for everyone, the ensuing situation will be one in which each is prepared to attempt to conquer each other. ... Hobbes concludes that the natural condition is a war of all against all, for every person is disposed to fight every other, and there is no established authority to prevent them from acting on this disposition. ... This general condition of enmity precludes the security and stability necessary to develop arts, letters, engineering, and durable collective enterprises; everyone lives in 'continual fear and danger of violent death,' and the life of natural man is 'solitary, poor, nasty, brutish, and short.'"[341]

Social Contract

To escape this state of war of all against all, people accept a social contract, a concept that Hobbes elaborated in his book *Leviathan,* published in 1651. Hobbes writes that a commonwealth may be formed when everyone agrees: *"I authorize and give up my right of governing myself to this man, or to this assembly of men, on this condition; that thou give up, thy right to him, and authorize all his actions in like manner."*

Hobbes goes on to distinguish three possible forms of government based on the social contract. *"When the representative is one man, then is the Commonwealth a monarchy; when an assembly of all that will come together, then it is a democracy, or popular Commonwealth; when an assembly of a part only, then it is called an aristocracy."* Of the three forms, Hobbes preferred a strong monarchy, a perhaps unsurprising conclusion given the recent experience of the English Civil War.

"He concluded that the only effective way out of the conflict caused by pride and various points of view was the absolute imposition of the will of one sovereign on all subjects and all contentious issues. For Hobbes, it was clear that even what many would call tyranny was preferable to the uncertainty and violence of civil war."[342]

Famous Frontispiece PLATE 13

In the introduction to the work Hobbes explains the metaphor he has chosen to represent a strong central government. *"For by Art is created that great Leviathan called a commonwealth, or state, ... which is but an Artificial Man; though of greater stature and strength than the Natural, for whose protection and defence it was intended; and in which, the Sovereignty is an Artificial Soul, as giving life and motion to the whole body."* "The *OED* tells us that Hobbes's *Leviathan* changed forever the meaning of the word, which originally connoted the biblical sea monster or whale, familiar from Isaiah and the Book of Job, but with Hobbes became an epithet for the all-powerful state."[343]

The frontispiece to the book depicts the torso and arms of a giant figure incorporating some three hundred smaller figures, as if to suggest that the all-powerful sovereign represents the people. "The upper half of the frontispiece portrays a landscape of rolling hills, dominated by the figure of a giant whose torso emerges from the crest of the hills and towers heavenward. The tip of the sword and the head of the crozier extend to the upper boader of the picture and obtrude into the phrase ... from the Book of Job [41:24] describing the towering strength of the sea monster Leviathan. The power of the Leviathan figure is characterized by the way that he spans the space, from the tip of his sword piercing the distant heaven, to the staff of his crozier reaching down into the foreground of the city. ... As an extension of the sword and bishop's crozier, the respective panels show the extent of the sovereign's secular and sacral spheres."[344]

Hobbes, pessimistic about human judgment, calls for an all-powerful benevolent monarch, ignoring history's lesson that those two adjectives seldom go hand in hand.

Locke, *Second Treatise on Government*, 1689

Equality and Natural Rights

John Locke took a more optimistic view of humanity. He believed that in the state of nature, the law of reason would prevent people from harming each other. According to Locke, people enter into a social contract to avoid the state of war and to protect property. In the social contract, people give up certain rights to the government, either a monarchy or a democracy. But legitimate authority must be derived by the consent of the governed. If the government, whether a monarchy or a legislative body, becomes tyrannical, the people have the right to rebel. Locke's ideas appear in his *Two Treatises of Government*, published in 1690. The second treatise, in particular, presented a number of ideas drawn on by Jefferson in the American Declaration of Independence, notably the concept of natural rights.

Locke insists, as a point of departure, on the equality of men in the state of nature. God created all of us in what was, morally speaking, *"a state of equality, wherein all the power and jurisdiction is reciprocal, no one having more than another."* (2nd T. 4). Locke, however, doesn't go so far as to accord equality to women. "Locke's position on the natural subjection of wives *is* an embarrassment for his general theory of equality."[345]

Labor Theory of Title

The state of nature, for Locke, offered virtually unlimited resources of land that any member of society could claim for his own provided he could use it advantageously. By general consent this then become his property which it is the responsibility of the state to protect.

In Section 32 of the *Second Treatise on Government* Locke writes, *"As much land as a man tills, plants, improves, cultivates, and can use the product of, so much is his property. He by his labour does, as it were, inclose it from the common. Nor will it invalidate his right, to say every body else has an equal title to it; and therefore he cannot appropriate, he cannot inclose, without the consent of all his fellow-commoners, all mankind. God, when he gave the world in common to all mankind, commanded man also to labour, and the penury of his condition required it of him. God and his reason commanded him to subdue the earth, i.e. improve it for the benefit of life, and therein lay out something upon it that was his own, his labour. He that in obedience to this command of God, subdued, tilled and sowed any part of it, thereby annexed to it something that was his property, which another had no title to, nor could without injury take from him."*

Social Contract and Right of Revolution

"Locke maintained that humans had originally lived in a state of nature characterized by absolute freedom and equality, in which there was no government of any kind. The only law was the law of nature (which Locke equated with the law of reason), by which individuals enforce for themselves their natural rights to life, liberty, and property. Soon, however, humans began to perceive that the inconveniences of the state of nature outweighed its advantages. Accordingly, they agreed first to establish a civil society based on absolute equality and then to set up a government to arbitrate the disputes that might arise within this civil society. But they did not make government's powers absolute. ... All powers not expressly surrendered to the government were reserved to the people themselves; as a result, governmental authority was both contractual and conditional."[346]

190

For Hobbes the social contract required permanent submission to the all-powerful sovereign. Locke, by contrast, considered the social contract to be a provisional measure. If the sovereign behaved like a tyrant, the people reserved the right to rebel against his authority. "Locke's argument is premised upon the assumption that popularly enacted laws establish limits to a ruler's exercise of power, and when these limits are exceeded, the ruler loses his authority, which then returns to the people as the original source of all political authority."[347]

Locke's optimistic yet pragmatic theory calls on government to protect "life, liberty and property," a ringing phrase that Jefferson tellingly modified to "life, liberty and the pursuit of happiness."

Connections: Rules

Rules appear throughout our survey of the seventeenth century, from the prescribed guides for conduct informing every aspect of life under Louis XIV, to the conflict over accepted procedures at the root of the English Civil War. The extension from rules to universal laws associated with the work of Isaac Newton marks the seventeenth century as the beginning of modern science.

Monteverdi was the first great composer to write in the new area of opera, a genre that emerged from academic study of the rules of ancient tragedy. Descartes in his *Discourse on the Method* elucidated the principles of the scientific method as well as rules of deduction. Velásquez slyly used the rules of reflection in a painting intended in part to alter his rank in court. Molière carefully observed the conventions governing French classic theater in creating a comedy that overthrew expectations of a happy ending while lampooning the rules of court society. Newton, by demonstrating that the force causing an apple to fall from the tree was identical to the force that governed planetary orbits, went from rules to universal laws. Newton's work spawned a search for general principles governing every aspect of human life, with Hobbes and Locke among the first to propose laws of political science.

18th Century

Context

Triangular Trade

"Molasses to rum to slaves" describes the seventeenth- and eighteenth-century pattern defined by need, greed and favorable trade winds in the absence of moral restraint. Molasses from the Caribbean would be shipped to New England to be turned into rum which could be shipped, along with other goods, to Africa to be exchanged for slaves. The dreaded "middle passage" in which slaves from Africa were transported to the New World, with many dying along the way, represents the human cost of this cynical commodification of life.

"Once mass slavery began, white Europeans soon saw that all slaves were Africans; from this they quickly developed the understanding that all black Africans were slaves. ... It was not only the ownership of people (something that was practiced in many societies) that was so grave, but the belief that because of their color they deserved nothing more than to be beasts of burden, combined with unusual cruelty."[348]

Natural Rights and American Revolution

For Hobbes and Locke, the state of nature and the social contract remained abstractions of political philosophy. For Thomas Jefferson and the other Founding Fathers who tried to frame a new model of government amid conflicting interests and seemingly irreconcilable differences, these issues were all too real. If "all men are created equal," as the Declaration of Independence proclaimed in 1776, how could slavery be justified? Did the birth of a new nation justify compromise on this point? *E pluribus unum* (out of many one) seemed like an unlikely motto for a contentious group of colonies but in the end accurately described the historical process.

England unwittingly played an essential role in unifying the colonies. From the perspective of the British parliament, the colonies, enjoying the protection of the mother country, should reasonably be expected to share the costs of maintaining a royal governor and a military presence. The colonists' cry of "No taxation without representation" concealed their actual position, no taxation under any circumstances. "The colonists' fury shows that, while they were subjects of the British crown, they already thought of themselves as autonomous political entities."[349] Greater vision on the British side might have eventually resulted in a relationship like that enjoyed with other nations in the Commonwealth. Instead, a revolutionary war led to complete independence, with the assistance of France and Spain, supporting "a cause which they would never have tolerated among their own colonies."[350]

Encyclopédie

The Enlightenment elevation of reason, inspired by Newton and fostered by Descartes, found supreme expression in the *Encyclopédie*, or Systematic Dictionary of the Arts, Sciences and Crafts, edited by Denis Diderot. The *Encyclopédie* "appeared in Paris in 17 volumes of 16,288 pages between 1751 and 1765, with further supplements, illustrations, and indexes appearing up to 1782. It was programmatic, opinionated, anticlerical, and highly critical of the regime; and its editors were regularly harassed by officialdom yet it was a monument to the age. It aimed at nothing less than a summary of the whole of human knowledge."[351]

The mania for encyclopedias reflected the confidence that knowledge would lead to perfection. "Following the example of Newton and his fellow scientists, people believed that if rationality was going to tell them *anything* about the world, it should be able to tell them *everything*. Unfettered rational enquiry would lead to a coherent body of knowledge, driven by underlying universal laws, that would reveal a benevolent pattern in all things."[352]

Euler, The Seven Bridges of Königsberg, 1735

Seven Bridges

Is mathematics invented or discovered? Do mathematicians create patterns or simply stumble onto relationships that are already "out there?" Clearly, mathematics *can* be invented: the simplest method is to take an existing body of mathematics, alter one fundamental assumption, and see where it leads you. But there's no denying that over and over, in the history of mathematics, an apparently abstract system eventually finds application in the physical world.

We can trace the invention of one branch of mathematics to a particular problem, known as "The Seven Bridges of Königsberg." The town of Königsberg was divided by the Pregel River, in the middle of which lay two large islands, connected to the mainland and to each other by seven bridges. In the 18th century the inhabitants of Königsberg would amuse themselves on a summer's afternoon with promenades that might take in one or more of the city's seven bridges. The most enthusiastic walkers tried to include as many of the bridges as possible, and it became a matter of some debate in the city whether one could invent a path that would cross all of the bridges exactly once. Nobody could find a solution, but then again, nobody could prove that a solution didn't exist.

Now Königsberg numbered among its inhabitants Leonard Euler, the greatest mathematician of the 18th century, but when the mayor of the city submitted the problem to Euler he initially refused to consider it. *"This type of solution bears little relationship to mathematics, and I do not understand why you expect a mathematician to produce it, rather than anyone else, for the solution is based on reason alone, and its discovery does not depend on any mathematical principle."*[353]

But Euler evidently changed his mind because in March 1736 he wrote to a fellow mathematician: *"A problem was posed to me about an island in the city of Königsberg, surrounded by a river spanned by seven bridges, and I was asked whether someone could traverse the separate bridges in a connected walk in such a way that each bridge is crossed only once. I was informed that hitherto no-one had demonstrated the possibility of doing this, or shown that it is impossible. This question is so banal, but seemed to me worthy of attention in that geometry, nor algebra, nor even the art of counting was sufficient to solve it. ... And so, after some deliberation, I obtained a simple, yet completely established, rule with whose help one can immediately decide for all examples of this kind, with any number of bridges in any arrangement, whether such a round trip is possible, or not."*[354]

Vertices of Odd Degree

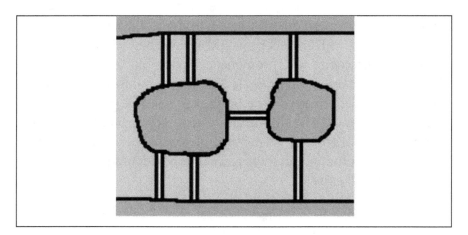

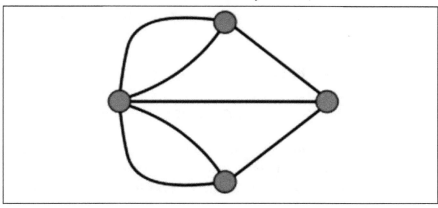

If we accept the upper figure as a sketch of the map problem, the lower figure reduces the problem to its critical elements, vertices and paths. Every time you enter and leave a vertex, you account for an even number of paths—one going in, one going out. When you think about the problem this way, you can appreciate that there can be *at most* two vertices with an *odd* number of paths, namely the starting point and the ending point. Every other vertex must have an even number of paths if you plan to cross every bridge exactly once. When you start counting the paths in the diagram you can see why nobody ever succeeded in traversing the seven bridges. Every vertex has an odd number of paths, going from left to right: 5, 3, 3 and 3.

Applications

Graph theory, which Euler essentially invented in order to deal with the problem, has led to many developments in mathematics, including topology and network theory. Practical applications of graph theory appear in the analysis of transportation networks, computer chip design, molecular biology, neuroscience and even linguistics and sociology.

A problem that Euler originally dismissed as too trivial to merit his attention, but lying just outside the boundaries of existing mathematical thought, eventually led him to invent a new branch of mathematics.

Bach, B Minor Mass, ca. 1748

Compendium

Toward the end of his life, J.S. Bach began compiling the works he particularly wanted to entrust to posterity into a series of compendia. He gathered his greatest works for organ and harpsichord into four volumes entitled *Clavierübung* ("keyboard practice") comprising six partitas, the French and Italian overtures, the Organ Mass, and the Goldberg Variations. Many years earlier Bach had composed settings of the Kyrie and Gloria of the Roman Catholic Mass as part of a job application for a post at the court of Dresden. Now he resolved to finish the mass setting with a Credo, Sanctus and Agnus Dei. "The completion of the mass had no external motivations that we know of. Rather, it was part of the encyclopedic series of works Bach created towards the end of his life, which represented different aspects of his style: the *Art of the Fugue* is his treatise on counterpoint while the B Minor Mass would become the crowning example of his vocal style."[355]

To some extent, such exhaustive treatments seem to have been an essential part of Bach's personality. In 1722 Bach composed the Well-Tempered Clavier, a series of 24 preludes and fugues in all twelve major and minor keys, in order to illustrate the benefits of a new tempering system. Twenty years later he composed another set of 24 preludes and fugues in all the major and minor keys. Clearly Bach had a predilection for completeness.

Most of the movements of the B Minor Mass are borrowed from earlier cantatas. Bach uses a chorus from Cantata 29, "Wir danken dir, Gott," (We thank you, God) to set the text "Gratias agimus tibi," (We give thanks to thee). This makes sense since the German and Latin texts are virtually synonymous. Why did Bach re-use these movement? Some scholars suggest that Bach had a pretty good idea that the B Minor Mass, even though it would never be performed in his lifetime, might have a better chance of surviving than individual cantatas. With good reason, he had a high opinion of the chorus "Wir danken dir, Gott" and wanted to preserve it in the Mass as a kind of showcase of his very best work. He liked the movement enough to use it again for the final movement of the mass, "Dona nobis pacem" (Grant us peace).

Chiasm

Artists of the eighteenth century had a particular fondness for symmetrical structures, notably in the form of wings on either side of a main building, a basic pattern underlying architecture as compact as Monticello or as vast as Versailles. "Balanced proportion and symmetry, which are the underlying principles of Versailles, were seen in a baroque worldview as signs of perfection, mirroring the beauty and perfection of divine creation."[356]

Bach's penchant for chiastic structures can be plainly observed in the nine movements that compose the Credo section of the mass, arranged in such a way that the Crucifixus movement comes at the very center. The outer "wings" of this musical palace embrace choruses in *stile antico* (the Renaissance style of writing for voices of equal importance, with carefully controlled treatment of dissonance) and *stile moderno* (contrasting instrumental and vocal voices, with a strong emphasis on the underlying bass line).

A	Credo in unum Deum *(Chorus: stile antico)*
	Patrem omnipotentem *(Chorus: stile moderno)*
B	Et in unum Dominum *(Aria)*
C	Et incarnatus *(Chorus)*
D	Crucifixus *(Chorus)*

C	Et resurrexit *(Chorus)*
B	Et in Spiritum sanctum *(Aria)*
A	Confiteor *(Chorus: stile antico)*
	Et expecto *(Chorus: stile moderno*

Bach's architectural scheme for the mass seems so right, even so inevitable, that we have to remind ourselves that the Roman Catholic liturgy in itself specifies no such structure, and that no composer before or since has treated the text in quite this way.

Counterpoint

Counterpoint, the juxtaposition of two or more melodic lines, represents an extraordinary musical challenge, as any music student required to complete counterpoint exercises will attest. The Dona Nobis Pacem, the final movement of the work, develops two themes, first separately and then together. "The vocalists are accompanied by the instruments, and Bach's aim is to reach the highest degree of transparency in the polyphonic texture by supporting every vocal voice with a different instrumental timbre."[357]

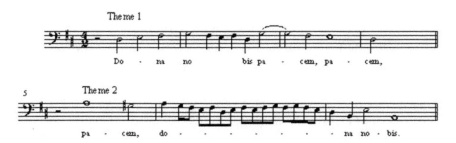

The trumpets begin by doubling the vocal parts and then expand the texture to six contrapuntal lines by making independent entries.

Bach took pleasure in the sheer virtuosity of overcoming extreme challenges of counterpoint, and I believe that the collections of works he made toward the end of his life, culminating in his masterpiece, the Mass in B Minor, represent a kind of statement to the world: this I have accomplished.

Fielding, *Tom Jones*, 1749

Symmetrical Structures

The overall theme of *Tom Jones* appears in the novel's full title: *The History of Tom Jones, a Foundling.* The question of Tom's parentage occupies much of the story, serves as an impediment to his marrying his true love, Sophia Western and, when finally resolved, permits a happy ending. The balance and symmetry of neoclassical architecture find their place in the novel's system of contrasting pairs of characters.

Squire Allworthy (generous, forgiving, sophisticated)	Squire Western (suspicious, grudging, crude)
Bridget Allworthy (the squire's sister)	Mrs. Western (the squire's unmarried sister)
Tom (generous, fun-loving)	Blifil (self-seeking, hypocriti-

Sophia Western (respectable, open)	cal)
Mr. Partridge (Tom's faithful servant)	Molly Seagram (unrespecta-ble, calculating)
	Mrs. Honour (Sophia's maid)

One critic conceives of *Tom Jones as* "shaped like a Palladian mansion. ... The novel is divided into eighteen books. As has often been pointed out, the first six of these deal with events in Somerset, at the homes of Allworthy and Western, and the last six with events in London. Tom and Sophia are separated in Book VI and do not see one another again until Book XIII. The central six books deal with events on the road while hero and heroine make their way from what had been home to London."[358]

Although the complicated plot takes many twists and turns, the novel has the clear three-part structure of many epics: a hero leaves home; he goes on a journey; after many adventures, he returns home. The novel also displays a two-part symmetry, with the episode at Upton Inn occurring at the exact middle. Before Upton Inn, Sophia pursues Tom; thereafter, Tom pursues Sophia.

Authorial Absolutism

Each of the eighteen books opens with an introductory chapter in which the narrator comments on the story, the act of writing, and the relationship of the author to the reader, as we see in this excerpt from Book II, Chapter 1: *"For I am, in reality, the Founder of a new Province of Writing, so I am at liberty to make what Laws I please therein. And these Laws, my Readers, whom I consider as my Subjects, are bound to believe in and to obey; with which they may readily and cheerfully comply, I do hereby assure them, that I shall principally regard their Ease and Advantage in all such Institutions."*

When the eponymous Jones first makes his appearance, in Book III, Chapter II, Fielding exercises an appropriate literary flourish. *"As we determined when we first sat down to write this History, to flatter no Man, but to guide our Pen throughout by the Directions of Truth, we are obliged to bring our Heroe on the Stage in a much more disadvantageous Manner than we could wish; and to declare honestly, even at his first Appearance, that it was the universal Opinion of all Mr. Allworthy's Family that he was certainly born to be hanged."*

Identity and Irony

Fielding continually asserts his authorial presence, not only in the introductory chapters to each book but also in the careful control of knowledge. One may regard the novel as an enormous exercise in dramatic irony, including both the usual definition, in which the audience knows something that a main character does not, and also the reverse, in which a character deliberately conceals information from the audience. While the true identity of Tom Jones himself lies at the core of the plot, the hidden or mistaken identities of various other characters adds to its intricacy. In particular, the identity of Mrs. Waters, who is not Captain Waters' wife, nor Fitzpatrick's wife, nor Tom's wife, has been described by one critic as the keystone of the plot.

Unlike a sonnet, a painting, or a piece of plainsong, which we can examine in their entirety in a few moments, Fielding's rollicking novel takes a fair bit of time to assimilate. But the spirit of *Tom Jones* inhabits the rationalistic world of cause and effect. If Newton undertook to formulate universal laws governing every object in God's creation, Fielding seems to enjoy his position as absolute monarch of a world he has created with every detail under his authorial control.

In this plot-driven novel, Fielding not only pulls the strings but continually appears on stage to revel in his role as puppet-master.

Jefferson, *Monticello*, 1772 PLATE 14

Neo-Palladianism

We have observed the influence of classical antiquity in the rules of French classic drama and in the scholarly speculation that led to the invention of opera. The neoclassic movement in architecture sought relief from over-ornamentation through a return to the simplicity of Greek and Roman art. Palladian architecture, derived from the designs of the 16th-century Italian architect Andrea Palladio, represented a return to architecture based on mathematical proportions. Palladio's work, with its pillars, arches and porticos, echoes the symmetry of Greek and Roman temple architecture.

Jefferson's careful study of European architecture during his time as ambassador to France in the 1780s left him dissatisfied with the first version of Monticello and he resolved to rework the building in the prevailing Palladian style. "The Palladian style is best expressed in his villas. They stood in contrast to the ornate style of the late Renaissance. Inside and out, the emphasis was on proportion, balance, and symmetry; the whole structure and

the rooms within were often based on mathematical ratios."[359]
To the basic Palladian concept of a central core with symmetrical
wings, Jefferson added octagonal forms, hidden stairs, and red
brick construction. One of the most striking features of Monticello is the octagonal dome that replaces a second-story portico.

Slavery Obscured

Slavery in the 18th and 19th centuries, followed by segregation in
the 19th and 20th, represented America's dirty secret, an acute
embarrassment to the man who had famously written "all men
are created equal." "Although Jefferson lived on a daily basis
with the reality of slavery, he shaped his life to have as few face-
to-face confrontations with slavery as possible. As with so much
of his life and thought, he arranged a system of neat compart-
ments to keep separate things that he believed ought to remain
separate. Some of Monticello's most distinctive features shield-
ed the plantation's slave life from Jefferson's gaze, in ways similar to those followed by other planters, but always bearing the
stamp of his own architectural ingenuity."[360]

A series of dumbwaiters connected to the kitchen in the lower
level permitted the delivery of food and wine to the dining area
where Jefferson and his guests could serve themselves. "Further,
the estate's landscaping and covered walkways blocked the main
house's direct view of the slave quarters."[361]

Ostentatious Modesty

"From the outset, Monticello was ostentatiously modest, with
window treatments that disguised its upper stories and created
the illusion of a single-story building. ... Though the entire complex would grow to contain forty-three rooms, thirty-three in the
house itself, it did not give the impression of a big house where
the master reaffirmed his exalted position in a hierarchy of orders
among whites by staging rituals of deference and subordination

at odds with the new republic's egalitarian ethos. Monticello was not meant to diminish awestruck visitors, but rather to arouse their interest in what interested Jefferson."[362]

"If any one particular detail within a residence represents an opulent symbol of everyday life, it is a grandiose staircase. In the marble halls and palaces of Europe, a staircase was more than a means of getting from one floor to the other—it was a symbol of aristocratic superiority. Within the aristocratic homes, it was also the first monumental element seen by a visitor upon entering. Noblemen often greeted visitors from the top of a grand, wide, often double-switchback staircase. Their welcoming gestures were from elaborate heights as they descended to the adoration of the guests. The grand staircase became a central feature of the mansions and palaces of Europe and later of the grand center-hall colonials in America. In essence, the grand staircase was a symbol of wealth and power. Jefferson, however, would have none of this and within his own home designed a radically different type of staircase, based in part on his European visit and Enlightenment ideals."[363]

This "ostentatious modesty" may have had an effect on visitors similar to that of fellow actors who Laurence, Lord Olivier insisted should address him as "Larry." Recalling John F. Kennedy's observation, "It has been said the greatest volume of sheer brainpower in one place occurred when Jefferson dined alone," we may wonder whether Jefferson's visitors would really have been put entirely at ease by his elaborate unpretentiousness.

The classical symmetry of Monticello embodies the Enlightenment belief in the power of the rational mind to overcome social contradictions.

Smith, *The Wealth of Nations*, 1776

Laws of Economics

The search for universal laws inspired by Newton's example extended to economics. In *The Wealth of Nations* Adam Smith explained the now-familiar law of supply and demand. *"When the quantity of any commodity which is brought to market falls short of the effectual demand, all those who are willing to pay the whole value of the rent, wages, and profit, which must be paid in order to bring it thither, cannot be supplied with the quantity which they want. Rather than want it altogether, some of them will be willing to give more. A competition will immediately begin among them, and the market price will rise more or less above the natural price, according as either the greatness of the deficiency, or the wealth and wanton luxury of the competitors, happen to animate more or less the eagerness of the competition."*[364] Conversely, when the supply exceeds the demand, the price will tend to fall. A similar law governs the wages offered labourers, which tend to vary with the supply of labour. Adam Smith effectively founded the science of political economy by considering the subject as an interdependent system, comparable to the movement of planets in the solar system

Smith also saw the efficiencies inherent in the division of labor. "People come to exchange goods when they see that specialization is beneficial to all parties. If one man grows corn while another bakes bread, their cooperation will bring them a greater stock of food than if each did both jobs for himself."[365] Smith illustrates the principle from an experience he had seen for himself. "A small pin factory, employing ten men on eighteen operations, produced about 50,000 pins a day; if one unskilled man were to set about pin-making on his own, a day's work would bring him no more than one or a few pins. The example is highly effective because everyone is familiar with pins and hardly anyone would guess that the difference in the amount produced is so enormous."[366] The factory assembly line can be seen as a direct application of Smith's principle.

Invisible Hand

Smith observed that a group of individuals, each motivated solely by self-interest, when viewed collectively will appear to be influenced by an "invisible hand" promoting the general good *"It is not from the benevolence of the butcher, the brewer, or the baker that we expect our dinner, but from their regard to their own interest. We address ourselves, not to their humanity but to their self-love, and never talk to them of our own necessities but of their advantages."*

"By acting according to the dictates of our moral faculties, *'we necessarily pursue the most effectual means for promoting the happiness of mankind, and may therefore be said, in some sense, to co-operate with the Deity, and to advance as far as in our power, the plan of Providence.'* These statements illustrate one of Smith's most characteristic theses: the view that man is led as if by an Invisible Hand to promote ends which were not part of his original intention."[367]

Free Markets vs. Mercantilism

Mercantile theory, as pursued under Colbert's direction in France, supposed that "the wealth of nations" resulted from protective tariffs that would reduce imports and thereby support local manufacturing. "A favourable balance of trade, that is to say, an excess of exports over imports, would add to the national stock of money, and so, it was thought, the government should regulate the pattern of trade to reach a favourable balance."[368] Adam Smith argued the opposite: that wealth would result from free trade in open markets. Open competition would allow the law of supply and demand to bring about lower prices that would act to the benefit of all.

Free trade can thus be viewed as a global extension of the division of labor. "The protection of a home industry from the competition of imports helps that industry but is harmful to the country as a whole because it promotes monopoly and high prices; like the individuals in the division of labour, a nation benefits more by producing what it can do best and exchanging its products with those of other countries."[369] "It will be apparent that the concept of the philosophical or analytical system as a kind of 'imaginary machine' is particularly apt as a description of Smith's contribution to theoretical economics."[370]

For Adam Smith, human behavior in the aggregate is as predictable and law-abiding as the motions of the planets. While his *laissez-faire* philosophy has been seized upon by conservative politicians, Smith consistently pointed to the role of government in providing public services.

Kant, *Groundwork for a Metaphysics of Morals*, 1785

Arguments for God's Existence

In his *Critique of Pure Reason* Kant sought to refute the classic arguments for the existence of God. With regard to Anselm's ontological argument Kant insists that "existence" is not a predicate, but simply another form of the verb "to be." Certain nouns may be used as attributes for God, such as omnipotence, omniscience, and the like, but "existence" is not a proper attribute in the same sense as the others. Kant argues that you cannot leap from concept to reality, as in "the thought of God" to "the existence of God." We cannot say that the idea of God implies God's existence.

Kant similarly refutes the Thomas Aquinas' cosmological argument, based on the necessity of a first cause. Kant insists that the concept of cause only makes sense for a phenomenon (something perceived by the senses), whereas God is a *noumenon* (something conceived in the mind rather than perceived by the senses). The cosmological argument proceeds from the "necessity" of a certain being to the fact of its existence, which is valid only if ideas and facts can be converted. But Kant's refutation of the ontological argument already shows that they cannot.

Morality and Reason

Christianity posits God's law as the basis for human morality. The Old Testament contains laws governing every aspect of human existence. Jesus reduced the legal apparatus to two principles: love God and love your neighbor. But God remains the source. "Morality thus becomes something external to our own nature ... It has to be imposed on us." Reduced to its most basic terms, "Morality is simply obedience."[371]

Kant insisted on a rational basis for morality without any dependence on external authority. "The conception of morality as autonomy was Kant's fundamental innovation in moral philosophy."[372] "It was a decisive step away from the spirit of moral authoritarianism when Kant considered our own rational will to be the author of morality's commands."[373]

Categorical Imperative

In *Groundwork for a Metaphysics of Morals* Kant undertook to establish a moral system based only on reason, rather than any effort to understand divine intention. The result has become known as Kant's Categorical Imperative: *So act that the principle underlying your action might become universal law.* Kant illustrates with an example: "Someone considering getting out of a financial scrape by promising to repay a loan even though he has no intention of doing so. He is proposing to act on the maxim 'If I believe myself to be in financial need I will borrow money and promise to pay it back [in order to get out of my difficulty] although I also know that this will never happen.' He is then supposed to ask 'How it could stand if my maxim were a universal law. ... In a world in which everyone made false promises ... no one in his right mind would accept a promise, and thus one's own plan of getting out of trouble by making a false promise would become impossible. ... That is, because a world of false promises is actually logically impossible, there would be a practical contradiction between one's own maxim of making a false promise and the universalization of that maxim: you could not will the universalization of the maxim and still successfully act upon the maxim."[374]

Referring to the Categorical Imperative as FUL (formula of universal law), Shelly Kagan points out that "of course this does not mean that all rational beings *will* obey FUL. As we have already noted, humans at least, are only imperfectly rational, and thus may often fail to conform to FUL, sometimes knowingly. But everyone *should* obey FUL: they have reason to do so, based on the mere fact that they are rational. If the argument is sound, then FUL is a categorical imperative."[375] The *Groundwork* displays both Kant's confident reliance on human reason and a characteristic Enlightenment search for universal philosophical principles in the style of Newton's laws of physics. In Kant we observe a fundamentally social philosophy consistent with Schiller's dream, "Alle Menschen werden Brüder," (All men will become brothers) that we will encounter again in Beethoven's Ninth Symphony.

Kant reflected Enlightenment optimism in his confidence that by following his model of morality everyone would come to the same conclusion, to their common benefit.

Connections: Rationalism

The thinkers of the eighteenth-century Enlightenment relied on reason, not emotions or religious beliefs, as the basis for action, believing reason to be superior to sense perception. Euler, perhaps the most prolific mathematician of all time, in applying logical principles to solve an apparently non-mathematical problem, ended up creating a new branch of mathematics. Bach's symmetrical structures in music, like the symmetrical structure of Jefferson's home at Monticello, and the careful symmetry of Fielding's novel *Tom Jones*, reflected the Enlightenment preference for rational design. Adam Smith, following the example of Newton, sought general laws, and an underlying rationality, for economics. Kant proposed a purely rational, non-theistic basis for morality.

19th Century

Context

French Revolution

It has been noted that revolution occurs less as a result of simple oppression and more as a result of rising expectations. The division between the privileged (notably the monarch, the nobles and clergy) and the poor (pretty much everybody else) prevailed in Europe for hundreds of years without a successful revolution. The 19th century, frequently considered as a "long" century running from 1789 to 1914, often seems like one continuous revolutionary period, with each success raising the expectations of oppressed peoples. From that perspective, one might even wish to begin the century with 1776, for the success of the American Revolution added one more factor to the series of circumstances leading to the French Revolution in 1789, conventionally the beginning of the revolutionary period.

The so-called causes of the French Revolution have engendered nearly as many theories as the reasons for the fall of the Roman Empire. The example of the American Revolution undoubtedly played a part, as did Enlightenment ideals turned into the battle cry of "Liberty, Equality, Fraternity." A scarcity of food in the 1780s, the result of crop failures, combined with a heavy tax burden, the result of poor financial management by the monarchy, made the economic situation of the lower classes practically intolerable. Whatever the exact causes, the political instability of the 19th century in France clearly appears in the succession of republics, dictatorships and restorations of the monarchy which followed the French Revolution. Mid-century, particularly the year 1848, saw revolutionary activity all across Europe.

"In the long run the Revolution probably had its greatest impact in the realm of pure ideas. ... The idea of revolution itself was

213

irrepressible, even where particular revolutionary movements were repressed. Prior to 1789 most Europeans held a static view of the political and social order, where change could at best be limited and gradual. After 1789 everyone knew that the world could be turned upside down. ...The concept of human rights, if not invented by the French revolutionaries, was certainly given its strongest modern impetus."[376]

Industrialization

The Industrial Revolution strikes us in retrospect as a two-edged sword. On the one hand, it raised the standard of living by producing goods at lower cost and increased availability. On the other hand, the factory system created new problems of unemployment, lower wages and poor living conditions. "The factory system changed the relationships of the workplace, as well as its physical setting. Discipline, time-keeping and application were made conditions of employment rather than self-imposed standards. The workers were still largely paid by piecework but the owners insisted on long hours to raise the productivity of their machines. ... The factory stands as the emblem of industrialization, not as a technical system, nor as an economic phenomenon, but as a new way of working and living. ... Industrialization subjected millions of people to virtual slave labour in factories and mines."[377]

"Apart from the dozen factors which contributed to the initial Industrial Revolution, some thirty others have to be taken into account as change fueled change in the economic, social, cultural, psychological, political, and military spheres."[378] These include scientific and mechanized agriculture; new sources of power: coal, steam, gas, oil, electricity; power-driven machinery and heavy industry; improved transport: canals, roads, railways, flight; communications: post, telegraph, telephone, radio; the money economy: wages, prices, taxes, paper money; science and technology: research and development; exploitation: child labour, female labour, sweatshops.

Nationalism

In addition to the Enlightenment ideals of self-determination, 19th-century revolutions were stimulated by sentiments of nationalism, the idealistic attempt to reunite people who shared the same language. The Austrian Empire, ruled from Vienna, was threatened by nationalist movements of many of the different language groups included in the empire's embrace, including the Hungarians, Poles, Czechs, Slovaks, Serbs and Italians. Cultural patriotism, the notion that each people had its own particular spirit, or *Volksgeist,* fostered collections of native legends and fairy tales such as those by the Grimm brothers. "All over Europe, every branch of art and literature was mobilized to illustrate and to embroider national themes. ... Musicians recruited the harmonies and rhythms of their native folk dance and folk-song to elaborate distinctive national styles that became the hallmark of numerous 'national schools.'"[379]

"Nationalism also underlined an important distinction between 'civilization' and 'culture.' Civilization was the sum total of ideas and traditions which had been inherited from the ancient world and from Christianity; it was grafted onto the native cultures of all the peoples of Europe from the outside, to form the common legacy. Culture, in contrast, grew from the everyday life of the people. ... In earlier times, civilization had been extolled and culture despised. Nationalism now did the opposite. National cultures were extolled, and common civilization downgraded."[380]

Gauss, *Theory of the Motion of the Heavenly Bodies,* 1809

Prince of Mathematics

Like many mathematicians, Carl Friedrich Gauss was a child prodigy. The story is told that when Gauss was in grade school, the teacher assigned the class to add up all the numbers from 1 to 100, assuming that this would give him a breather for the better part of an hour. Imagine his astonishment when Gauss, in less than a minute, without applying pencil to paper, produced the correct answer. You can do this yourself: arrange the numbers from 1 to 100 in an imaginary line. Now arrange the numbers from 100 to 1 directly beneath them. The sum of each pair of numbers will then be 101, and the sum of all the groups will be 100 times this or 10100. But since you have now counted each number twice, you need to divide by 2 to get the correct result, 5050. The astonishing thing is not that Gauss did the math, or that he did it while still in grade school, but that he could see *how* to do it.

Non-Euclidean Geometry

"Through a point not on a given straight line, one and only one line can be drawn parallel to the given line." Ancient mathematicians, including Euclid, found this axiom troubling, and Euclid spent a great deal of time trying to deduce it from the preceding axioms. It turns out that the parallel postulate is not only not self-evident; it is not even necessarily true. Gauss worked out the mathematics for non-Euclidean geometries using alternatives to the parallel postulate, but so feared the consequences that, like Copernicus or Darwin, he kept his findings secret for many years. Yet Gauss dared to think the unthinkable.

Suppose we replace Euclid's parallel postulate with this version: "Through a point not on a given straight line, *no* lines can be drawn parallel to the given line." This is the geometry of a sphere. If we understand a line to be the shortest distance between two points, then a line on a sphere will be part of a great circle, and any "parallel" line will meet the original line at the poles, so no parallel lines are possible.

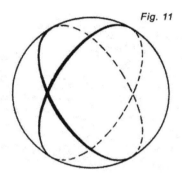

Fig. 11

Another variant of the parallel postulate states: "Through a point not on a given straight line, *an infinite number of lines* can be drawn parallel to the given line." Clearly this doesn't work on a plane and it doesn't work on a sphere. But it does work on a saddle shape (or hyperbolic paraboloid, to give its proper name). If parallel lines are lines that do not intersect, then on a saddle shape an infinite number of lines can be drawn parallel to a given line.

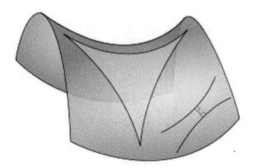

Normal Distribution

Gauss also made important contributions to statistics by showing that measurement errors followed a normal distribution that could be graphed using what is sometimes called a bell-shaped curve.

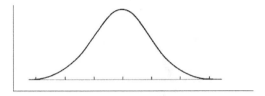

The normal curve describes virtually every human measure—height, weight, head size, arm span—as well as vast numbers of physical measurements. The curve has several notable properties: the midpoint of the curve coincides with the mean or average value. The mode, or most frequently appearing value, and the median, or middle value, also fall at this spot. The further you get away from the mean, the fewer values appear: the great bulk of the values occur not far from the mean. Moreover, since the area under the curve is 1, we can describe the likelihood of discovering any particular value in terms of probabilities. We are much less likely to encounter values in the tails of the curve than in the middle.

Statistics students learn a rule of thumb concerning the shape of the curve:

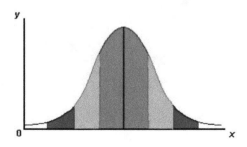

Roughly 68% of the data fall in the middle shaded sections; roughly 95% of the data fall in the dark and light middle sections taken together; and roughly 99% of the data fall in all six shaded sections taken together. This diagram allows us to illustrate the trade-off between confidence interval and margin of error. We can be 95% certain that the actual mean of a data set (let us say, a poll of voters taken before an election) falls in four middle shaded areas taken together. That may seem like an awfully wide margin of error. We can reduce the margin of error and say that we are 68% certain that the actual mean falls in just the two middle shaded sections. So we've reduced our margin of error, but we also have less confidence in the result. Of course, we are 99% confident that the actual result lies somewhere in all the shaded areas taken together, but we obtain that high level of confidence at the expense of a very wide margin of error.

Gauss' gifts to the twentieth century include the statistical notion that populations may be predictable even if individual data are not, and that non-Euclidean geometry has physical applications.

Austen, *Pride and Prejudice*, 1815

Irony

"Irony, which essentially is saying one thing while meaning another, is Austen's characteristic mode."[381] Jane Austen's "blend of ironic wit and drama may be seen in its simplest form in the first chapter of the novel, in the dialogue between Mr. and Ms. Bennett on the topic of Mr. Bingley's leasing Netherfield Park. Every remark which each makes, Mrs. Bennet petulantly, and Mr. Bennet perversely, bounces off the magnificent opening sentence: *"It is a truth universally acknowledged, that a single man in possession of a good fortune, must be in want of a wife.""*[382]

Austen's "characteristic mode" finds its most sympathetic exponent in her protagonist, Elizabeth Bennet. "Elizabeth sets herself up as an ironic spectator, able and prepared to judge and classify, already making the first large division of the world into two sorts of people: the simple ones, those who give themselves away out of shallowness ... and the intricate ones, those who cannot be judged and classified so easily, who are 'the most amusing to the ironic spectator because they offer the most formidable challenge to his powers of detection and analysis. Into one of these preliminary categories, Elizabeth fits everybody she observes."[383]

Free Indirect Discourse

"When Jane Austen began to write her novels, she did something extremely innovative in the world of English literature. She incorporated into her narration a new technique, which has become known as 'Free Indirect Discourse', and this soon became a hallmark of her writing style. ... Other writers followed—Flaubert, Kafka, James Joyce and Virginia Woolf were each in their time, praised for the modernity of their styles using this narrative technique—but it was Jane Austen who led the way and showed them all how it was done."[384]

"Perhaps Austen's most remarkable stylistic achievement is her subtle and sustained use of free indirect discourse (or free indirect speech), a technique through which the speech or thought-processes of her characters are blended with the narrator's descriptions. Typically, free indirect discourse serves one of two main purposes. In the first case, it can be used to provide economical summaries of conversations, whether made by individuals or multiple speakers. ... Alternately, the technique is employed to compress an individual's thoughts or speech with dramatic and/or ironic purpose."[385] This device gives Austen the perfect tool for exploring the misapprehensions that lie at the root of *Pride and Prejudice*.

Pride and Prejudice

The pride of the title attaches to Mr. Darcy, whose preoccupation with his wealth and social position leads him to utter one of the most bizarre marriage proposals in all of English literature: *"In vain have I struggled. It will not do. My feelings will not be re-pressed. You must allow me to tell you how ardently I admire and love you."* Austen moves into indirect discourse for the astonishing continuation. *"His sense of her inferiority—of its being a degradation—of the family obstacles which judgment had always opposed to inclination, were dwelt on with a warmth which seemed due to the consequence he was wounding, but was very unlikely to recommend his suit."*

The prejudice of the title attaches to Elizabeth, who early in the novel allows the opinions of others to unduly affect her opinion of Mr. Darcy before she can make a proper estimation, a misstep which affects their relationship well past the mid-point of the book, so that she reads a letter from Mr. Darcy *"with a strong prejudice against every thing he might say."* Rereading the letter Elizabeth sees, with embarrassment, how she has misjudged him.

"But pride is not confined to Darcy, nor prejudice to Elizabeth. Darcy's social pride is itself fed by his prejudice against people of her rank, while Elizabeth's pride in her judgment and wit spurs her dislike of Darcy—both through her offense at his scorn of her and at his air of superiority and through her enjoyment of the opportunity to exercise her cleverness and wit by abusing such a tempting target. In their respective reformations they must each shed both pride and prejudice."[386]

Austen's denouement requires alteration on the part of both pro-tagonists. "In *Pride and Prejudice*, the resolution of the romance does not hinge on the capitulation of either lover to the other. ... At the end of *Pride and Prejudice*, though both lovers gallantly assume a more than equal share of the blame, the true portion of responsibility for their initial misery and later happiness is in equilibrium. Equality of errors leads to equality of education."[387]

The interiority of ironic detachment and free indirect discourse permit Austen to invest her characters with passionate self-awareness.

Beethoven, Symphony No. 9, 1824

Striving Toward the Ideal

Beethoven spent thirty years trying to figure out how best to translate Schiller's poem *An die Freude* (Ode to Joy) into music. The poem has been described as "an Enlightenment document filled with the hopes and expectations of an era that had yet to suffer the disappointment and disillusionment of the French Revolution, the Reign of Terror, and the Napoleonic era."[388] In the end, Beethoven introduced a chorus to sing Schiller's paean to universal brotherhood. "The key to the finale is the 'Joy' theme. It sounds as effortlessly natural as a folk song. But it gave Beethoven an enormous amount of trouble; there are literally dozens of versions of the last eight bars in the sketchbooks."[389]

The initial presentation of the theme is followed by two variations. Beethoven sets the text "Like a conquering hero" to a new variation of theme in the form of a Turkish march.

Beethoven introduces a new melody to set "Seid umschlungen, Millionen!" (You millions, I embrace you.)

For moments of high seriousness Beethoven typically writes a fugue, as if invoking the spirit of J. S. Bach, master of that challenging contrapuntal style. At the climax of the fourth movement Beethoven presents a *double* fugue combining this new theme with the Joy theme.

Pushing Limits

If we think of Bach as a composer who excelled all others working within prescribed limits, Beethoven in his mature works seems determined to push beyond existing limits. The average Haydn symphony lasts around twenty-five minutes. Beethoven's Ninth Symphony is three times that long. Beethoven shocked contemporary audiences by adding a chorus to the instrumental forces. "The Ninth Symphony calls for the largest orchestra that Beethoven ever used, one including four horns, three trombones, piccolo, and contrabassoon in addition to the normal pairs of winds, trumpets and timpani, and strings. These instruments are augmented in the finale by the bass drum, triangle, cymbals, and vocal forces."[390] Beethoven also pushed his performers to their limits. Instrumentalists, soloists and choristers can attest to the technical difficulties encountered by anyone undertaking to perform the work.

Audiences accustomed to the transparency and clarity of Mozart and Haydn must have been thoroughly confounded by the opening of Beethoven's Ninth Symphony which conceals melody, rhythm and tonality. "It would be no exaggeration to state that the mysterious beginning of the first movement of the Ninth Symphony is the work's most striking feature. The murmuring sextuplets of the second violins and cellos and the open fifth (A-E) of the horns of the first two measures are couched in a soft dynamic that obscures any clear sense of time, space, or tonality."[391]

Apposing Opposites

The classical tradition that Beethoven inherited favored contrast over the uniformity that marked the earlier Baroque style. Beethoven carried the process a step further, replacing contrast with conflict. Part of the drama associated with Beethoven's music lies in the composer's fondness for juxtaposing opposites: fast vs. slow, loud vs. soft, high vs. low, dissonant vs. consonant, major vs. minor. The final movement of the Ninth Symphony opens with a grinding dissonance, played *fortissimo*, that Wagner described as a *Schreckenfanfare* (horror fanfare).

Beethoven favors sudden shifts and clashing styles. The sublime moment of "Vor Gott" (before God) is followed immediately by the mundane Turkish March quoted earlier, complete with bass drum, cymbals and triangle.

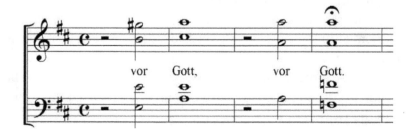

Beethoven prefers "both/and" over "either/or." The last movement of the Ninth Symphony opens with unprecedented musical
"reminiscences" of each of the preceding movements, leading to
a musical structure that has confounded description. "Its fusion
of styles and procedures is matched by the multivalence of its
forms, which constitute a palimpsest of superimposed hybrid
structures—a set of variations; one or another sonata form; a
four-movement cycle superimposed on a sonata-allegro concerto
form with double exposition; a cantata; a through-composed text-
derived form; a suite; a divertimento; an operatic finale; and even
a free fantasy."[392]

Beethoven's penchant for juxtaposing strongly contrasting elements provides a vehicle for expressing Schiller's idealistic message of universal brotherhood.

Turner, *The Slave Ship*, 1839 PLATE 15

Romanticism and Abolitionism

The so-called Romantic Revolution in the arts of the 19th century
may be viewed as a reaction against the concentration on rationality that characterized the Enlightenment. In place of works
based on structures apprehended and appreciated by the mind,
Romantic artists created works emanating from and appealing to
the emotions. Instead of nature as a source of order and universal law, Romantic artists offered nature as a refuge from the dep-
redations of the Industrial Revolution. In place of a pursuit for
objective truth, Romantic artists unabashedly celebrated the subjective reality of the individual ego.

These qualities appear clearly displayed in William Turner's *The
Slave Ship* (1839). Anyone seeing this painting for the first time
may have reactions similar to those of early viewers: where is
the linear perspective? Where are the lines defining the subject?
And what's happening, anyway? The formal title refers to the

historical events behind the painting: "Slavers Throwing Overboard the Dead and Dying—Typhoon Coming On." The painting "has often been linked to the story of the *Zong*, a Liverpool vessel whose captain deliberately drowned 132 diseased and dying slaves *en route* from West Africa to Jamaica in 1781, so that the ship-owners could claim insurance for them as goods lost at sea."[393] Turner anticipated the painting in these lines, written in 1812:

Aloft all hands, strike the top-masts and belay;
Yon angry setting sun and fierce-edged clouds
Declare the Typhon's coming.
Before it sweeps your decks, throw overboard
The dead and dying – ne'er heed their chains
Hope, Hope, fallacious Hope!
Where is thy market now?"

Contemporary viewers may have had a stronger emotional response than we do, inured as we are to television coverage of genocide in Bosnia or Rwanda or Darfur or the Congo, but can we fail to be affected by the sight of a visible limb in the lower right corner, still bearing its shackles?

Human Powerlessness before Nature

Nature as portrayed here seems far from the symmetrical gardens of Versailles or the orderly procession of the planets as described by Newton's laws. Turner seizes on the majesty and destructive power of nature as summed up in an apocalyptic storm. Nature for the romantics was vast, terrifying and cataclysmic, mysterious, beyond man's comprehension rather than the ordered source of natural law. Instead of man, the master of all he surveys, we see man, vulnerable and impotent before the elements, as represented in the tiny foreground figure. The sinking ship, meanwhile, seems practically insignificant compared to the sky and water, whose boundaries are erased.

"The main tenets of the Romantic movement opposed everything which the Enlightenment had stood for. Where the Enlightenment had stressed the power of Reason, the Romantics were attracted by all in human experience that is irrational: by the passions, by the supernatural and paranormal, by superstitions, pain, madness, and death. Where the Enlightenment had stressed man's growing mastery of nature, the Romantics took delight in trembling before nature's untamed might: in the terror of storms and waterfalls, the vastness of mountains, the emptiness of deserts, the loneliness of the seas. Where the Enlightenment had followed the classical taste for harmony and restraint, and for the rules which underlay civilized conventions, the Romantics courted everything which defied established convention: the wild, the quaint, the exotic, the alien, the deranged."[394]

Emotion over Reason

In place of line, communicating rational, linear thinking, the romantics exploited colour, conveying emotion and the intensity of personal feelings. Turner leaves out solid objects in order to concentrate on the play of light on water. Elevating the importance of color over the traditional elements of form and structure asserts the power of the artist to transcend logical processes of thought and break through to states of mind beyond or below man's conscious control. A century before Freud, artists explored the possibility of pushing aside the rational mind in order to delve into the subconscious mind. Subjective emotion could take the place of objective reason in a polemical appeal. Turner's *The Slave Ship* represents an emotional rather than a reasoned argument for the abolitionist campaign.

Turner's revolution lay in promoting color—heretofore considered decorative—to the primordial status of line, shape and perspective.

Kierkegaard, *Either/Or*, 1843

Existential Choice

Often described as the "father of existentialism," Søren Kierke-gaard argued that individuals bear the obligation of formulating their own answers to the problem of human existence. In *Fear and Trembling* he offers multiple perspectives on the biblical sto-ry in which Abraham has been commanded to sacrifice his son Isaac, as if compelling the reader—by choosing among conflict-ing alternatives—to arrive at a personal response.

"The title *Either/Or* presents us with a choice between the aes-thetic and the ethical. The first volume is written from the point of view of the reflective aesthete. The second volume, on the other hand, is written by a judge, who advocates transparency and openness in communication. It is written in the form of let-ters, as a direct communication to the aesthetic author of the first volume." [395]

The final word belongs to an anonymous parson in a sermon en-titled, "The Edifying In The Thought That Against God We Are Always In The Wrong." With a taste for the paradoxical, Kier-kegaard, in the guise of a parson, writes, *"You loved God, and therefore your soul could only find repose and joy in the thought that you must always be in the wrong. ... For what does it ex-press other than that God's love is always greater than our love?"*[396]

Indirect Communication

From Kierkegaard's perspective, the Danish State Church, by offering preconceived solutions to existential dilemmas, deprived individuals of the right, indeed the obligation, to think on their own. Determined not to perpetuate this error in his own writ-ings, Kierkegaard deliberately placed obstacles in the reader's way—what he referred to as "indirect communication"—in the hope that readers would work out their own personal solutions and not simply adopt his.

"Kierkegaard struggled to find appropriate means of communication that would address the inward nature of Christian faith.... Everything was made too easy for people, with the press providing ready-made opinions, popular culture providing ready-made values, and speculative philosophy providing promissory notes in place of real achievements.... Kierkegaard's task as a communicator was, initially, to make things more difficult. In order to do this, he devised a method of indirect communication."[397]

To this end, Kierkegaard invented multiple pseudonyms and spurious elements of scholarly apparatus. "*Either/Or* is exemplary in this respect, wrapped as it is in several layers of pseudonymity. The two main parts are assigned to two fictitious authors, the first part containing what is at least made to look like a diary by a third author, and the second containing a sermon by a fourth. On top of that the work is as a whole presented as a pseudonymous editor in a fictitious preface."[398]

Christianity and the Absurd

In addition to works addressed to non-Christian audiences, Kierkegaard also published a number of "edifying discourses," reflecting his own belief in God without ever wavering from his insistence on individual solutions to existential questions. "Kierkegaard likened himself to a missionary whose responsibility it was to reintroduce Christianity into Christendom. ... He believed that men had forgotten not only what it means to exist Christianly, but also humanly."[399]

Kierkegaard used the word "absurd" to describe elements of Christian belief that seemed to defy rationality. "What, then, is the absurd? The absurd is that the eternal truth has come into existence in time, that God has come into existence, has been born, has grown up. etc., has come into existence exactly as an individual human being, indistinguishable from any other human being." "The absurdity of atonement requires faith that we believe that for God even the impossible is possible, including the forgiveness of the unforgivable."[400] Yet Søren Kierkegaard remained a believer. *"When the believer has faith, the absurd is not the absurd — faith transforms it, but in every weak moment it is again more or less absurd to him."*[401]

Kierkegaard contradicted nearly two millennia of Church doctrine in asserting that God exists but that each individual must decide what that means.

Marx, *The Communist Manifesto*, 1848

Class Struggle

The year 1848 saw the publication of a rationale for revolution, *The Communist Manifesto* by Karl Marx. Marx proposes a new view of human history. *"The history of all hitherto existing societies is the history of class struggles. ... In the earlier epochs of history, we find almost everywhere a complicated arrangement of society into various orders, a manifold gradation of social rank. In ancient Rome, we have patricians, knights, plebeians, slaves; in the Middle Ages, feudal lords, vassals, guild-masters, journeymen, apprentices, serfs; in almost all of these classes, again, subordinate gradations. ... Our epoch, the epoch of the bourgeoisie, possesses, however, this distinctive feature; it has simplified the class antagonisms. Society as a whole is more and more splitting up into two great hostile camps, into two great classes directly facing each other: Bourgeoisie and Proletariat."*[402]

Capitalism

Marx continues with a prescient portrait of modern capitalism describing the globalization of raw materials, labour, and culture, and the concentration of property in the hands of the few. Capitalism subverts inherited cultural beliefs and destroys established values. *"The bourgeoisie, wherever it has got the upper hand, has put an end to all feudal, patriarchal, idyllic relations. It has pitilessly torn asunder the motley feudal ties that bound man to his 'natural superiors,' and has left remaining no other nexus between man and man than naked self-interest, than callous 'cash payment.' It has drowned the most heavenly ecstasies of religious fervour, of chivalrous enthusiasm, of philistine sentimentalism, in the icy water of egotistical calculation. It has resolved personal worth into exchange value, and in place of the numberless indefeasible chartered freedoms, has set up that single, unconscionable freedom—Free Trade. In one word, for exploitation, veiled by religious and political illusions, it has substituted naked, shameless, direct, brutal exploitation."*

Capitalism disregards all boundaries in its effort to globalize markets. *"The bourgeoisie has through its exploitation of the world market given a cosmopolitan character to production and consumption in every country. ... All old-established national industries have been destroyed or are daily being destroyed. They are dislodged by new industries ... that no longer work up indigenous raw material, but raw material drawn from the remotest zones; industries whose products are consumed, not only at home, but in every quarter of the globe. In place of the old wants, satisfied by the production of the country, we find new wants, requiring for their satisfaction the products of distant lands and climes."*

Marx's criticism of the commoditization of labour in the factory system seems all the more remarkable for having been written even before the invention of the assembly line. *"The workman*

... becomes an appendage of the machine, and it is only the most simple, most monotonous, and most easily acquired knack, that is required of him. ... In proportion as the use of machinery and division of labour increases, in the same proportion the burden of toil also increases, whether by prolongation of the working hours, by increase of the work exacted in a given time, or by increased speed of the machinery. Modern industry has converted the little workshop of the patriarchal master into the great factory of the industrial capitalist." "In short, what might in 1848 have struck an uncommitted reader as revolutionary rhetoric or, at best, as plausible prediction can now be read as a concise characterization of capitalism at the start of the new millennium. Of what other document of the 1840s can this be said?"[403]

Communism

The *Communist Manifesto* concludes with demands that also strike us as remarkably modern.

1. Abolition of property in land and application of all rents of land to public purposes.

2. A heavy progressive or graduated income tax.

3. Abolition of all right of inheritance.

4. Confiscation of the property of all emigrants and rebels.

5. Centralization of credit in the hands of the State, by means of a national bank with State capital and an exclusive monopoly.

6. Centralization of the means of communication and transport in the hands of the State.

7. Extension of factories and instruments of production owned by the State.

8. Equal liability of all to labour.

9. Combination of agriculture with manufacturing industries; gradual abolition of the distinction between town and country, by a more equable distribution of the population over the country.

10. Free education for all children in public schools. Abolition of children's factory labour in its present form.

Marx's stirring phrase has entered the common vocabulary of political discourse: "Working men of all countries, unite. [You] have nothing to lose but your chains."

Surveying the hierarchical nature of social arrangements throughout history, Marx calls for a revolution that would at last produce a truly egalitarian model.

Darwin, *On the Origin of Species*, 1859

Intelligent Design

The prevailing wisdom in the nineteenth century held that, based on information contained in the Bible, the earth was around 6,000 years old, God created each species individually, and human beings were set apart from the natural world. Contemporary ideas of natural theology maintained that "the adaptation of living beings to their surroundings was so perfect that it proved the existence of God. How could such perfect design have come about … except from the careful hands of a designer. If a watch were accidentally found on a path, we would be entirely justified in thinking that it had been constructed by a skilled craftsman according to some design or plan. Such intricate mechanisms do not suddenly appear out of nothing, like magic. They are made by a maker."[404]

Charles Darwin, born in 1809, initially subscribed to these beliefs. But Darwin, fascinated by natural science, discovered evidence that made these conventional beliefs untenable. Layers of rock showed that the world was not static or fixed and that the earth must be much older than 6,000 years. Connections between the fossils of extinct giant mammals and smaller living animals suggested that species were not unchanged after all.

In 1831 Darwin signed on as an unpaid naturalist for a voyage of exploration on the H.M. S. Beagle, a five-year adventure that included visits to the Galapagos Islands. On each island, Darwin discovered species specifically adapted for life there and found nowhere else: tortoises, giant daisies, iguanas, and flightless cormorants. These findings made it impossible to sustain the position that God had created each species individually. It seemed more likely that species had adapted to survive in different environments. Darwin concluded, *"Each species had not been independently created, but had descended like varieties, from other species."* But Darwin still needed a mechanism to explain these modifications.

Natural Selection

Three principles—the struggle for existence, chance variation (what we would call mutation), and survival of the fittest—lay at the basis of Darwin's theory of evolution, as contained in his book *On the Origin of Species by Means of Natural Selection* (1859). *"As more individuals are produced than can possibly survive, there must in every case be a struggle for existence. ... Owing to the struggle for life any variation, however slight ... if it be in any degree profitable ... will tend to the preservation of that individual, and will generally be inherited by its offspring. The offspring, also, will thus have a better chance of surviving. ... I have called this principle, by which each slight variation, if useful, is preserved, by the term of Natural Selection."* He named it 'natural selection' because he saw it as an analogy to 'artificial selection.' The breeding of plants and animals for desired properties was widely practiced in the England of his time, so it was a process that was well known to his intended readership."[405]

Darwin argued that tiny modifications in a basic structure can, over a long period of time, lead to quite different manifestations. *"The framework of bones being the same in the hand of a man, wing of a bat, fin of the porpoise and leg of the horse, —the same number of vertebrae forming the neck of the giraffe and of the elephant,—and innumerable other such facts, at once explain themselves on the theory of descent with slow and slight successive modifications."*

Darwin respectfully rejected the notion of each species being created separately. *"When I view all beings not as special creations, but as the lineal descendants of some few beings which lived long [ago] ... they seem to me to become ennobled. ... And as natural selection works solely by and for the good of each being, all corporeal and mental endowments will tend to progress towards perfection."* Subsequently, in *The Descent of Man*, Darwin extended the principle of evolution to human beings.

Social Darwinism

Before long, Darwin's ideas were perverted to justify racism and imperialism, the "survival of the fittest" was applied to nations instead of species. Moreover, the theory of evolution could be twisted into a rationale for eliminating social assistance to the poor, the infirm and the handicapped, whom nature must have intended to die in the "struggle for existence." "A welfare state or subsidized industry, it was assumed, would encourage idleness and permit an increasing number of 'unfit' people or firms to survive, thereby undermining economic and social progress and national health."[406]

Those who insist on a model of continual human progress may want to reflect that some of the same objections to evolution that Darwin encountered 150 years ago are still being presented today.

Connections: Rebellion

The word rebellion connotes a refusal to obey rules or accept normal standards, or a general opposition to authority. The nineteenth century saw an overturning of political authority in the French Revolution, followed by a succession of nationalist uprisings. Gauss, by daring to reject the limitations of Euclidean geometry, articulated the principles for new ways of conceiving space. Jane Austen, both in her life and in her work, rejected the limitations of female social conformity. Beethoven boldly exceeded the limitations of the classical style that he inherited. In his paintings, Turner rejected both conventional subject matter and the traditional manner of treating it. Kierkegaard, while remaining a believer, rejected the easy answers of religious authority and demanded individual responsibility for addressing existential questions. Marx boldly called for opposition to the ruling class and declared the historical inevitability of class struggle. Darwin rejected prevailing notions of intelligent design in proposing a theory of evolution through natural selection.

20ᵗʰ Century

Context

World Wars

Prior to 1914 Europe enjoyed nearly a century of peace. Nationalist uprisings stayed contained within political borders; whenever conflicts between states threatened to break into war pressure was brought to bear, either from within or from without, to contain them. Yet the same period was marked by increasing distrust that led both to the formation of defensive alliances, to be activated in the event of war, and a growing militarization that increased the likelihood of war. "Europe's very success in surviving those earlier crises paradoxically led to a dangerous complacency in the summer of 1914 that, yet again, solutions would be found at the last moment and the peace would be maintained. And if we want to point fingers from the twenty-first century we can accuse those who took Europe into war of two things. First, a failure of imagination in not seeing how destructive such a conflict would be and second, their lack of courage to stand up to those who said there was no choice left but to go to war. There are always choices."[407]

One assumes that those who spoke favorably of war could not have envisioned the catastrophe that lay ahead. One would have to go back to the 14ᵗʰ century to find a comparable era of cataclysms. World War I (1914-1918) cost more than 40 million casualties in a conflict characterized by trench warfare and waves of soldiers advancing into machine gun fire. In 1918 a pandemic known as the "Spanish flu" wiped out roughly one-third the population of Europe, more than double the number killed in the world war, a catastrophe on the scale of the Black Death that ravaged Europe in the 14ᵗʰ century. The Great Depression, initiated by the American stock market crash of 1929, had a devastating effect on both developed and developing countries. The Second World War, from 1939 to 1945, introduced "total warfare" resulting in the activation of a nation's entire economic and industrial capacity and causing over 70 million deaths, most of them civilian. The Cold War that followed, an arms race between the United States and the Soviet Union, created fear of world annihilation by atomic and hydrogen weapons.

Totalitarianism and Genocide

The 20th century learned a terrifying new word, "genocide," starting with the Holocaust, the murder of approximately six million European Jews and tens of thousands of other people deemed undesirable during World War II, as part of a program of deliberate extermination planned and executed by the Nazi regime in Germany led by Adolf Hitler. Later in the century came the discovery of other genocides. In Russia, the policies of Joseph Stalin led to 10 to 20 million deaths attributable to execution, forced collectivization, and imprisonment in gulags. Stalin "is the clearest example in history of a pathological criminal who rose to supreme power through the exercise of his criminal talents. In *The Guinness Book of Records* he holds the top place under 'mass murder.'... The total tally of his victims can never be exactly calculated; but it is unlikely to be much below 50 million."[408] In China the famine during, and partly caused by the Great Leap Forward, caused the death of tens of millions of peasants, while millions more perished in the violence of the Cultural Revolution.

Globalization

The twentieth century saw the extension of consciousness from the earliest level of the tribe or village past the level of the nation-state to encompass the entire planet. Positive aspects of this globalization include a broadening of empathy to embrace victims of war or natural disaster in distant lands. "What really has expanded is not so much a circle of empathy as a circle of rights—a commitment that other living things, no matter how distant or dissimilar, be safe from harm and exploitation."[409] And Adam Smith proved correct in asserting that unrestricted free trade would both increase the availability and bring down the prices of consumer goods.

Yet globalization has also meant overriding "customary intricate ways of allowing and restraining authority, and instead handed enormous power to whichever individual or small group could control its centre. ... Since 1980 the so-called 'Washington Model' of free trade has been imposed on America and, through international agreements and agencies, the rest of the world. Family loyalties, local customs, mutual support, non-economic networks, all of which were embedded in different ways in different societies, have had to be crushed or marginalized in the name of economic efficiency."[410]

Freud, *The Interpretation of Dreams*, 1899

Model of the Mind

Artists and writers of the 19th century intuitively gave expression to the subconscious, or unconscious, mind. It awaited Sigmund Freud to offer a more formal scheme. Freud proposed a three-part model of the psyche consisting of the id, the ego, and the super-ego.

- id: instinctive drives and impulses, the "child mind," amoral, egocentric, ruled by the pleasure/pain principle
- ego: the part of the mind that contains consciousness, mediator between the id and super-ego
- super-ego: the conscience, in Freud's model the internalization of the father figure

Contemporary theory has altered this model somewhat, separating the functions of the oldest or reptilian brain; the mammalian brain, that humans share with all other mammals; and the neocortex, or human brain. We would associate the mammalian brain, or amygdala, with Freud's id. So far have Freud's ideas pervaded popular culture that we have difficulty imagining a time before the recognition of the unconscious mind as an active force in determining human behaviour.

The Language of Dreams

Where do dreams come from? Earlier peoples considered dreams to have a supernatural origin. "Freud argued for a different idea, one that is so common today that we may not realize how radical it once was: that dreams are not messages from an external force or being, but that they are instead reflections of thoughts and feelings in our own minds, thoughts and feelings of which we might be partially or completely unaware. The study of our dreams will lead us to understand these thoughts and feelings better. If we take our dreams seriously, we will know things about ourselves that we might not be able to learn any other way."[411]

Freud described dreams as the "royal road to the unconscious," as developed in his book *The Interpretation of Dreams,* first published in 1899. Nowadays we tend to reject Freud's over-reliance on symbolism to provide a code for deciphering dreams. Yet we still recognize the role of wish fulfillment in dreams and the possibility of understanding dreams as expressions of repressed feelings—experiences too painful for the conscious mind to bear. Ideas in dreams appear in the form of images, rather than concepts, which the analyst must interpret.

"Now the dream thinks mainly in images, and it can be observed that as sleep approaches, to the degree that voluntary activity becomes more sluggish, so involuntary ideas emerge, which all belong to the class of images. This incapacity for the kind of thinking that we feel is intentional, and the emergence of images that is regularly associated with this absent state of mind, are two features which persist in the dream, and which psychological analysis compels us to recognize as essential characteristics of the dream-life."[412]

"Dreams that directly express wishes ... are commonest among children. Undisguised dreams also occur to people subjected to extreme privation. ... Turning to the great majority of dreams which do not overtly express wishes, Freud adduced evidence to show that these dreams are disguises. ... If we now assume that dreams are disguises and that they can be undisguised along paths of association, and we then proceed to undisguise them— or 'interpret' them, as the activity is usually called—we find that we are led to a wish whose existence can be independently established."[413]

Freud and Oedipus

In *The Interpretation of Dreams* Freud offers a number of observations on Sophocles' play *Oedipus Rex* that have come to be incorporated into the phrase "Oedipus complex." *"His destiny moves us only because it might have been ours—because the oracle laid the same curse upon us before our birth as upon him. It is the fate of all of us, perhaps, to direct our first sexual impulse towards our mother and our first hatred and our first murderous wish against our father. Our dreams convince us that this is so."*

"Oedipus did have one freedom: he was free to find out or not find out the truth. ... And of this freedom he makes full use. Against the advice and appeals of others, he pushes on, searching for the truth, the whole truth and nothing but the truth. And in this search he shows all those great qualities that we admire in him—courage, intelligence, perseverance, the qualities that make human beings great."[414]

Freud offered a theoretical groundwork for understanding the role of the unconscious mind, articulated the pervasive role of sexuality in human thought and behavior, and proposed a new frame of reference for understanding dreams.

Picasso, *Les Demoiselles d'Avignon*, 1906-1907
PLATE 16

Sexual Imagery

The title, given by one of the artist's friends, refers to the denizens of Barcelona's red-light district. Picasso himself preferred the more straightforward "Mon bordel." The artist's original sketches contained a medical student and a sailor among the figures, so that the interaction between the prostitutes and the clients takes place within the painting. Removing the clients and having the figures stare out of the painting turns the spectators into clients.

Leo Steinberg published a provocative essay on the painting, commenting in particular on its sexual imagery. "Beginning with the raised, pointed edge of the foreground table, 'a visual metaphor of penetration,' the space and the figures and objects in it were seen by Steinberg as expressively and symbolically in the service of the sexual content of the picture. ... In this one work Picasso discovered that the demands of discontinuity could be met on multiple levels: by cleaving depicted flesh; by elision of limbs and abbreviation; by slashing the web of connecting space;

by abrupt changes of vantage; and by a sudden stylistic shift at the climax."[415]

William Rubin finds in the painting references to syphilis, still a fatal disease at the time Picasso created *Les Demoiselles.* "The Medusa crouching on the right, whose asymmetrical distortions invoke—quite without illustrating—the atrocious structural deformations of *syphilis osseuse,* to which the rotting human head is subject, especially in the advanced congenital form of the disease."[416]

"Of all the whores in the early ensemble sketches, the one whose torso is seen finally from the back is the only one in an obscene posture: she is shown from the beginning spreading her legs to exhibit her sex to the sailor. As she is the only whore not totally nude in the first ensemble exercise—Picasso endowed her with a belted, filmy peignoir—one might wonder whether he had second thoughts concerning propriety."[417]

Discontinuity

The principle of geometric perspective that evolved in the Renaissance adopted a single point of view which gave a single point of reference to every aspect of the visual experience. The twentieth century challenged the concept of a single wisdom. Anthropological studies of various societies of the world required accepting a relativism of values. Einstein's challenge to traditional notions of space denied the idea of a fixed reference point while his challenge to traditional notions of time produced uncertainty as to whether one event precedes or follows another. In contrast to the three-dimensional space created by geometric perspective, Picasso has deliberately flattened the space of the painting.

In place of single-point perspective, Picasso presents several different perspectives simultaneously. In place of a single consistent style, Picasso employs multiple styles within the same painting, including evocations of early Iberian art and of African tribal masks which inspired the "mysterious 'masks' that expressed otherness, savage sexuality, violence, and, finally, horror."[418] We observe an "extraordinary dislocation of the frontward staring head from the rearview shoulders of the croucher."[419] The women seem unaware of each other. They all stare at the viewer. It is as if the viewer has become the single point of perspective.

Picasso and Rubens

The apple on the table offers a hint that Picasso hoped viewers would notice the resemblance between *Les Demoiselles* and *The Judgment of Paris* by Rubens. In Greek myth Eris, the goddess of discord, angry at not being invited to a wedding, shows up at the ceremony and tosses a golden apple—the apple of discord—into the throng, inscribed with the words "for the fairest one." Three goddesses claimed the apple—Hera, Athena and Aphrodite. Zeus called upon Paris to make the judgment. Each of the goddesses shamelessly offered bribes. Paris could not resist Aphrodite's offer of the love of the most beautiful woman in the world, Helen of Troy. No matter that she was already married to the Greek king Menelaus. So Aphrodite got the apple, Paris got Helen, and when the Greeks tried to retrieve her, the Trojan War began.

In Picasso's painting, the goddesses from the Greek myth have become prostitutes. And why not: didn't the goddesses essentially prostitute themselves for the sake of their vanity? Picasso's ironic perspective directs the women's gaze outwards: they are judging us, the viewers, as potential clients willing to pay for their favours, just as Paris was willing to rig the contest in order to win the love of Helen.

Einstein's refutation of an absolute frame of reference has its counterpart in Picasso's juxtaposition of multiple perspectives, multiple styles and multiple sources in a single painting.

Einstein, General Theory of Relativity, 1915

Relativity

In 1908 Albert Einstein published what has become known as the special theory of relativity. [Einstein] "started with two simple postulates. The first was that the laws of nature remain the same no matter how fast you are moving, and so no one can claim to be truly at rest and all motion is relative."[420] We experience relativity in common situations such as looking out the window of a subway train at another train, observing motion, and being unable to determine whether it is our train that is moving, or the other train, or both. "A clearer example is that of two rockets travelling at constant speeds towards each other in space. If both the rockets' engines are off and they are just 'cruising' they could never decide whether they were both moving towards each other or whether one was stationary and the other approaching it."[421]

"The second was that the speed of light through empty space is a fundamental constant of nature measured to have the same value no matter what speed the observer is travelling at."[422]

Consequences of a Constant c

"Einstein also proved that the speed of light is the maximum speed possible in the Universe. Special relativity ... leads to Einstein's best-known equation, relating mass and energy: $E = mc^2$."[423] If nothing can exceed the speed of light c, odd things happen when you approach c. "When you're moving very fast: 1. Time flows more slowly for you; 2. Distance shrinks ahead of you; 3. You become more and more massive."[424]

We must accept the speed of light as a fundamental property of nature. "Asking how you can go faster than light is somewhat akin to asking how you can walk north from the North Pole. ... It's a question that doesn't really make any sense."[425]

Gravity: Newton and Einstein

In 1915 Einstein published his general theory of relativity, extending his redefinition of space and time to account for gravity. According to Einstein, gravity results from the way that space curves in the vicinity of large objects. "The gravitational field is not *diffused through* space; the gravitational field is *that space* itself. ... Space ... is an entity that undulates, flexes, curves, twists. ... The sun bends space around itself, and Earth does not turn around it because of a mysterious force but because it is racing directly in a space that inclines, like a marble that rolls in a funnel. There are no mysterious forces generated at the center of the funnel; it is the curved nature of the walls that causes the marble to roll. Planets circle around the sun, and things fall, because space curves."[426] The curvature of space affects everything. "Due to this curvature, not only do planets orbit around the star but light stops moving in a straight line and deviates. ... But it isn't only space that curves; time does too. Einstein predicted that time passes more quickly high up than below, nearer to Earth. .. If a person who has lived at sea level meets up with his twin who has lived in the mountains, he will find that his sibling is slightly older than he."[427]

Any sound scientific theory should be able to make testable predictions. Newton's theory of gravity successfully predicted the existence of the planet Neptune whose subsequent discovery supported the theory. "Einstein had suggested that the Sun's gravity would bend the path of light reaching us from distant stars if the light had to pass close enough to the Sun on its way to Earth."[428] Einstein's prediction was supported by an experiment in 1919. A number of consequences follow from Einstein's theory of relativity, including the existence of gravitational waves (ripples in the curvature of space-time), black holes (regions of space with a gravitational attraction so strong that not even light can escape), and the Big Bang Theory, in which equations for an expanding universe, when carried backward, mark the formation of the universe 14 billion years ago. The existence of gravitational waves was confirmed experimentally only in early 2016.[429]

While Copernicus showed that the earth is not the center of the solar system, Einstein showed that there are *no* absolute reference points for space or time. Einstein went on to posit the speed of light as an absolute speed limit in the universe and to reconceive gravity not as a force but as a shape.

Joyce, *Ulysses*, 1922

Ulysses and the *Odyssey*

James Joyce's *Ulysses* self-consciously evokes Homer's *Odyssey*. The novel recounts the travels of its main character, Leopold Bloom, about the city of Dublin in the course of a single day, June 16, 1904. During this day Bloom encounters a second protagonist, Stephen Daedalus, while his wife Molly, a professional singer, begins an affair with her manager, Blazes Boylan. We observe obvious parallels between Joyce's main characters and Homer's.

The Odyssey	Ulysses
Ulysses	Leopold Bloom
Telemachus	Stephen Daedalus
Penelope	Molly Bloom
The suitors	Blazes Boylan

These parallels extend to the overall structure of the novel, which comprises eighteen episodes named after incidents in Homer's epic, each covering roughly one hour in a day that extends from 8 a.m. to around 2 a.m. the following morning.

Wordplay in *Sirens*

The *Sirens* chapter of *Ulysses* shows how Joyce favors musicality over immediate clarity of language. "With this episode, we embark on the novel's real 'odyssey of style.' The style of 'Sirens' is startlingly innovative. From the initial list of disjointed phrases to the concluding 'Pprrpffrrppffff' of Bloom's fart, language is teased, twisted, inverted, perverted in order to create an acoustic surround."[430]

Line 17 reads: "Avowal. *Sonnez.* I could. Rebound of garter. Not leave thee. Smack. *La cloche!* Thigh smack. Avowal. Warm. Sweetheart, goodbye." The expression "*Sonnez la cloche!*" is broken up, as if this were a four-part madrigal with one person trying to sing all four parts. A similar separation occurs with "Rebound of garter. ... Smack. ... Thigh smack."

The full "explanation" of this expression appears only in line 412:

"--Sonnez!

Smack. She set free sudden in rebound her nipped elastic garter smackwarm against her smackable a woman's warmhosed thigh.

--La cloche!"

In the background at the bar can be heard the song, "Goodbye, Sweetheart, Goodbye," whose final words--"I could not leave thee though I said Goodbye, Sweetheart, Goodbye"--appear scattered through line 17.

Joyce pushes onomatopoeia to its limits in evoking musical sounds: "jingle jingle jaunted jingling" for bells; "coin rang clock clacked" for percussion; "Clapclop. Clipclap. Clappyclap" for applause; "Her wavyavyeavyheavyeavyevyevy hair" for a trill; "the endlessnessnessness" for a fermata.

Joyce refers to musical instruments, he makes puns on their names, he includes actual musical notation, and he quotes fragments of long-forgotten songs, all in the interest of making us hear the sounds that Bloom hears while he eats.

Jingle. Bloo.
Boomed crashing chords. When love absorbs. War! War! The tympanum.
A sail! A veil awave upon the waves.
Lost. Throstle fluted. All is lost now.
Horn. Hawhorn.
When first he saw. Alas!
Full tup. Full throb.
Warbling. Ah, lure! Alluring.
Martha! Come!
Clapclap. Clipclap. Clappyclap. (11: 19-28)

"*Sirens* creates a complete sound world, a surrounding ambiance through which the characters move and which is prior to anything they might think, say, feel or even sing. Style is beginning to be foregrounded."[431]

Interior Monologue

Like Picasso, Joyce incorporates a number of different styles into a single work, with straightforward, logical language for normal narration and a rapid "stream of consciousness" style to enter a character's mind, not with complete sentences, as in Austen, but in a mishmash of sensations and associations. An extract from Episode 4 traces one part of Bloom's journey.

Wander through awned streets. Turbaned faces going by. Dark caves of carpet shops, big man, Turko the terrible, seated cross-legged, smoking a coiled pipe. Cries of sellers in the streets. Drink water scented with fennel, sherbet. Dander along all day. Might meet a robber or two. Well, meet him. Getting on to sundown. The shadows of the mosques among the pillars; priest with a scroll rolled up. A shiver of the trees, signal, the evening wind. I pass on. Fading gold sky. A mother watches me from her doorway. She calls her children home in their dark language. High wall: beyond strings twanged. Night sky, moon, violet, colour of Molly's new garters. Strings. Listen. A girl playing one of those instruments what do you call them: dulcimers. I pass. (4/89-98)

One of the many challenges of *Ulysses*—and Joyce has deliberately written the novel like a puzzle to be solved—lies in the associations the author expects the reader to make. In the *Sirens* episode Bloom listens to singing while having dinner in a hotel. Joyce expects us to remember the reference to dulcimers in the earlier passage.

Through the hush of air a voice sang to them, low, not rain, not leaves in murmur, like no voice of strings or reeds or whatdoyoucallthem dulcimers touching their still ears with words, still hearts of their each his remembered lives. (11/675-677)

Joyce has constructed his puzzle in such a fashion that one cannot possibly solve it in a single reading, no matter how attentive. But the novel amply rewards multiple readings for, as one critic remarks, "It is as impossible to imagine 20th century literature without *Ulysses* as to imagine 20th century physics without relativity."[432]

Like Virgil, Joyce turned to Homer for a model, describing his novel as "a modern Odyssey," with modernity lying in the stream of consciousness technique, the juxtaposition of multiple styles, and the extreme exploration of the musicality of language.

Heisenberg, Uncertainty Principle, Quantum Mechanics, 1927

Uncertainty Principle

Just as relativity theory offered a new perspective on the vast distances of interstellar space, so quantum theory offered a new perspective on the infinitesimal distances of subatomic space, with results even more challenging to the traditional Newtonian model. In 1930 Werner Heisenberg published a paper on one important aspect of quantum mechanics, the uncertainty principle. *"Our ordinary description of nature, and the idea of exact laws, rests on the assumption that it is possible to observe the phenomena without appreciably influencing them. To co-ordinate a definite cause to a definite effect has sense only when both can be observed without introducing a foreign element disturbing their interrelation. ... The uncertainty principle may be expressed in concise and general terms by saying that every experiment de-*

stroys some of the knowledge of the system which was obtained by previous experiments."[433]

According to Heisenberg's Uncertainty Principle, you can determine the position of a particle or the velocity of a particle, but not both. The more accurate your determination of the position, the more inaccurate your determination of the velocity. This leads to a probabilistic model for subatomic particles. If this model seems strange from a Newtonian perspective, it may seem more familiar if we look at it from the perspective of statistics, which we now accept as an everyday part of our lives. Well-designed polls give us an idea of how a mass of people will behave without being able to specify the behaviour of any single individual

Newtonian Determinism

Newtonian mechanics describes a closed system which has been described as a "clockwork" universe in which the future can be completely determined if we have complete knowledge of the present. The uncertainty principle denies this. "In one fell swoop, Heisenberg removed the conceit that the workings of Nature should necessarily accord with common sense. ... We should be prepared to abandon the prejudice that small things behave like smaller versions of big things."[434] "One of the most profound changes in human thinking brought about by the quantum revolution was the notion of indeterminism—that is, the disappearance of determinism, along with the concept of the clockwork universe."[435]

Classical physics	Relativistic physics
• there exists one absolute time shared by all observers • electrons are discrete entities like planets that circle the nucleus in definite orbits • given properties (e.g., the speed of an object, the temperature of a gas), can be measured to any desired degree of accuracy. • space has three dimensions; space and time are independent	• rates of time run differently in different places • electrons are thought of as probabilistic waves • measurement results not in a single number but in a probability distribution that specifies the likelihoods that the various possible results will be obtained • there is a single entity called spacetime, which has four dimensions

Quantum Indeterminism

In the quantum world, the very concept of causality does not exist. Heisenberg declared: "In the strict formulation of the causal law—if we know the present, we can calculate the future—it is not the conclusion that is wrong but the premise."[436] "The indeterminacy of quantum events means that one can never determine exactly the outcome of a single observation of any atomic process; the scientist can predict only the *probability* of each outcome among a wide range of possibilities. However, for a large number of observations, the probabilities do lead to precise statistical predictions, which the experimental results will display."[437]

If we insist on thinking of an electron as a particle, it seems reasonable to imagine its position and velocity at two different times. Heisenberg, however, tells us we must learn to develop a new way of thinking. "Quite generally there is no way of describing what happens between two consecutive observations. It is of course tempting to say that the electron must have been somewhere between the two observations and that therefore the electron must have described some kind of path or orbit even if it may be impossible to know which path. This would be a reasonable argument in classical physics. But in quantum theory it would be a misuse of the language which ... cannot be justified."[438] Contemporary theory says that there is no position and velocity inherent in the electron.

Einstein "could not accept what quantum mechanics seemed to be suggesting, that our world is, at its most fundamental level, inherently unpredictable. Indeed, one of Einstein's most famous quotes is that he did not believe 'that God plays dice,' in the sense that he could not accept that Nature is probabilistic. However, Einstein was wrong."[439]

Perhaps the simplest example of the queerness of quantum mechanics is that the statement "If a subatomic particle appears first at point A and then at point B, it must have travelled some path between the two," is *false*.

Bartók, *Music for String, Percussion and Celesta*, 1936

Folkloric Elements

The musical counterpart to cultural patriotism took the form of historical editions such as *Denkmäler der Tonkunst in Österreich*, a collection of Austrian art music from the Renaissance, Baroque and Classical periods. Countries such as Hungary, without a well-established tradition of art music, focused on folk music, the research of which led to a new discipline, ethnomusicology. Béla Bartók became infected with the wave of nationalist sentiment in 1903. He adopted national dress, spoke Hungarian rather than German, and dropped the prefix "von" from his family name."[440] A chance encounter with authentic Hungarian folk music in 1904 led Bartók to an investigation that lasted several decades. "Bartók began serious study of Magyar folksong in 1905, when he undertook the first of a series of journeys to collect folk melodies and use them in his own composed setting. By the end of his life he had also studied Romanian, Slovak, Serbian, Croatian, Arabic, and Turkish folk musics and had published several volumes of melodies, each organized and with a commentary based on his own system of classification."[441] Bartók wrote vocal and choral settings of dozens of these folk melodies.

"Various composers in the late nineteenth and early twentieth centuries turned to the modalities of their native folk music as the basis for composition, but it was Bartók who most thoroughly and extensively transformed these modes into the materials of a new musical language."[442] The last movement of Bartók's *Music for Strings, Percussion and Celesta* has been described as "a rondo-like suite of folk dances."[443] Unlike the steady duple or triple meter encountered in classical music, the dances in this movement display the so-called Bulgarian rhythm, irregular meters with exceptionally short note values. Bartók writes, "*the most frequent Bulgarian rhythms are as follows: 5/16 (subdivided into 3 + 2 or 2 + 3); 7/16 (2 + 2 + 3) ...; 8/16 (3 + 2 + 3); 9/16 (2 + 2 + 2 + 3); and about sixteen other less common rhythmic types, not counting the rhythmically-mixed formulas.*"[444]

The melody is in neither the major nor minor scales encountered in classical music but in the Lydian mode, like a major scale with a raised 4th degree.

Sonority

Twentieth-century composers devoted unprecedented attention to sonority, the pure sound of a work of music. They employed less familiar instruments, with particular attention to the hitherto neglected percussion section, or used familiar instruments in unusual ways. The "strings" in Bartók's composition are asked to play *sul ponticello* (with the bow kept near the bridge so as to bring out the higher harmonics and thereby produce a nasal tone) or *glissando* (sliding the finger along the strings). The third movement in particular contains all manner of eerie sonorities such as repeated high xylophone notes against *glissandi* in the timpani; muted string trills; harp *glissandi*; and the unearthly sound of the celesta.

Bartók also addressed the spatial aspects of sound. "The commission received from Paul Sacher in 1936 gave Bartók the opportunity to explore an unusual combination of instruments (double string orchestra with celesta, harp, piano, xylophone, timpani and percussion) and to reconsider their traditional roles. The antiphonal use of two string orchestras justifies Bartók's symmetrical layout in which he divides the strings into two groups on each side of the central group of piano, celesta, harp and percussion."[445] In the orchestral score Bartok includes directions for the unconventional layout of the instruments.

Approximate Position of the Orchestra			
Violoncello I Viola I Violin II Violin I	Double Bass I Timpani Side Drums Celesta Pianoforte	Double Bass II Bass Drum Cymbals Xylophone Harp	Violoncello II Viola II Violin IV Violin III

Symmetrical Structures

The opening movement takes the form of an unusual fugue in which alternate entries move by 5ths above and below the original tonal center of A. As Bartók writes in an introduction to the orchestral score: *"The second entry appears a fifth higher; the 4th again a fifth higher than the 2nd; the 6th, 8th, and so on, again a fifth higher than the preceding one. The 3rd, 5th, 7th, and so on, on the other hand, each enter a fifth lower. After the remotest key—E flat—has been reached (the climax of the movement) the following entries render the theme in contrary motion until the fundamental key—A—is again reached, after which a short coda follows."*

The final measures of the movement present a summary of this basic idea—movement from A to E ♭ , and the symmetrical treatment of the theme.

If twentieth-century music represents a breaking away from an outworn classical tradition, Bartók discovered in the asymmetrical rhythms and modal melodies of traditional folk music the resources for creating a new musical language.

Sartre, *Being and Nothingness*, 1943

Existence Precedes Essence

In the absence of God, we have no pre-determined nature or pre-established goals. We simply exist. Our "essence," how we define ourselves, what we become, now becomes our own responsibility. We must create our own values and determine our own meaning in life.

"Man first of all exists, encounters himself, surges up in the world – and defines himself afterwards. ... To begin with he is nothing. He will not be anything until later, and then he will be what he makes of himself. ... Man is nothing else but that which he makes of himself. That is the first principle of existentialism."[446]

Sartre and Kant

Both Kant and Sartre speak for individual moral responsibility as opposed to obedience to external authority. But where Kant says everyone should come to the same conclusion, given the premises, Sartre says each one comes to his own conclusion. "If I regard a certain course of action as good, it is only I who choose to say that it is good and not bad."

In his lecture "Existentialism is a Humanism" Sartre presents a very Kantian idea: *"The existentialist frankly states that man is in anguish. His meaning is as follows: When a man commits himself to anything, fully realizing that he is not only choosing what he will be, but is thereby at the same time a legislator deciding for the whole of mankind – in such a moment a man cannot escape from the sense of complete and profound responsibility."*

Sartre then offers a moral dilemma for which, he maintains, Kant's Categorical Imperative fails to offer guidance. A young man in 1940, living alone with his mother, had *"the choice between going to England to join the Free French Forces or of staying near his mother and helping her to live. ... He found himself confronted by two very different modes of action; the one concrete, immediate, but directed towards only one individual; and the other an action addressed to an end infinitely greater, a national collectivity."*[447]

What will assist the young man in making a decision? Christian doctrine calls for loving one's neighbor. But *"To whom does one owe the more brotherly love, the patriot or the mother?"* Nor does Kant provide a solution. *"The Kantian ethic says, Never regard another as a means, but always as an end. Very well; if I remain with my mother, I shall be regarding her as the end and not as a means: but by the same token I am in danger of treating as means those who are fighting on my behalf; and the converse is also true, that if I go to the aid of the combatants I shall be treating them as the end at the risk of treating my mother as a means."*

Condemned to Freedom

Sartre writes, *"The existentialist finds it extremely embarrassing that God does not exist, for there disappears with Him all possibility of finding values in an intelligible heaven. ... For if indeed existence precedes essence, one will never be able to explain one's action by reference to a given and specific human nature; in other words, there is no determinism—man is free, man is freedom. ... Thus we have neither behind us, nor before us in a luminous realm of values, any means of justification or excuse. We are left alone, without excuse. That is what I mean when I say that man is condemned to be free. Condemned, because he did not create himself, yet is nevertheless at liberty, and from the moment that he is thrown into this world he is responsible for everything he does."*[448]

Being condemned to freedom means being required to make one's own choices in the absence of pre-determined rules. *"What is not possible is not to choose. I can always choose, but I must know that if I do not choose, that is still a choice."* Finally, *"existentialism is nothing else but an attempt to draw the full conclusions from a consistently atheistic position."*[449]

"Sartre sometimes talks as if any choice could be authentic so long as it is lived with a clear awareness of its contingency and responsibility. But his considered opinion excludes choices that oppress or consciously exploit others."[450] Thus Sartre, like Kant, operates consistently within a context of community. Although in *No Exit* Sartre notoriously wrote, "Hell is other people," his autonomous existentialist finally accepts the necessity of a social framework.

In the absence of God, Sartre argues, each individual is responsible not only for personal decisions but also for the effect of those decisions on the rest of society.

Connections: Uncertainty

The word uncertainty, the state of being indeterminate, indefinite or problematical, describes the general state of mind of those enduring the cataclysms of the twentieth century. Unsurprisingly, this same attitude of doubt or variability runs through the cultural products of this era. Freud upset supreme confidence in the rational mind by demonstrating the power and inaccessibility of the unconscious mind. Picasso upset expectations of consistency by juxtaposing different styles and perspectives in a single work. Einstein overthrew assumptions of absolute time and space that had served as the bedrock of science for centuries. In *Ulysses* Joyce combined variability of style with a radical dislocation of syntax. Heisenberg overthrew established principles of order and predictability by demonstrating the probabilistic nature of the subatomic universe. Bartók composed music in which mode and meter were no longer constant but variable. Sartre, arguing for the absence of absolutes, depicted the human condition as "condemned to freedom."

Through the Matrix

The Monomyth

In 1949 Joseph Campbell, in a book called *The Hero with a Thousand Faces,* proposed the notion of the Monomyth, or Hero's Journey, a basic pattern that Campbell detected in narratives from around the world. According to Campbell, important myths share a common structure whose individual elements may receive greater or lesser emphasis, or may be omitted altogether.

Monomyth, the Hero's Journey
Departure
• Peculiarity of parentage
• Call to adventure
• Supernatural aid
Initiation
• Road of trials
• Meeting with goddess
• Knowledge
Return
• Difficulties en route
• Supernatural aid
• Reward

Aspects of the Monomyth seem to appear in a number of the works included in our repertoire of literature.

Peculiarity of Parentage

- Odysseus: son of King Laertes and Anticleia, both tracing lineage to the gods
- Oedipus: royal birth, abandoned by Laius and Jocasta, raised by Polybus and Merope
- Aeneas: son of mortal (prince Anchises) and the goddess Venus.
- Beowulf: son of a warrior and a princess
- Lancelot: son of King Ban, carried off and raised by the Lady of the Lake
- Tristan: conceived out of wedlock to royal parents, orphaned
- Tom Jones: mystery of parentage the central issue of the novel

---

Call to Adventure

- Odysseus: caught in terrible winds and sent to distant lands
- Oedipus: leaves Corinth for Thebes in an effort to avoid his terrible fate
- Aeneas: travels to Italy to the future site of Rome
- Beowulf: leaves his homeland to assist Hrothgar
- Lancelot: called upon to rescue Guinevere after her abduction by Meleagant
- Tristan: sent by King Mark to bring back his bride Isolde
- Knight in Wife of Bath's Tale: sent by Queen on a quest to find out "what women really want"
- Tom Jones: banished from Squire Allworthy's estate

Supernatural Aid

- Odysseus: receives frequent assistance from the goddess Athena
- Oedipus: receives ambiguous information about his parentage and fate from the Delphic Oracle
- Aeneas: receives aid from his mother, the goddess Venus
- Beowulf: uses a magical sword to kill Grendel's mother when his own sword loses its power
- Lancelot: receives a ring from the Lady of the Lake
- Tristan: ingests magic love potion intended for King Mark
- Knight: receives assistance from woman who at first appears to be an old hag

---

Road of Trials

- Odysseus: survives encounters with Cyclops, Scylla and Charybdis, the Sirens, etc.
- Oedipus: kills Laertes, not recognizing him as his father
- Aeneas: a love affair with Dido delays his mission
- Beowulf: kills Grendel, Grendel's mother, and later, an unnamed dragon
- Lancelot: survives the Sword Bridge and countless combats in tournament
- Tristan: wounded by a poisoned lance as he attempts to rescue a maiden from six knights
- Knight: travels widely but cannot discover an answer to the Queen's question
- Tom Jones: Fielding substitutes amorous adventures for knightly combat

---

Meeting with Goddess
- Odysseus: kept captive by Circe for a year
- Oedipus: meets the Sphinx
- Aeneas: meets the Sibyl
- Lancelot: locates Queen Guinevere
- Tristan: love affair with Isolde
- Knight: meets old hag

Knowledge
- Odysseus: Circe gives advice on the remaining stages of his journey
- Oedipus: answers the Sphinx's riddle, thereby releasing the city of Thebes from her curse
- Aeneas: Sibyl instructs him on how to get to the underworld
- Lancelot: Lancelot and Guinevere, hearing false reports of the other's death, try to kill themselves
- Knight: learns the secret of what women really want

Difficulties in Returning Home
- Odysseus: kept captive by Calypso for seven years
- Aeneas: combat with the inhabitants of Latium
- Lancelot: victim of a trick, imprisoned
- Tristan: exiled (depending on version)

Supernatural Aid

- Odysseus: Hermes, sent by Zeus, persuades Calypso to release him; Athena helps Odysseus disguise his identity
- Oedipus: blind prophet Tiresias tells Oedipus, seeking his father's murderer, that he is looking for himself
- Aeneas: the river Tiber tells Aeneas where to find an ally; Venus heals Aeneas' wound so that he can return to battle with Turnus
- Lancelot: Meleagant's sister, returning a favour he did for her, arranges Lancelot's release
- Tom Jones: Mrs. Waters discloses the truth of Tom's birth to Squire Allworthy

---

Reward

- Odysseus: reunion with his wife Penelope
- Oedipus: awarded the kingship of Thebes and marriage to Jocasta, but learning the truth, he blinds himself and becomes an exile
- Aeneas: succeeds in taking the city that will become Rome
- Lancelot: overcomes Meleagant (story incomplete)
- Knight: old hag becomes beautiful maiden
- Tom Jones: marries Sophia Western

Having observed a degree of similarity among these stories, extending over a millennium, we may inquire how they differ. I should like to suggest a division into three categories: playing by the rules, playing with the rules, and an ironical treatment of the rules. According to this division, *The Odyssey, Oedipus Rex, The Aeneid* and *Beowulf* play by the rules, with an obvious difference in the tragic ending that characterizes *Oedipus Rex*. We may also wish to note that supernatural intervention plays a minimal role in *Beowulf,* whose hero relies primarily on his extraordinary physical strength.

Our examples from the Middle Ages seem to play with the rules. Chrétien de Troyes departs from the simple heroic tradition, as indicated in the title of his work, *Lancelot of the Cart.* The hero Lancelot must repeatedly endure humiliation, and must fight badly, on the orders of the queen, in order to demonstrate his complete subservience. Gottfried von Strassburg depicts the conflict between love and honour in *Tristan,* whose hero employs deceit and trickery to preserve the appearance, but not the spirit, of honour, notably the ploy that enables Isolde to pass the trial by ordeal. In the Wife of Bath's Tale, from *The Canterbury Tales,* the Knight succeeds only when he leaves the most important decision of his life up to the woman, thereby demonstrating the subservience of men that the Wife of Bath advocates.

Examples from the Renaissance to the present display an ironical treatment of the rules of literature. Hamlet employs a play within the play in an attempt to trap the king. Hamlet's self-consciousness has been described as the creation of human personality—the ability to see ourselves. Molière communicates his mockery of social convention within the strict rules of French classic drama. In *Tom Jones,* the author constantly intrudes on the tale, insisting that it is entirely his own creation, even as he acknowledges and mocks the heroic tradition. Jane Austen replaces the stereotypical characters of contemporary popular literature with protagonists capable of remarkable self-awareness. Joyce's *Ulysses* presupposes a reader's intimate familiarity with *The Odyssey,* replacing heroic deeds with everyday events in an intricate structure that constitutes a loving parody of literary style and content.

Symbolism, Realism, Abstraction

I propose two perspectives for surveying the works of art included in the matrix. The first follows the format we have just employed in looking at literature: how artists respond to the rules of
their domain. Classical architecture, tapestry and sacred illumination can be described as "playing by the rules," a description
that would probably apply as well to the work of Giotto. But in
the Renaissance artists began playing with the rules. Robert
Campin sets the Annunciation in a bourgeois kitchen while
maintaining many elements of medieval symbolism. Velásquez
places the artist in the middle of a formal painting, plays games
with mirrors, and calls attention to the theatrical convention of
the "fourth wall" by situating a royal audience beside the contemporary viewer of his painting. Jefferson's Monticello plays
games with aesthetics: the difference between classical columns
and pediments and neo-classical columns and pediments lies in
the unspoken assumption that "the Greeks had it right," a sentiment in keeping with Jefferson's political views, which favoured
a democratic confidence in the will of the common people over
an aristocratic fear of the general population. Picasso, by incorporating several different styles in the same painting, looks ironically at the rules governing style and perspective, as he does by
replacing mythological deities with Spanish prostitutes.

A second way of looking at the history of art is through the lens
of representation. Classical sculpture, such as the statue of
Athena housed in the Parthenon, offered an idealized view. Later sculptors and painters gave more realistic representations of
their subjects, and one can judge figurative art on this scale between idealism and realism. Representation for medieval artists
meant including the accompanying symbols or context, not producing a life-like form. The development of linear perspective
offered a tool of illusion—that a two-dimensional surface could
represent a three-dimensional subject—in the service of realism
in representation. In the work of Turner, we find a goal not of

representing a realistic image but rather of representing the emotions that such a scene evokes, as well as the artist's ideas about the relationship between man and nature. Twentieth-century art, like music and science, dares to think the unthinkable: what if there isn't any representation at all? Turner's painting *The Slave Ship* already takes us to the brink. What if there is no representation? Twentieth-century artists explored two paths: some experimented with non-representational art; others found ways to "abstract" some essential element of form from a subject. We can look at Picasso's "*Les Demoiselles d'Avignon*" both as a story and as a pure exercise in juxtaposing angular shapes and surfaces.

Art, Literature and Music

Can we find some general principle that accounts for changes in style in art, literature and music through the roughly three thousand years we have been studying? The aesthetician Colin Martindale, in his book *The Clockwork Muse: The Predictability of Artistic Change*, enunciates a "law of novelty," a universal human desire to avoid repetition and boredom. According to this principle, any artistic style gradually increases in emotion, complexity or ornamentation until it reaches some breaking point, after which a new style appears. The "law of novelty" accounts for the major shift in style which occurred after J.S. Bach, whose perfection of counterpoint effectively left no further territory to explore. Bach represents the end of an era in music. Beethoven, by contrast, opened various avenues of expression that composers spent the rest of the 19th century exploring. The so-called "law of novelty" rests on the psychological principle of habituation, which Martindale describes as the universal mainspring of artistic change.

If a "law of novelty" propels stylistic change in the arts, can we articulate any general principles that apply to all the arts throughout the history of western culture? Philosopher Denis

Dutton proposes seven universal features of art to cover not only the repertoire we have chosen but also non-western cultures.

1.   Expertise or virtuosity: the exercise of a specialized skill
2.   Non-utilitarian pleasure: the art object is viewed as a source of pleasure in itself
3.   Style: recognizable sets of characteristics of form and composition
4.   Criticism: development of a critical vocabulary and criteria for excellence
5.   Imitation: art objects imitate real and imaginary experiences of the world
6.   "Special focus": art is bracketed off from ordinary life
7.   Imagination: the work of art is raised from the mundane practical world[451]

I find numbers 2, 6 and 7 to be a bit too similar for my taste, and would have preferred some way of conflating them, but Dutton does appear to have captured fundamental principles that underlie the works in our repertoire, even if his features may not encompass every work of the avant-garde in the latter years of the 20th century.

God: Faith and Reason

To survey some 2500 years of philosophical thought I propose to focus on a single issue: the existence of God. The so-called cosmological argument begins with Aristotle, who used motion and existence almost interchangeably. A "mover" for Aristotle could be considered a "cause." Any effect has a cause, and yet the chain of causes and effects cannot be infinitely long. Therefore, there must be a first cause, or prime mover, in Aristotle's phrase, something which moves other things without itself being moved." This so-called "unmoved mover" may be considered the ultimate cause.

St. Anselm, the first of the medieval scholastic philosophers, took a somewhat different approach to the existence of God. The so-called ontological argument owes a good deal to Plato, who posited the existence of ideal forms, reflected or represented in everyday reality. St. Anselm argues that we cannot call something "good" if there were not some absolute standard of goodness, what Plato would call the ideal form of The Good. According to Anselm, the absolute Being, who incorporates Goodness, Justice and Greatness, is God. In paraphrase, Anselm argues:

1. By definition, God is a being greater than anything that can be imagined.
2. Existence in both reality and imagination is greater than existence in imagination alone.
3. Therefore, God must exist in reality, because if God did not, God would not be a being greater than anything which can be imagined.

The scholastic philosophers undertook, among others things, to reconcile Christianity and classical thought. St. Thomas Aquinas' cosmological argument for God follows Aristotle's model. In paraphrase:

1. Every effect has a cause.
2. An effect cannot cause itself.
3. The chain of causes cannot be infinitely long.
4. There must be a first cause, and that is God.

Fifty years later William of Ockham, endeavoring to reform scholasticism, published a textbook on logic whose title, *Summa Logicae* (Sum of Logic), appears as a direct response to St. Thomas Aquinas. Ockham denies the existence of universals, and thus rejects the Platonist position. For William, a universal existed in the mind, nothing more. He argued that human reason alone cannot prove the existence of God. This knowledge, he maintains, can come only through revelation. William rejected proofs of the existence of God, which he considered to be a matter of faith rather than knowledge. For William, universals were no more than linguistic devices that we use to try to understand reality: universals have no actual existence in themselves.

Nonetheless, variations on the cosmological and ontological arguments persisted. Descartes, in the third of his Meditations, maintains that a finite being could not conceive of an infinite being, namely God, unless God existed. *"By the name God, I understand a substance infinite, eternal, immutable, independent, all-knowing, all-powerful, and by which I myself, and every other thing that exists, if any such there be, were created. But these properties are so great and excellent, that the more attentively I consider them the less I feel persuaded that the idea I have of them owes its origin to myself alone. And thus it is absolutely necessary to conclude, from all that I have before said, that God exists. For though the idea of substance be in my mind owing to this, that I myself am a substance, I should not, however, have the idea of an infinite substance, seeing I am a finite being, unless it were given me by some substance in reality infinite."*[452]

Descartes offers a form of the ontological argument in his Fifth Meditation which, paraphrased, reads:

1. Whatever I clearly and distinctly perceive to be contained in the idea of something, is true of that thing.
2. I clearly and distinctly perceive that necessary existence is contained in the idea of God.
3. Therefore, God exists.

Modern philosophy, as distinct from scholastic philosophy, has been said to begin with the work of Immanuel Kant in the 17th century who, as we have seen, presents refutations for both the cosmological and the ontological arguments. Instead, he offers a Categorical Imperative designed to offer moral guidance without reference to a deity. Denying the existence of universal and absolute values requires each person to create an individual moral code, essentially the position of the Existentialist philosophers of the 20th century. The rejection of universal values leaves one in a state of moral uncertainty on a footing with the political, artistic and scientific uncertainty characteristic of our modern age.

Many believers would say that their faith does not depend on the validity or non-validity of philosophical arguments. They might find greater affinity with the mystics, like Hildegard von Bingen, whose faith came from a direct experience of God's presence.

Conclusion

"Only connect," E. M. Forster wrote. In these pages, I have tried to draw connections between aspects of western culture extending over more than three millennia. Harold Bloom, in *The Western Canon*, describes the way writers speak to each other across generations. I would suggest that not just writers but all artists in some fashion speak to each other, if not within the same generation, at least within the same century. I believe that that our appreciation of Notre-Dame Cathedral is deepened by coming to understand Gottfried von Strassburg, Perotin, Thomas Aquinas and Fibonacci; that we can make better sense of Velasquez by coming to know Molière, Monteverdi, Descartes, Newton, Hobbes and Locke; that our understanding of Fielding is enhanced by becoming acquainted with Jefferson, Bach, Kant, Euler and Smith. "Don't take any course where they make you read *Beowulf*," the Woody Allen character tells the Diane Keaton character in *Annie Hall*. But *Beowulf* offers a terrific experience that informs and benefits from a knowledge of Gregory of Tours, and both cast light on the Book of Kells, the writings of St. Augustine and plainsong.

I leave the last word to Aristotle, who began his *Metaphysics* with the sentence, "All human beings by nature desire knowledge," an apt description of my motivation in writing these words and your willingness to read them.

Repertoire

1. Prologue
Paleolithic Art: Cave Paintings at Lascaux, ca 15,000 BC
Egyptian art: Imhotep, The Pyramid of King Zoser, ca 2650 BC

2. Ancient Greece
Homer, *The Odyssey,* 800-600 BC
Pythagoras. fl.ca.500 BC
Parthenon, 448-432 BC
Herodotus, *Histories,* 450s BC
Sophocles, *Oedipus Rex*, 428 BC
Plato, *The Republic,* 360 BC
Aristotle, *Nichomachean Ethics*, ca 330 BC
Euclid, *Elements*, 300 BC

3. Ancient Rome
Caesar, *Commentaries on The Gallic Wars*, ca.50-40 BC
Virgil, *The Aeneid*, 19 BC
Paul of Tarsus, *Epistle to the Romans*, 60 AD
Colosseum, 80 AD
Ptolemy, *Almagest*, ca. 150 AD

4. Early Middle Ages (5th-10th Centuries)
St. Augustine, *The City of God*, ca 420 AD
Gregory of Tours, *Ten Books of History,* 594 AD
Beowulf, ca. 700 AD
The Book of Kells, ca. 800
Plainsong, *Kyrie orbis factor*, 9th century

5. 11th Century
St. Anselm, *Proslogion*, ca.1078
Bayeux Tapestry, ca.1100
Song of Roland, ca. 1100
Alleluia Justus ut palma, ca. 1100

6. 12th Century
Basilica of St. Sernin, Toulouse, 1080-1120
Peter Abelard, *Sic et non,* 1121
Leonin, *Viderunt omnes,* ca 1160
Chrétien de Troyes, *Lancelot, The Knight of the Cart*, 1168

7. 13th Century
Notre Dame Cathedral, 1163-ca.1270
Pérotin, *Viderunt omnes*, ca 1200
Fibonacci, *Liber abaci,* 1202
Gottfried von Strassburg, *Tristan*, 1210
Thomas Aquinas, *Summa Theologica*, 1274

8. 14th Century
Giotto, *Entrance of Christ into Jerusalem*, 1306
William of Ockham, *Sum of Logic*, 1323
Machaut, *Ma fin est mon commencement*, ca 1360
Chaucer, *The Canterbury Tales*, 1380-1390

9. 15th Century
Robert Campin, *Merode Altarpiece*, ca.1425-1438
Ockeghem, *Missa prolationum* (Sanctus), mid-15th century
Villon, *Ballade des dames du temps jadis*, 1461
Leonardo da Vinci, *Notebooks* [various]

10. 16th Century
Erasmus, *In Praise of Folly*, 1511
Luther, *95 Theses*, 1517
Michelangelo, Sistine Chapel Ceiling ("The Creation of Adam"),
1511
Machiavelli, *The Prince,* 1513
Castiglione, *The Book of the Courtier,* 1528
Copernicus, *On the Revolutions of the Heavenly Spheres,* 1543
Lassus, *De Profundis*, 1584

Shakespeare, *Hamlet*, ca. 1600

11. 17th Century

Monteverdi, *Orfeo* (Possente spirto), 1607
Descartes, *Discourse on the Method*, 1637
Velásquez. *Las Meninas*, 1656
Molière, *Le Misanthrope,* 1666
Newton, *Principia Mathematica*, 1687
Hobbes, *Leviathan*, 1651
Locke, *2nd Treatise on Government*, 1689

12. 18th Century

Euler, *The Seven Bridges of Königsberg*, 1735
Bach, *B Minor Mass* (Dona nobis pacem), ca. 1748
Fielding, *Tom Jones*, 1749
Jefferson, *Monticello*, 1772
Smith, *The Wealth of Nations,* 1776
Kant, *Groundwork* for a *Metaphysics of Morals*, 1785

13. 19th Century

Gauss, *Theory of the motion of the heavenly bodies*, 1809
Austen, *Pride and Prejudice*, 1813
Beethoven, Symphony No. 9 (last movement), 1824
Turner, *The Slave Ship,* 1839
Kierkegaard, *Either/Or*, 1843
Marx, *The Communist Manifesto,* 1848
Darwin, *On the Origin of Species*, 1859
Freud, *Interpretation of Dreams*, 1899

14. 20th Century

Picasso, *Les Demoiselles d'Avignon*, 1906-1907
Einstein, General Theory of Relativity, 1915
Heisenberg, Uncertainty Principle, Quantum Mechanics, 1927
Joyce, *Ulysses*, 1922
Bartók, *Music for Strings, Percussion and Celesta*, 1936
Sartre, *Being and Nothingness*, 1943

Plates

PLATE 1: Lascaux Cave Paintings, ca.17,000 BC

PLATE 2: Imhotep, The Pyramid of King Djoser, ca.2650 BC

PLATE 3: Parthenon, 448-432 BC

PLATE 4: Colosseum 80 AD

PLATE 5: The Book of Kells, ca. 800

PLATE 6: Bayeux Tapestry, ca. 1100

Plates
PLATE 8: Notre Dame Cathedral, 1163-ca. 1269

PLATE 9: Giotto, Entrance of Christ into Jerusalem, 1306

PLATE 10: Robert Campin, *Merode Altarpiece*, ca.1425-1438

PLATE 11: Michelangelo, "The Creation of Adam," Sistine
Chapel Ceiling, 1511

PLATE 12: Velásquez, *Las Meninas*, 1656

PLATE 13: Hobbes, *Leviathan*, 1651

Plates

PLATE 14: Jefferson, *Monticello*, 1772

PLATE 15: Turner, *The Slave Ship*, 1839

PLATE 16: Picasso, *Les Demoiselles d'Avignon*, 1907

Bibliography

Print Materials

Aczel, Amir D. (2005). *Descartes' Secret Notebook: A True Tale of Mathematics, Mysticism, and the Quest to Understand the Universe.* New York: Broadway Books.

Al-Khalili, Jim (1999). *Black Holes, Wormholes and Time Machines.* Philadelphia: Institute of Physics Publishing.

Al-Khalili, Jim (2003). *Quantum: A Guide for the Perplexed.* London: Weidenfeld & Nicolson.

Atlas, Allan W. (1998) *Renaissance Music: Music in Western Europe, 1400-1600.* New York: W. W. Norton

Antokoletz, Elliott and Susanni, Paolo (2011). *Béla Bartók: A Research and Information Guide.* 3rd edition. New York: Routledge Music Bibliographies.

Aristotle (1996). *Poetics.* Translated by Malcolm Heath. New York: Penguin Books

Attridge, Derek, ed. (2004). *James Joyce's Ulysses: A Casebook.* New York: Oxford University Press.

Bagby, Laurie M. Johnson (2007). *Hobbes's Leviathan: Reader's Guide.* London: Continuum.

Baker, Sheridan (1995). Editor, critical edition of Fielding, *Tom Jones.* New York: W. W. Norton

Barbero, Alessandro (2004). *Charlemagne: Father of a Continent.* Berkeley: University of California Press.

Barnes, Jonathan (2004). Introduction to Aristotle, *The Nichomachean Ethics*, trans. J.A.K. Thomson. New York: Penguin Books.

Bibliography

Barnes, Timothy D. (1981). *Constantine and Eusebius*. Cambridge, Massachusetts: Harvard University Press.

Bartlett, Robert C. and Collins, Susan D. (2011). *Aristotle's Nicomachean Ethics*. Chicago: University of Chicago Press.

Barzun, Jacques (2000). *From Dawn to Decadence: 1500 to the Present—500 Years of Western Cultural Life*. New York: HarperCollins.

Batts, Michael S. (1971). *Gottfried von Strassburg*. New York: Twayne Publishers, Inc.

Bayley, Amanda, ed. (2001). *The Cambridge Companion to Bartók*. Cambridge: Cambridge University Press.

Beard, Mary (2010). *The Parthenon*. Revised edition. Cambridge, Massachusetts: Harvard University Press.

Bennett, Jeffrey (2014). *What Is Relativity? An Intuitive Introduction to Einstein's Ideas, and Why They Matter*. New York: Columbia University Press.

Bennett, Judith M. and Hollister, C. Warren (2006). *Medieval Europe: A Short History*. 10th ed. New York: McGraw-Hill.

Bermel, Albert (1990). *Molière's Theatrical Bounty: A New View of the Plays*. *Carbondale: Southern Illinois University Press*.

Bernstein, Jeremy (2009). *Quantum Leaps*. Cambridge, Massachusetts: Harvard University Press.

Bernstein, R. B. (2003). *Thomas Jefferson*. New York: Oxford University Press.

Biggs, Norman, *et al.* (1986) *Graph Theory 1736-1936*. New York: Oxford University Press.

Bisson, Lillian M. (1998). *Chaucer and the Late Medieval World*. New York: St. Martin's Press.

Blechner, Mark J. (2001). *The Dream Frontier*. New York: Routledge.

Bloom, Harold, ed. (1987a). *Beowulf.* New York: Chelsea House Publishers.

Bloom, Harold, ed. (1987b). *Henry Fielding's Tom Jones*. New York: Chelsea House Publishers.

Bloom, Harold, ed. (1987c). *Sigmund Freud's The Interpretation of Dreams.* Philadelphia: Chelsea House Publishers.

Bloom, Harold, ed. (1988). *Sophocles' Oedipus Rex*. New York: Chelsea House.

Bloom, Harold, ed. (1996a). *Homer's Odyssey.* Broomall, Pennsylvania: Chelsea House Publishers.

Bloom, Harold, ed. (1996b). *Vergil's Aeneid.* Broomall, Pennsylvania: Chelsea House Publishers.

Bloom, Harold (1998). *Shakespeare: The Invention of the Human.* New York: Riverhead Books.

Bloom, Harold (2003a). *Hamlet: Poem Unlimited.* New York: Riverhead Books.

Bloom, Harold (2005). *Jane Austen's Pride and Prejudice.* Philadelphia: Chelsea House.

Bony, Jean (1983). *French Gothic Architecture of the 12th and 13th Centuries.* Berkeley: University of California Press.

Boyer, Carl B. (1991) *A History of Mathematics,* 2nd ed. New York: John Wiley & Sons.

Brault, Gerard J. (1978). *The Song of Roland: An Analytical Edition.* University Park: The Pennsylvania State University Press.

Bibliography

Bridgehead, Andrew (2005). *1066: The Hidden History in the Bayeux Tapestry*. New York: Walker & Company.

Brinton, Crane, Christopher, John B., and Wolff, Robert Lee (1976). *A History of Civilization*. 5th edition. Englewood Cliffs, New Jersey: Prentice-Hall.

Brower, Jeffrey and Guilfoy, Kevin (2004). *The Cambridge Companion to Abelard*. Cambridge: Cambridge University Press.

Brown, Howard Mayer and Stein, Louise K. (1999). *Music in the Renaissance*. Upper Saddle River, New Jersey: Prentice-Hall.

Brown, Raymond E. (1997). *An Introduction to the New Testament*. New Haven: Yale University Press.

Browne, Janet (2006). *Darwin's Origin of Species: A Biography*. New York: Atlantic Monthly Press.

Budgen, Frank (1960). *James Joyce and the Making of Ulysses*. Bloomington, Indiana: Indiana University Press. (Originally published 1934)

Bull, George (1976). Introduction to Baldesar Castiglione, *The Book of the Courtier*. London: Penguin Books.

Bull, George (1999). Introduction to Niccolo Machiavelli, *The Prince*. London: Penguin Books.

Burkholder, J. Peter and Palisca, Claude V., eds. (2006). *Norton Anthology of Western Music*. New York: W. W. Norton.

Burton, David M. (2003). *The History of Mathematics: An Introduction*. 5th edition. New York: McGraw Hill.

Butt, John (1991). *Bach: Mass in B Minor*. New York: Cambridge University Press.

Calinger, Ronald S. (2016). *Leonard Euler: Mathematical Genius in the Enlightenment.* Princeton: Princeton University Press.

Campbell, Joseph (1949). *The Hero with a Thousand Faces.* New York: Bollingen Foundation.

Cantor, Norman F. (1993). *The Civilization of the Middle Ages.* New York: Harper Perennial.

Cantor, Paul (2004). *Shakespeare: Hamlet.* 2nd edition. Cambridge: Cambridge University Press.

Capra, Fritjof (2007). *The Science of Leonardo: Inside the Mind of the Great Genius of the Renaissance.* New York: Doubleday.

Capra, Fritjof (2013). *Learning from Leonardo: Decoding the Notebooks of a Genius.* San Francisco: Berrett-Koehler Publishers, Inc.

Cassidy, David C. (2009). *Beyond Uncertainty: Heisenberg, Quantum Physics, and the Bomb.* New York: Bellevue Literary Press.

Chandrasekhar, S. (1995). *Newton's Principia for the Common Reader.* New York: Oxford University Press.

Chappell, Vere (1994). *The Cambridge Companion to Locke.* Cambridge: Cambridge University Press.

Chinca, Mark (1997). *Gottfried von Strassburg: Tristan.* New York: Cambridge University Press.

Christ-von Wedel, Christine (2013). *Erasmus of Rotterdam: Advocate of a New Christianity.* Toronto: University of Toronto Press.

Connell, William J. (2005). *The Prince by Niccolò Machiavelli with Related Documents.* Boston: Bedford/St. Martin's.

Bibliography

Connelly, Joan Breton (2014). *The Parthenon Enigma: A new understanding of the West's most iconic building and the people who made it.* New York: Alfred A. Knopf.

Cook, Nicholas (1993). *Beethoven: Symphony No. 9.* Cambridge: Cambridge University Press.

Cooper, David (2015). *Béla Bartók.* New Haven: Yale University Press.

Copeland Edward and McMaster, Juliet, eds. (2011). *The Cambridge Companion to Jane Austen.* Second edition. New York: Cambridge University Press.

Copley, Stephen and Sutherland, Kathryn, eds. (1995). *Adam Smith's Wealth of Nations: New Interdisciplinary Essays.* Manchester: Manchester University Press.

Cox, Brian and Forshaw, Jeff (2011). *The Quantum Universe (And Why Anything That Can Happen, Does).* New York: DaCapo Press.

Coyle, John, ed. (1997). *James Joyce: Ulysses; A Portrait of the Artist as a Young man.* Cambridge: Icon Books.

Curtis, Gregory (2006). *The Cave Painters: Probing the Mysteries of the World's First Artists.* New York: Alfred A. Knopf.

Dahmus, Joseph (1968). *A History of the Middle Ages.* New York: Barnes & Noble.

D'Arcais, Francesca Flores (1995). *Giotto.* New York: Abbeville Press Publishers.

Davies, Brian and Leftow, Brian, eds. (2004). *The Cambridge Companion to Anselm.* Cambridge: Cambridge University Press.

Davies, Norman (1996). *Europe: A History.* London: The Bodley Head.

Devlin, Keith (2011). *The Man of Numbers: Fibonacci's Arithmetic Revolution.* New York: Walker & Company.

Donaldson, E. Talbot (1966). *Beowulf: A New Prose Translation.* New York: W. W. Norton.

Donnelly, Dorothy F., ed., (1995). *The City of God: A Collection of Critical Essays.* New York: Peter Lang.

Duggan, Joseph J. (1997). *Lancelot: The Knight of the Cart.* Afterword. New Haven: Yale University Press.

Dunham, William, ed. (2007). *The Genius of Euler: Reflections on his Life and Work.* Washington, D.C.: The Mathematical Association of America.

Dutton, Denis (2002). "Aesthetic Universals" in *The Routledge Companion to Aesthetics*, edited by Berys Gaut and Dominic McIver Lopes. New York: Routledge.

Elsen, Albert E. (1967). *Purposes of Art: An Introduction to the History and Appreciation of Art.* 2nd edition. New York: Holt, Rinehart and Winston, Inc.

Erlande-Brandenburg, Alain (1997). *Notre-Dame de Paris.* New York: Harry N. Abrams, Inc., Publishers.

Evans, James Allan (2006). *The Beginnings of History: Herodotus and the Persian Wars.* Toronto: University of Toronto Press.

Eves, Howard (1969). *An Introduction to the History of Mathematics.* 3rd ed. New York: Brooks Cole.

Fabbri, Paolo (1994). *Monteverdi.* Trans. Tim Carter. Cambridge: Cambridge University Press.

Farr, Carol (1997). *The Book of Kells: Its Function and Audience.* Toronto: University of Toronto Press.

Fein, David A. (1997). *François Villon Revisited.* New York: Twayne Publishers.

Fitch, Fabrice (1997). *Johannes Ockeghem: Masses and Models.* Paris: Honoré *Champion* Éditeur.

Fitts, Dudley (1960). Introduction to *Greek Plays in Modern Translation.* New York: Holt, Rinehart and Winston.

Fitzmyer, Joseph A., S.J. (1992). *Romans: A New Translation with Introduction and Commentary.* New Haven: Yale University Press.

Fleming, William (1974). *Arts and Ideas: New and Brief Edition.* New York: Holt, Rinehart and Winston, Inc.

Fleming, William (1974). *Arts and Ideas: New and Brief Edition.* New York: Holt, Rinehart and Winston, Inc.

Foster, Thomas C. (2008). *How to Read Novels Like a Professor.* New York: Harper Perennial.

Foster, Thomas C. (2014). *How to Read Literature Like a Professor.* Rev. ed. New York: Harper Perennial.

Foucault, Michel (1966). *"Las Meninas,"* in *The Order of Things: An Archeology of the Human Sciences.* New York: Pantheon, pp.1-15.

Fowler, Robert (2004). *The Cambridge Companion to Homer.* Cambridge: Cambridge University Press.

Fowlie, Wallace (1973). *French Literature: Its history and its meaning.* Englewood Cliffs, NJ: Prentice-Hall, Inc.

Foys, Martin K., Karen Eileen Overbey and Dan Terkla (2009). *The Bayeux Tapestry: New Interpretations.* Woodbridge, England: The Boydell Press.

Franzén, Torkel (2005). *Gödel's Theorem: An Incomplete Guide to Its Use and Abuse.* Wellesley, Massachusetts: A. K. Peters.

Fratantuono, Lee (2007). *Madness Unchained: A Reading of Virgil's Aeneid.* Lanham, Maryland: Rowman & Littlefield.

Freeman, Charles (2004). *Egypt, Greece and Rome: Civilizations of the Ancient Mediterranean.* 2nd edition. New York: Oxford University Press.

Freeman, Philip (2008). *Julius Caesar.* New York: Simon & Schuster.

Fullerton, Susannah (2013. *Happily Ever After: Celebrating Jane Austen's Pride and Prejudice.* London: Frances Lincoln Limited.

Gaines, James R. *Evening in the Palace of Reason: Bach meets Frederick the Great in the Age of Enlightenment.* New York: HarperCollins.

Galfard, Chris (2015). *The Universe in Your Hand.* New York: Flatiron Books.

Gardner, Sebastian (2009). *Sartre's Being and Nothingness: A Reader's Guide.* New York: Continuum International Publishing Group.

Gemes, Ken and Richardson, John (2013). *The Oxford handbook of Nietzsche.* Oxford: Oxford University Press.

Georgi, David (2013). *Poems: François Villon.* Evanston, Illinois: Northwestern University Press.

Ghiselin, Michael T. (2006). Introduction to Darwin, *On the Origin of Species by Means of Natural Selection.* Mineola, NY: Dover Publications.

Bibliography

Gilbert, Stuart (1955). *James Joyce's Ulysses: A Study.* New York: Vintage.

Gillespie, Michael Patrick and Fargnoli, A. Nicholas (2006). *Ulysses in Critical Perspective.* Gainesville: University Press of Florida.

Giordano, Ralph G. (2012). *The Architectural Ideology of Thomas Jefferson.* Jefferson, North Carolina: McFarland & Company, Inc., Publishers.

Giulini, Domenico (2005). *Special relativity: A First Encounter.* New York: Oxford University Press.

Godden, Malcolm and Lapidge, Michael (1991). *The Cambridge Companion to Old English Literature.* Cambridge: Cambridge University Press.

Godden, Malcolm and Lapidge, Michael (2013). *The Cambridge Companion to Old English Literature.* 2nd edition. Cambridge: Cambridge University Press.

Goldsworthy, Adrian (2006). *Caesar: Life of a Colossus.* New Haven: Yale University Press.

Gordon-Reed, Annette, and Onuf, Peter S. (2016). *'Most Blessed of the Patriarchs': Thomas Jefferson and the Empire of the Imagination.* New York: Liveright Publishing Company.

Graham-Dixon, Andrew (2009). *Michelangelo and the Sistine Chapel.* New York: Skyhorse Publishing.

Grayling, A. C. (2005). *Descartes: The Life and Times of a Genius.* New York: Walker & Company.

Green, Christopher, ed. (2001). *Picasso's Les Demoiselles d'Avignon.* Cambridge: Cambridge University Press.

Greenblatt, Stephen (1997). "Introduction to Hamlet" in *The Norton Shakespeare.* New York: W. W. Norton

Grene, David, ed. (1991) *Sophocles I.* Chicago: The University of Chicago Press.

Griffiths, Paul (1984). *Bartók.* London: J. M. Dent.

Grun, Bernard (1975). *The Timetables of History: A Horizontal Linkage of People and Events.* New York: Simon and Schuster.

Giucciardini, *Niccolò* (2005). "Isaac Newton: *Philosophiae Naturalis Principia Mathematica*, First Edition (1687)," in Grattan-Guinness, I., ed., *Landmark Writings in Western Mathematics, 1640-1940.* Amsterdam: Elsevier, pp.59-87.

Guyer, Paul (2006). *The Cambridge Companion to Kant and Modern Philosophy.* New York: Cambridge University Press.

Guyer, Paul (2007). *Kant's Groundwork for the Metaphysics of Morals: A Reader's Guide.* New York: Continuum.

Hale, John (1993). *The Civilization of Europe in the Renaissance.* New York: Simon and Schuster.

Hannay, Alastair (1992). Introduction to *Søren Kierkegaard: Either/Or: A Fragment of Life.* London: Penguin Books.

Hatto, A. T. (2004). Introduction to Gottfried von Strassburg, *Tristan,* trans., A. T. Hatto. New York: Penguin Books.

Hawking, Stephen (2001). *The Universe in a Nutshell*, New York: Random House.

Heinzelmann, Martin (2001). *Gregory of Tours: History and Society in the Sixth Century.* Cambridge: Cambridge University Press.

Heisenberg, Werner (1949). *The physical principles of the quantum theory.* Translated by Carl Eckart and F. C. Hoyt. New York: Dover.

Hobsbawm, Eric (2011). *How to Change the World: Reflections on Marx and Marxism.* New Haven: Yale University Press.

Bibliography

Hogan, Craig J. (1998). *The Little Book of the Big Bang: A Cosmic Primer.* New York: Springer-Verlag.

Holme, Paul L. (1958). Introduction to *Edifying Discourses: A Selection: Søren Kierkegaard.* New York: Harper Torchbooks.

Honour, Hugh and Fleming, John (1982). *The Visual Arts: A History.* Englewood Cliffs, N.J.: Prentice-Hall, Inc.

Hopkins, Keith and Beard, Mary (2005). *The Colosseum.* Cambridge, Massachusetts: Harvard University Press.

Hoppin, Richard H. (1978). *Medieval Music.* New York: W. W. Norton.

Hughes, Robert (1982). *The Shock of the New.* New York: Alfred A. Knopf.

Icher, François (1998). *Building the Great Cathedrals.* New York: Harry N. Abrams. Trans. From the French by Anthony Zielonka.

Jacobus, Laura (2008). *Giotto and the Arena Chapel: Art, Architecture & experience.* Turnhout, Belgium: Harvey Miller Publishers.

Javitch, Daniel, ed. (2002). *Baldesar Castiglione: The Book of the Courtier.* New York: W. W. Norton.

Johnson, Paul (1983). *Modern Times: The World from the Twenties to the Eighties.* New York: Harper & Row.

Johnston, Ian (2001). "Introductory Lecture on Shakespeare's *Hamlet.*" [Public domain]

Joll, Evelyn, Martin Butlin, and Luke Hermann (2001). *The Oxford companion to J. M. W. Turner.* New York: Oxford University Press.

Jones, Gareth Stedman (2002). Introduction to Marx and Engels, *The Communist Manifesto.* New York: Penguin Books.

Keele, Rondo (2010). *Ockham Explained: From Razor to Rebellion.* Chicago: Open Court.

Kenner, Hugh (1987). *Ulysses*, revised edition. Baltimore: The Johns Hopkins University Press

Killeen, Terence (2014). *Ulysses Unbound: A reader's companion to James Joyce's Ulysses.* Dublin: Wordwell.

Kleiner, Fred S., *et al.* (2003). *Gardner's Art Through the Ages: The Western Perspective.* Eleventh edition. Belmont, CA: Wadsworth/Thomson Learning.

Knox, Bernard (1982). Introduction to Sophocles, *Oedipus the King*, trans. Robert Fagles. New York: Penguin Books.

Knox, Bernard (1996). Introduction to Homer, *The Odyssey*, trans. Robert Fagles. New York: Penguin Books.

Knox, Bernard (2006). Introduction to Virgil, *The Aeneid,* trans. Robert Fagles. New York: Penguin Books.

Lacy, Norris J. and Grimbert, Joan Tasker (2005). *A Companion to Chrétien de Troyes.* Rochester, New York: D. S. Brewer

Ladis, Andrew (2008). *Giotto's Narrative, Figuration, and Pictorial Ingenuity in the Arena Chapel.* University Park, Pennsylvania: The Pennsylvania State University Press.

Lane, Barbara (1984). *The Altar and the Altarpiece: Sacramental Themes in Early Netherlandish Painting.* New York: Harper & Row.

Lane, Melissa (2007). Introduction to Plato, *The Republic*, trans. Desmond Lee. New York: Penguin Books.

Lawrence, Karen (1981). *The Odyssey of Style in Ulysses.* Princeton, New Jersey: Princeton University Press.

Leach, Elizabeth Eva (2003). *Machaut's Music: New Interpretations.* Rochester, NY: The Boydell Press.

Bibliography

Lehner, Mark (1997). *The Complete Pyramids*. London: Thames and Hudson.

Levy, David Benjamin (2003). *Beethoven: The Ninth Symphony*. New Haven: Yale University Press.

Lewis-Williams, David (2002). *The Mind in the Cave: Consciousness and the Origins of Art*. New York: Thames & Hudson.

Linton, Christopher M. (2004). *From Eudoxus to Einstein: A History of Mathematics Astronomy*. Cambridge: Cambridge University Press.

Livio, Mario (2002). *The Golden Ratio: The Story of Phi, the World's Most Astonishing Number*. New York: Broadway Books.

Logan, Ian (2009). *Reading Anselm's Proslogion: The History of Anselm's Argument and its Significance Today*. Burlington, Vermont: Ashgate.

MacMillan, Margaret (2013). *The War that Ended Peace: The Road to 1914*. Toronto: Penguin Canada.

Marenbon, John (1999). *The Philosophy of Peter Abelard*. New York: Cambridge University Press.

Marincola, John (2003). Introduction to Herodotus, *The Histories*, trans. Aubrey de Sélincourt. London: Penguin Books.

Marozzi, Justin (2008). *The Way of Herodotus: Travels with the Man Who Invented History*. Philadelphia: DaCapo Press.

Martindale, Colin (1990). *The Clockwork Muse: The Predictability of Artistic Change*. Toronto: HarperCollins Canada.

Marty, Martin (2004). *Martin Luther*. New York: Viking Penguin.

McGinn, Bernard (2014). *Thomas Aquinas's Summa theologiae: A Biography*. Princeton, N.J.: Princeton University Press.

McGrady, Deborah and Bain, Jennifer (2012). *A Companion to Guillaume de Machaut*. Boston: Brill.

McKim, Donald K., ed. (2003). *The Cambridge Companion to Martin Luther*. New York: Cambridge University Press.

McKitterick, Rosamond (2008). *Charlemagne: The Formation of a European Identity*. Cambridge: Cambridge University Press.

Meehan, Bernard (1994). *The Book of Kells: An Illustrated Introduction to the Manuscript in Trinity College Dublin*. London: Thames & Hudson.

Mermin, N. David (1990). *Boojums All the Way Through: Communicating Science in a Prosaic Age*. Cambridge: Cambridge University Press.

Mermin, N. David (2005). *It's About Time: Understanding Einstein's Relativity*. Princeton: Princeton University Press.

Merton, Thomas (2000). Introduction to Saint Augustine, *The City of God*. New York: The Modern Library.

Mitchell, Kathleen and Wood, Ian, eds. (2002). *The World of Gregory of Tours*. Boston: Brill.

Moo, Douglas J. (2002). *Encountering the Book of Romans: A Theological Survey*. Grand Rapids, Michigan: Baker Academic.

Musgrove, John, ed. (1987). *Sit Banister Fletcher's A History of Architecture*. 19th ed. London: Butterworths.

Nabokov, Vladimir (1980). *Lectures on Literature*. New York: Harcourt Brace Jovanovich.

Nichols, J. K. B. M. (1962). *An Introduction to Roman Law. Oxford: At the Clarendon Press.*

Bibliography

Nighan, Raymond (2001). *Hamlet and the Daemons: An Inquiry into the Nature of the Ghost and Its Mission.* [Public domain]

Oakes, Kenneth (2011). *Reading Karl Barth: A Companion to Karl Barth's Epistle to the Romans.* Eugene, Oregon: Cascade Books.

O'Daly, Gerald (1999). *Augustine's City of God: A Reader's Guide.* Oxford: Clarendon Press.

O'Donnell, James. J. (2005). *Augustine: A New Biography.* New York: HarperCollins.

Osborne, Roger (2006). *Civilization: A New History of the Western World.* New York: Pegasus.

Overbye, Dennis (2016). "Gravitational Waves Detected, Confirming Einstein's Theory." *New York Times*, Feb. 11, 2016.

Orchard, Andy (2003). *A Critical Companion to Beowulf.* Suffolk: D. S. Brewer.

Pakaluk, Michael (2005). *Aristotle's Nicomachean Ethics: An Introduction.* New York: Cambridge University Press.

Palmer, R. R. and Colton, Joel (1971). *A History of the Modern World.* New York: Alfred A. Knopf.

Partridge, Loren (1996). *Michelangelo: The Sistine Chapel Ceiling, Rome.* New York: George Braziller.

Pedretti Carlo (2004). *Leonardo Art and Science.* Surrey, England: TAJ Books.

Pelletier, Jenny E. (2013). *William Ockham on Metaphysics: The Science of Being and God.* Boston: Brill.

Pietrangeli, Carlo *et al* (1986). *The Sistine Chapel: The Art, the History, and the Restoration.* New York: Harmony Books.

Pinker, Seven (2011). *The Better Angels of our Nature*. New York: Viking.

Pirrotta, Nino and Povoledo, Elena (1975). *Music and Theatre from Poliziano to Monteverdi*. Cambridge: Cambridge University Press.

Raphael, D. D. (1991). Introduction to *The Wealth of Nations*. New York: Alfred A. Knopf.

Rathey, Markus (2003). "Johann Sebastian Bach's Mass in B Minor: The Greatest Artwork of All Times and All People." Lecture

Rathey, Markus (2016). *Bach's Major Vocal Works: Music, Drama, Liturgy*. New Haven: Yale University Press.

Reed, J. D. (2007). *Virgil's Gaze: Nation and Poetry and the Aeneid*. Princeton, New Jersey: Princeton University Press.

Repcheck, Jack (2007). *Copernicus' Secret: How the Scientific Revolution Began*. New York: Simon & Schuster.

Reznick, David N. (2010). *The Origin Then and Now: An Interpretive Guide to the Origin of Species*. Princeton: Princeton University Press.

Rice, Daryl H. (1998). *A Guide to Plato's Republic*. New York: Oxford University Press.

Richter, Irma A., ed. (1952). *The Notebooks of Leonardo da Vinci*. Oxford: Oxford University Press.

Ringer, Mark (2006). *Opera's First Master: The Musical Dramas of Claudio Monteverdi*. Pompton Plains, New Jersey: Amadeus Press.

Roberts, Andrew (2014). *Napoleon: A Life*. New York: Penguin Books.

Bibliography

Robertson, Ritchie (1999). Introduction to Freud, *The Interpretation of Dreams*. New York: Oxford University Press.

Rovelli, Carlo (2016). *Seven Brief Lessons on Physics*. New York: Riverhead Books.

Rubin, William *et al* (1994). *Les Demoiselles d'Avignon*. New York: The Museum of Modern Art.

Russell, John, (1981). *The Meanings of Modern Art*. New York: Harper & Row, Publishers.

Sandifer, C. Edward (2007). *How Euler Did It*. [n.p.]: The Mathematical Association of America.

Santas, Gerasimos (2010). *Understanding Plato's Republic*. West Sussex: Wiley-Blackwell.

Sayers, Dorothy L. (1957). Introduction to *The Song of Roland*, trans. Dorothy Sayers. New York: Penguin Books.

Sayers, Sean (1999). *Plato's Republic: An Introduction*. Edinburgh: Edinburgh University Press.

Schapiro, Meyer (1979). *Late Antique, Early Christian and Medieval Art: Selected Papers*. New York: George Braziller, Inc.

Shapard, David M., ed. (2012). *The Annotated Pride and Prejudice*. New York: Random House.

Skinner, Andrew, ed. (1999). *Adam Smith: The Wealth of Nations*. Analytical Introduction. London: Penguin Books.

Solomon, Maynard (2003). *Late Beethoven: Music, Thought, Imagination*. Berkeley, California: University of California Press.

Solomon, Robert C. and Higgins, Kathleen M., eds. (1988). *Reading Nietzsche*. New York: Oxford University Press.

Spade, Paul Vincent (1999). *The Cambridge Companion to Ockham.* New York: Cambridge University Press.

Springborg, Patricia, ed. (2007). *The Cambridge Companion to Hobbes's Leviathan.* New York: Cambridge University Press.

Stauffer, George F. (2003). *Bach, the Mass in B Minor: The Great Catholic Mass.* New Haven: Yale University Press.

Stevens, Halsey (1953). *The Life and Music of Béla Bartók.* New York: Oxford University Press.

Stratton-Pruitt, Suzanne L., ed. (2003). *Velásquez's Las Meninas.* Cambridge: Cambridge University Press.

Stuhlmacher, Peter (1994). *Paul's Letter to the Romans: A Commentary.* Louisville, Kentucky: Westminster/John Knox Press.

Suchoff, Benjamin, ed. (1976). *Béla Bartók Essays.* New York: St. Martin's Press.

Suchoff, Benjamin (2004). *A Bartók Celebration.* Lanham, Maryland: Scarecrow Press.

Taddei, Mario and Zanon, Edoardo, eds. (2006). *Leonardo's Machines: Da Vinci's Inventions Revealed.* Cincinnati, Ohio: David and Charles.

Taruskin, Richard (1989). "Resisting the Ninth." *19th-Century Music*, Vol. 12, No. 3: 241-256

Temko, Allan (1955). *Notre Dame of Paris.* New York: Time Incorporated.

Throop, Priscilla (2007). *Yes and No: the complete English translation of Peter Abelard's Sic et Non.* Charlotte, Vermont: MedievalMS.

Todd, Janet, ed. (2005). *Jane Austen in Context.* New York: Cambridge University Press.

Bibliography

Todd, Janet (2006). *The Cambridge Introduction to Jane Austen.* New York: Cambridge University Press.

Toman, Rolf, ed. (1997). *Romanesque: Architecture; Sculpture; Painting.* Köln: Könemann.

Toomer, G. J. (1998). *Ptolemy's Almagest.* Princeton, New Jersey: Princeton University Press.

Torrell, Jean-Pierre (2005). *Saint Thomas Aquinas. Volume 1: The Person and His Work. Revised Edition.* Trans. By Robert Royal. Washington, D.C.: The Catholic University of America Press.

Tuchman, Barbara (1978). *A Distant Mirror: The Calamitous 14th Century.* New York: Ballantine Books.

Uitti, Karl D. and Freeman, Michelle A. (1995). *Chrétien de Troyes Revisited.* New York: Twayne Publishers.

Vaughan Williams, Ralph (1953). *Some Thoughts on Beethoven's Choral Symphony and other Essays.* Oxford: Oxford University Press.

Venning, Barry (2003). *Turner.* London: Phaidon.

Verner, Miroslav (1997). *The Pyramids: The Mystery, Culture, and Science of Egypt's Great Monuments.* New York: Grove Press.

Virgil (2006). *The Aeneid.* Translated by Robert Fagles. New York: Penguin Books.

Waldron, Jeremy (2002). *God, Locke and Equality: Christian Foundations of John Locke's Political Thought.* Cambridge: Cambridge University Press.

Walker, Hallam (1971). *Moliere.* New York: Twayne Publishers.

Warne, Christopher (2006). *Aristotle's Nicomachean Ethics; Reader's Guide.* New York: Continuum.

Watson, Richard (2002). *Cogito, Ergo Sum: The Life of René Descartes.* Boston: David R. Godine.

Watt, Ian, ed. (1963). *Jane Austen: A Collection of Critical Essays.* Englewood Cliffs, N.J.: Prentice-Hall, Inc.

Wenk, Arthur B. (1984). *La Musique et les grandes époques de l'art.* Québec : Les Presses de l'Université Laval.

Wenk, Arthur B. (1985). *Une Esquisse de la pensée musicale.* (Unpublished text)

Whenham, John, ed. (1986). *Claudio Monteverdi: Orfeo.* Cambridge: Cambridge University Press.

Wills, Chuck (2008). *Thomas Jefferson Architect: The Interactive Portfolio.* Philadelphia: Running Press.

Wilson, Paul (1992). *The Music of Béla Bartók.* New Haven: Yale University Press.

Wofford, Susanna L., ed. (1994) *William Shakespeare: Hamlet.* Boston: Bedford/St. Martin's.

Wood, Allen W., ed. (2002). *Groundwork for the Metaphysics of Morals: Immanuel Kant.* New Haven: Yale University Press.

Wood, Ian (1994). *Gregory of Tours.* Oxford: Headstart History.

Wood, Loraine (2007). "Joyce's Ineluctable Modality: (Re)Reading the Structure of 'Sirens.'" *Joyce Studies Annual,* Volume 2007, pp.67-91. (Published by Fordham University Press.)

Wright, Craig (1989). *Music and Ceremony at Notre Dame of Paris 500-1550.* New York: Cambridge University Press.

Bibliography

Wright, David (1984). Introduction to Chaucer, *The Canterbury Tales*, trans. David Wright. New York: Oxford University Press.

Internet Materials

Brown, Eric, "Plato's Ethics and Politics in *The Republic*", *The Stanford Encyclopedia of Philosophy* (Winter 2011 Edition), Edward N. Zalta (ed.), http://plato.stanford.edu/archives/win2011/entries/plato-ethics-politics/.

Cartwright, Mark. "Roman Law." *Ancient History Encyclopedia.* http://ancient.eu

Flynn, Thomas, "Jean-Paul Sartre", *The Stanford Encyclopedia of Philosophy* (Fall 2013 Edition), Edward N. Zalta (ed.), http://plato.stanford.edu/archives/fall2013/entries/sartre/

Fordham University Medieval Sourcebook. Thomas Aquinas. http://sourcebooks.fordham.edu/source/aquinas3.asp

Fordham University Modern History Sourcebook: Nicolas Copernicus: From *The Revolutions of the Heavenly Bodies*, 1543. http://sourcebooks.fordham.edu/mod/1543copernicus2.asp

Letter from Sir Isaac Newton to Robert Hooke. Historical Society of Pennsylvania Digital Library. http://www.digitallibrary.hsp.org

McDonald, William. "Søren Kierkegaard (1813-1855)." *The Internet Encyclopedia of Philosophy*. ISSN 2161-0002. http://www.iep.utm.edu.

McDonald, William. "Søren Kierkegaard." *The Stanford Encyclopedia of Philosophy*. (Fall 2016 Edition). Edward N. Zalta (ed). http://plato.stanford.edu/archives/fall2016/entries/kierkegaard.

Perkins, Leeman L. (2015). "Ockeghem" in *Grove Music Online*. Oxford: Oxford University Press.

Roesner, Edward H. (2015). "Perotinus" and "Leoninus" in *Grove Music Online*. Oxford: Oxford University Press.

Thornton, Bro. Andrew, translator (1983). "Martin Luther: Preface to the Letter of St. Paul to the Romans." St. Anselm College Humanities Program. http://www.ccel.org/l/luther/romans/pref_romans.html

Tuttle, Margaret Kathleen (2014). "The Influence of Ovid's *Servitium Amoris* on Chrétien de Troye's Lancelot, Knight of the Cart." www.academia.edu

Wright/Simms (2010). *Music in Western Civilization.* "In Their Own Words" (Source Readings). http://www.cengage.com/music

Notes

---

[1]Curtis, pp.127, 237
[2] Lewis-Williams, p.133
[3] Curtis, p.225
[4] Curtis, p.20
[5] Bataille, p.49
[6] Bataille, p.50
[7] Verner, pp.108-109
[8] Lehner, p.6
[9] Lehner, p.87
[10] Lehner, pp, 30, 22
[11] Freeman, p.45
[12] Verner, p.45
[13] Beard, p.37
[14] Davies, p.100
[15] Connelly, p.xx-xxi
[16] Connelly, p.xxi
[17] Connelly, pp.253, 254
[18] Freeman, pp.255, 257
[19] Davies, p.130
[20] Neil Dolan, "Thematic and Structural Analysis" in Bloom 1996a, p.12
[21] Michael Silk, "The *Odyssey* and its explorations" in Fowler, p.41
[22] Dolan, p.16
[23] Burton, p.86, 88
[24] Livio, p.26
[25] Eves, pp.52-53
[26] Burton, p.89
[27] Eves, p.61
[28] Connelly, p.72
[29] Connelly, p.83
[30] Connelly, p.85
[31] Beard, p.36
[32] Beard, p.67
[33] Connelly, p.95
[34] Connelly, p.93
[35] Connelly, p.254
[36] Connelly, p.251
[37] Marincola, p.xiv
[38] Marozzi, p.20
[39] Herodotus, *Histories*, p.401
[40] Herodotus, *Histories*, p.490
[41] Herodotus, *Histories*, p. 530

[42] Herodotus, *Histories*, pp.419-420
[43] E. R. Dodds "On Misunderstanding the *Oedipus Rex*" in Bloom 1988, p.41
[44] Bernard Knox, "Sophocles' Oedipus" in Bloom, 1988, p.6
[45] Knox in Bloom 1988, p.16
[46] Osborne, pp.67-69
[47] Aristotle, pp.18-19
[48] Knox in Bloom, 1988, pp.7-8
[49] Osborne, p.81
[50] Davies, p.111
[51] Sayers, p.125
[52] Rice, p.79
[53] Santas, p.3
[54] Sayers, p.2
[55] Sayers, p.3
[56] Sayers, p.98
[57] Rice, pp.51-52
[58] Pakaluk, p.21
[59] Warne, p.14
[60] Bartlett, p.x
[61] Bartlett, p.56
[62] Bartlett, p.34
[63] Osborne, p.84
[64] Bartlett, pp.296, 298
[65] Bartlett, P. 226
[66] Burton p.139
[67] Livio, p. 268
[68] Davies, p.149
[69] Nichols, p.1
[70] Cartwright
[71] Cartwright
[72] Davies, p.195
[73] Dahmus, p.50
[74] Dahmus, pp.48-49
[75] Goldsworthy, pp.189-190
[76] Freeman, p.118
[77] Goldsworthy, p.187
[78] Freeman, p.216
[79] Freeman, p.218
[80] Freeman, pp.224-225
[81] Caesar, *Commentaries*
[82] Fagles in Virgil, p.393
[83] Virgil, *The Aeneid*, trans. Robert Fagles
[84] Osborne, p.101
[85] Virgil, pp.378-379

[86] Brown, p.448
[87] Moo, p.24
[88] Stuhlmacher, p.181
[89] Fitzmyer, p. xiii
[90] Moo, p.25
[91] Moo, p.86
[92] Brown, p.437
[93] Hopkins and Beard, p.2
[94] Hopkins and Beard, pp. 32, 36, 41
[95] Hopkins and Beard, p.109
[96] Cassius Dio 66.25: trans.E. Cary
[97] Hopkins and Beard, pp. 75, 78, 81, 83
[98] Hopkins and Beard, pp.94, 103
[99] Hopkins and Beard, p.103
[100] Burton, p.181
[101] Toomer, p.39
[102] Toomer, p.141
[103] Toomer, pp. ix, viii
[104] Burton, p.184
[105] Osborne, p.110
[106] Osborne, p.136
[107] Dahmus, p.72
[108] Bennet, p.59
[109] Dahmus, p.199
[110] Davies, p.276
[111] McKitterick, p.237
[112] O'Daly, p.27
[113] Saint Augustine, *The City of God*, trans. Marcus Dods
[114] Osborne, p.129
[115] Osborne, p.130
[116] Augustine, *The City of God*, Book XIV
[117] Osborne, pp.130, 132
[118] Ian Wood, "The Individuality of Gregory of Tours" in Mitchell, p.46
[119] Wood, pp, 48, 54
[120] Heinzelmann, p.102
[121] Heinzelmann, p.112
[122] Heinzelmann, p.125
[123] Bennett, p.44
[124] Heinzelmann, p.125
[125] Heinzelmann, p.134
[126] Donaldson, p.ix
[127] Donaldson, p.x
[128] Donaldson, p.x
[129] Fred C. Robinson, "Beowulf," in Godden 1991, p.146

[130] Robinson in Godden 1991, p.153
[131] Andy Orchard, "Beowulf" in Godden 2013, p.143
[132] Donaldson, p.xii
[133] Orchard pp. 61, 76
[134] Farr, p.13
[135] Meehan, p.29
[136] Meehan, pp.9, 22
[137] Meehan, p.36
[138] Meehan, p.86
[139] Pulliam, pp.180, 186
[140] Pulliam, p.185
[141] Davies, p.271
[142] Davies, p.313
[143] Dahmus, pp. 231, 239
[144] Bennett, p.180
[145] Davies, p.339
[146] Bennett, p.268
[147] Bennett, p.205
[148] Dahmus, p.327
[149] Davies and Leftow, p.158
[150] Logan, p.37
[151] Davies and Leftow, p.169
[152] Bridgehead, p.57
[153] Bridgehead, p.73
[154] Bridgehead, p.60
[155] Bridgehead, p.109
[156] Bridgehead, p.8
[157] Bridgehead, p.308
[158] Bridgehead, pp.16-17
[159] Sayers, p.30
[160] Brault, pp. 27, 29
[161] Brault, p.43
[162] Sayers, p.16
[163] Brault, p.55
[164] Sayers, p.19
[165] Brault, pp.40, 42
[166] Hoppin, p.187
[167] Hoppin, p.187
[168] Bennett, p.226
[169] Davies, p.358
[170] Bennett, p.315
[171] Toman, p.146
[172] Musgrove, p.173
[173] Bennett, p.301

[174] Toman, p.120
[175] Toman, p.121
[176] Kleiner, p.343
[177] Brown, p.1
[178] Peter Abelard, *Sic et non*, trans. James Harvey Robinson
[179] Uitti and Freeman, p.73
[180] Lacy, p.141
[181] Chrétien de Troyes, *Lancelot, the Knight of the Cart*, trans. Burton Raffel
[182] Duggan, p.228
[183] Wright, p.273
[184] Roesner
[185] Wright, p.282
[186] Hoppin, p.221
[187] Davies, p.371
[188] Bennett, p.213
[189] Osborne, p.218
[190] Bennett, p.194
[191] Dahmus, p.314
[192] Bennett, pp. 235-236
[193] Isher, p.20
[194] Isher, p.24
[195] Temko, p.10
[196] Isher, pp. 130-131
[197] Erlande-Brandenburg, p.147
[198] Wright, p.7
[199] Isher, p.40
[200] Isher, p.46
[201] Burton, p.257
[202] Devlin, p.144
[203] Devlin, p.201
[204] Devlin, pp. 99-100
[205] Batts, p.45
[206] Batts, p.55
[207] Wright, p.288
[208] Wright, pp.290-291
[209] Hoppin, pp.240-241
[210] Wright, p.290
[211] Hoppin, p.240
[212] Wright, p.290
[213] Osborne, p.220
[214] Bennett, p.317
[215] McGinn, pp. 45-46
[216] Fordham University, Thomas Aquinas
[217] Tuchman

[218] Bennett, p.327
[219] Davies, p.409
[220] Davie, pp.419, 440
[221] Bennett, p.348
[222] Jacobus, p.131
[223] Ladis, p.3
[224] Ladis, p.116
[225] D'Arcais, pp.140-141
[226] Ladis, p.117
[227] Keele, p.161
[228] Spade, p.101
[229] Keele, p.96
[230] Keele, p.15
[231] Keele, pp.21, 22
[232] Jennifer Bain. "'... Et mon commencement ma fin': genre and Machaut's musical language in his secular songs," in McGrady, p.81
[233] Jacqueline Cerquiglini-Toulet, "'Ma Fin est mon commencement': the essence of poetry and song in Guillaume de Machaut," in McGrady, p.72
[234] Bain, pp.81-83
[235] Bain, p. 83
[236] Bain, p.83
[237] Bisson, p.99
[238] Bisson, p.107
[239] Bisson, p.108
[240] Bisson, p.110
[241] Bisson, p.250
[242] Bisson, p.255
[243] Bennett, p.339
[244] Dahmus, p.348
[245] Dahmus, p.349
[246] Schapiro, p.9
[247] Georgi, p.xi
[248] Fein, p.1
[249] Georgi, p.xiv
[250] Fein, p.93
[251] Georgi, p.235
[252] Brown, p.69
[253] Atlas, p.153
[254] Atlas, p.153
[255] Perkins
[256] Brown, p.70
[257] Capra 2007, p.27
[258] Capra 2013, p.xi
[259] Richter, p.6

260 Capra 2007, pp.1-2
261 Capra 2013, pp.183-186
262 Capra 2013, p.121
263 Capra 2007, p.28
264 Osborne, p.227
265 Davies, p.497
266 Hale, 123
267 Davies, p.508
268 Partridge, p.14
269 Partridge, p.15
270 Graham-Dixon, p.1
271 Graham-Dixon, p.59
272 John O'Malley, S. J. "The Theology Behind Michelangelo's Ceiling," in Pietrangeli, p.92
273 Graham-Dixon, p.80
274 Graham-Dixon, p.82
275 Pietrangeli, p.148
276 Partridge, p.48
277 Graham-Dixon, p.26
278 Graham-Dixon, p.26
279 Davies, p.478
280 Christ-von Wedel, p.75-76
281 Desiderius Erasmus, *In Praise of Folly*, trans. John Wilson
282 Davies, p.478
283 Connell, p.16
284 Niccolo Machiavelli, *The Prince*, trans. George Bull
285 Connell, pp.1, 3
286 Osborne, p.208
287 Marty, p.29
288 Marty, p.31
289 McKim, p.182
290 Marty, 68
291 Moo, p.24
292 Thornton
293 Baldesar Castiglione, *The Book of the Courtier*, trans. George Bull
294 Harry Berger, Jr., "Sprezzatura and the Absence of Grace," in Javitch, pp.295-296
295 Berger in Javitch, pp.297-298
296 Javitch, pp. xii-xiii
297 Berger in Javitch, pp.305-306
298 Repcheck, p. xiii
299 Fordham University Modern History Sourcebook
300 Repcheck, p. xiv
301 Linton, p.206

[302] Repcheck, p.190
[303] Repcheck, p.190
[304] Wright/Simms, Zarlino, p.4
[305] Atlas, p.629
[306] Brown, p.297, 300
[307] Brown, p.309
[308] Cantor, pp.25, 28, 3-4
[309] Cantor, p.23
[310] Bloom 2003, p.59
[311] Davies, p.616
[312] Osborne, pp.292-293
[313] Osborne, p.270
[314] Osborne, p.280
[315] Ringer, p.11
[316] Ringer, p.13
[317] Pirrotta, p.263
[318] Ringer, p.26
[319] Fabbri, p.65
[320] Ringer, p.66
[321] Ringer, p.69
[322] Grayling, p.11
[323] Burton, p.340
[324] Watson, p.19
[325] Quoted in Watson, p.193
[326] Watson, p.3
[327] Stratten-Pruitt, p.130
[328] Stratten-Pruitt, p.4
[329] Stratten-Pruitt, p.140
[330] Estrella de Diego, "Representing Representation: Reading *Las Meninas*, Again," in Stratten-Pruitt, pp.153-154.
[331] Stratten-Pruitt, p.128
[332] Walker, p.114
[333] Walker, p.114
[334] Walker, pp.120-121
[335] Bermel, p.250
[336] Chandrasekhar, pp. 22-23
[337] Burton, p.375
[338] Chandrasekhar, p.370
[339] Burton p.374
[340] Historical Society of Pennsylvania Digital Library
[341] Kinch Hoekstra, "Hobbes on the Natural Condition of Man," in Springborg, p.110
[342] Bagby, p.8
[343] Springborg, p.3

[344] Horst Bredekamp, "Thomas Hobbes's Visual Strategies," in Springborg, p. 32

[345] Waldron, p.40

[346] Coffin, p.545

[347] Richard Ashcraft, "Locke's political philosophy," in Chappell, p.230

[348] Osborne, p.280

[349] Osborne, p.318

[350] Davies, p.637

[351] Davies, pp.599-601

[352] Osborne, p.309

[353] Dunham, p.266

[354] Dunham, pp.267-268

[355] Rathey, p.189

[356] Rathey, p.176

[357] Rathey, p.183

[358] Frederick W. Hilles, "Art and Artifice in *Tom Jones,*" in Baker, p.789

[359] Wills, p.17

[360] Bernstein, p.110

[361] Bernstein, p.110

[362] Gordon-Reed, p.248

[363] Giordano, p.164

[364] Adam Smith, *The Wealth of Nations*

[365] Raphael, p.xxiii

[366] Raphael, p.xxiii

[367] Skinner, p.24

[368] Raphael, p.xxi

[369] Raphael, p.xxix

[370] Skinner, p.80

[371] J. B. Schneewind. "Why study Kant's Ethics?" in Wood, pp.85-86

[372] Schneewind, p.88

[373] Wood, p.158

[374] Guyer, pp.85-86

[375] Shelly Kagan. "Kantianism for Consequentialists," in Wood, p.119

[376] Davies, p.713

[377] Osborne, p.347

[378] Davies, p.767

[379] Davies, p.819

[380] Davies, p.821

[381] Bloom 2005, p.8

[382] Watt, p.63

[383] Marvin Mudrick, "Irony as Discrimination: *Pride and Prejudice,*" in Watt, pp.76-77

[384] Fullerton, p.39

[385] Anthony Mandal, "Language," in Todd 2005, p.30

386 Shapard, p.xxxvi
387 "Laura G. Mooneyham on Darcy and Elizabeth as Hero and Heroine," in Bloom 2005, p.68
388 Levy, p.10
389 Cook, p.34
390 Levy, p.181
391 Levy, p.41
392 Maynard Solomon, p.226
393 Venning, 246
394 Davies, p.783
395 McDonald, IEP
396 Kierkegaard, *Either/Or,* pp.604, 607
397 McDonald, IEP
398 Hannay, p.6
399 Holme
400 McDonald, SEP
401 Kierkegaard, *Journals*
402 Karl Marx, *The Communist Manifesto*, trans. Samuel Moore
403 Hobsbawm, pp. 112-113
404 Browne, p.17
405 Reznick, p.34
406 Browne, p.106
407 MacMillan, p.645
408 Davies, p.964
409 Pinker, pp.591-592
410 Osborne, pp.465, 481
411 Blechner, p.6
412 Freud, *The Interpretation of Dreams*
413 Richard Wollheim, "Dreams," in Bloom, 1987c, pp.84-85
414 Freud
415 Rubin, pp.30-31, quoting Steinberg
416 Rubin, p.58
417 Rubin, p.81
418 Rubin, p.16
419 Green, p.13
420 Al-Khalili 2003, p.40
421 Al-Khalili 1999, p.147
422 Al-Khalili, p.40
423 Al-Khalili 2003, p.40
424 Galfard, pp.131-132
425 Bennett, p.29
426 Rovelli, p.8
427 Rovelli, p.10
428 Al-Khalili, p.32

[429] Overbye

[430] Kileen, p.123

[431] Kileen, p.123

[432] Kenner, p.12

[433] Heisenberg

[434] Cox and Forshaw, p.13

[435] Al-Khalili 2003, p.56

[436] Cassidy, p.162

[437] Cassidy, p.163

[438] Mermin 1990, p.115

[439] Al-Khalili 2003, p.61

[440] Antokoletz, p.xvii

[441] Wilson, p.2

[442] Antokoletz, p. xxii

[443] Suchoff, A Celebration, p.36

[444] Suchoff, Essays, p.44

[445] Amanda Bayley, p.169

[446] Sartre, lecture, "Existentialism is a Humanity"

[447] Sartre, lecture, "Existentialism is a Humanity"

[448] Sartre, lecture, "Existentialism is a Humanity"

[449] Sartre, lecture, "Existentialism is a Humanity"

[450] Flynn

[451] Denis Dutton, "Aesthetic Universals" (2002)

[452] René Descartes, *Meditations on First Philosophy*, trans. John Veitch

THE MATRIX	Art	Literature	Music	Philosophy Theology	Science Mathematics	History Social Sciences
Ancient Greece: Proportion	Parthenon	Homer; Sophocles		Plato; Aristotle	Pythagoras; Euclid	Herodotus
Ancient Rome: *Virtus*	Colosseum	Virgil		Paul of Tarsus	Ptolemy	Caesar
5th–10th centuries Dichotomy	Book of Kells	Beowulf	Plainsong	St. Augustine		Gregory of Tours
11th century: Faith	Bayeux Tapestry	Song of Roland	Rise of polyphony	St. Anselm		
12th century: Rediscovery	St. Sernin de Toulouse	Chrétien de Troyes	Leonin	Peter Abelard		
13th century: Consolidation	Notre-Dame de Paris	Gottfried von Strassburg	Perotin	Thomas Aquinas	Fibonacci	
14th century: Self-Awareness	Giotto	Chaucer	Machaut	William of Ockham		
15th century: *Janus*	Robert Campin	Villon	Ockeghem		Leonardo da Vinci	
16th century: Humanism	Michel-angelo	Shakespeare	Gibbons	Erasmus; Luther	Copernicus	Machiavelli; Castiglione
17th century: Rules	Velasquez	Molière	Monteverdi	Descartes	Newton	Hobbes; Locke
18th century: Rationality	Jefferson	Fielding	Bach	Kant	Euler	Smith
19th century: Rebellion	Turner	Austen	Beethoven	Kierkegaard	Darwin; Gauss	Marx
20th century: Uncertainty	Picasso	Joyce	Bartók	Sartre	Einstein; Heisenberg	Freud

Index

Abelard, Peter, 86, 87, 88, 95, 136

Ad organum faciendum, 78

Aeneid, The, 39, 41, 50, 265

Alaric, 54, 58

Albigensian Crusade, 98

Alesia, 37

Alleluia Justus ut palma, 79, 80

Almagest, 49, 50

American Revolution, 212

An die Freude, 221

Anonymus 4, 92

Anselm, 69, 70, 71, 80, 208, 270

Aquinas, Thomas, 110, 113, 209, 270

Arena Chapel, 117, 118

Aristotle, xii, 21, 24, 25, 26, 31, 86, 110, 120, 121, 142, 180, 269, 270, 273

Augustine, 54, 55, 66, 88, 113

Augustus, 33

Austen, Jane, 218, 220, 235, 266

B Minor Mass, 197

Babylonian Captivity, 115

Bach, Johann Sebastian, 197, 198, 199, 211, 222, 268

Ballade des dames du temps jadis, 135, 142

Bartók, Béla, 254, 256, 257, 260

Battle of Hastings, 68, 80

Battle of Roncevaux Pass, 75

Bayeux Tapestry, 73, 80

Beethoven, Ludwig van, 221, 222, 224, 235

Benedict of Nursia, 52

Beowulf, 59, 60, 61, 66, 75, 77, 265

Black Death, 114, 115, 236

Book of Kells, 62, 66, 128

Book of the Courtier, The, 156, 168

Caesar, Julius, 36, 38, 46, 50

Camino de Santiago, 83, 125

Campbell, Joseph, 261

Campin, Robert, 131, 142, 267

Canterbury Tales, The, 125, 128, 266

Carolingian minuscule, 53

Carolingian renaissance, 53

Castiglione, 156, 157, 158, 168

Categorical Imperative, 209, 210, 258, 272

Catharism, 97

chanson de geste, 75, 77

Charlemagne, 53, 64, 76, 77, 80

Chaucer, Geoffrey, 125, 126, 128

Chrétien de Troyes, 90, 91, 104, 266

City of God, The, 54

Clement V, 115

Clotilde, 58

Clovis, 52, 58

Colbert, 169, 207

Colosseum, 44, 45, 46, 47, 50

Columbus, Christopher, 49, 129

Commentaries on the Gallic Wars, 36, 37, 50

Communist Manifesto, 229, 231

Constantine, 35

Copernican Revolution, 168

Copernicus, 49, 120, 145, 159, 168, 184, 215, 246

Council of Florence, 130

Council of Nicaea, 35

Council of Trent, 144

Creation of Adam, The, 147, 168

Critique of Pure Reason, 208

Damascus, 42

Darwin, Charles, 215, 233, 234, 235

De Profundis, 162

De revolutionibus, 49

Declaration of Independence, 188, 192

Deisidaimonia, 6

Demoiselles d'Avignon, 243, 268

Demoiselles d'Avignon, 242

Descartes, René, 140, 174, 176, 177, 191, 193, 271

Diderot, Denis, 193

Discourse on the Method, 175, 176, 191

Djoser, xiii, 3, 4

Domesday Book, 68

Edict of Milan, 35

Edward, 72, 73, 74

Einstein, Albert, 120, 242, 244, 245, 246, 253, 260

Either/Or, 227, 228

Eleanor of Aquitaine, 88, 89, 90, 91

Elements, 32

Encyclopédie, 193

English Civil War, 170, 186, 191

Entrance of Christ into Jerusalem, 117, 128

Erasmus, Desiderio, 148, 149, 150, 168

Euclid, 27, 28, 29, 30, 32, 215

Euler, Leonard, 195, 197, 211

Fear and Trembling, 227

Fibonacci, 101, 102, 103, 113

Fielding, Henry, 202, 203, 211

Florentine Cameratas, 171

Francis of Assisi, 96, 97, 119

French Revolution, 212, 221, 235

Freud, Sigmund, 226, 238, 239, 240, 241, 260

Galileo Galilei, 140, 160, 168, 183, 184

Gauss, Carl Friedrich, 215, 218, 235

Giotto, 116, 117, 118, 119, 128, 267

Gottfried von Strassburg, 104, 105, 106, 113, 266

Great Famine, 114

Great Schism, 115

Gregory, 64

Gregory of Tours, 56, 57, 58, 66

Gregory VII, 69

Groundwork for a Metaphysics of Morals, 209

Guido of Arezzo, 64

Hamlet, 164, 167, 168

Harold, Earl of Wessex, 68, 72, 73, 74, 80

Heisenberg, Werner, 250, 252, 260

Henry IV, 69

Hero with a Thousand Faces, The, 261

Herodotus, 17, 19, 56

Hildegard von Bingen, 82, 272

Hobbes, Thomas, 185, 186, 188, 190, 191, 192

Homer, 8, 10, 39, 41, 75, 246, 250

Hundred Years' War, 115, 116

Imhotep, 3

Industrial Revolution, 213, 224

Innocent III, 96, 119

Interpretation of Dreams, 239

Jefferson, Thomas, 188, 190, 192, 204, 205, 211, 267

Joan of Arc, 136

Joyce, James, 219, 246, 247, 248, 249, 260, 266

Judgment of Paris, The, 243

Julius II, 146

Kant, Immanuel, 208, 209, 210, 211, 258, 271

Kepler, Johannes, 145, 160, 168, 184

Kierkegaard, Søren, 227, 229, 235

Lancelot, 89, 90, 95, 266

Las Meninas, 178, 179

Lascaux, xiii, 1, 3

Lassus, 162, 164

Le Misanthrope, 181

Leo X, 154, 155

Leonardo da Vinci, 139, 140, 141, 142

Leonardo of Pisa, 101, 113

Leonin, 92, 93, 94, 95, 107

Letter to the Romans, 155

Leviathan, 186

Liber abaci, 101, 102

Little Ice Age, 114

Locke, John, 185, 188, 189, 191, 192

Louis XIV, 169, 170, 191

Luther, Martin, 143, 144, 153, 154, 155

Ma fin est mon commencement, 122, 128

Machaut, Guillaume de, 122, 123, 124, 128

Machiavelli, 151, 152, 153, 158, 168

Magellan, Ferdinand, 129

Magnus liber, 92, 93

Marathon, 14, 17, 18

Marx, Karl, 229, 231, 232, 235

Medici, Lorenzo, 151

Merode Altarpiece, 134, 142

Michelangelo, 146, 147, 148, 168

Miltiades, 17

Missa prolationum, 136, 137, 139, 142

Molière, 180, 181, 182, 191, 266

Monteverdi, Claudio, 173, 174, 191

Monticello, 198, 204, 205, 211

Music for Strings, Percussion and Celesta, 254

Musica enchiriadis, 78

Nationalism, 214

Newton, Isaac, 140, 141, 182, 183, 185, 191, 193, 194, 206, 211, 225, 245, 251

Nichomachean Ethics, 25

Ninety-five Theses, 154

Norman Conquest, 68, 74

Notre Dame Cathedral, 99, 107, 109, 113

Occam's Razor, 120, 161

Ockeghem, Johannes, 136, 137, 139, 142

Ockham, William of, 119, 120, 270

Ode to Joy, 221

Odyssey, The, 8, 9, 31, 39, 246, 265, 266

Oedipus Rex, 19, 21, 31, 240, 265

Orfeo, 173, 174

Palladio, Andrea, 203

Panathenaic Games, 16

Parthenon, 15, 16, 31, 32, 103, 267

Paul of Tarsus, 34, 42, 43, 44, 50, 51, 56, 148, 149, 155

Pax Romana, 34

Peace of Augsburg, 144

Peloponnesian Wars, 8, 19

Penitential Psalms, 162

Pericles, 14, 15

Perotin, 107, 109, 113

Persian Wars, 6

Philip IV of Spain, 178

Picasso, Pablo, 241, 242, 243, 249, 260, 267, 268

Plato, 22, 23, 24, 32, 55, 70, 121, 171, 270, 271

Poetics, 21, 31

Possente spirto, 173

Praise of Folly, The, 149

Pride and Prejudice, 219, 220

Prince, The, 151, 152, 168

Principia Mathematica, 183

Proslogion, 70, 80

Ptolemy, Claudius, 47, 48, 49, 50, 120, 159

Ptolemy. Claudius, 50

Pythagoras, 11, 12, 31, 160

R*epublic, The*, 24

Roi Soleil, 169

Roman Empire, 33, 41, 51, 55, 152

Roman Republic, 36

Rubens, Peter Paul, 243

Salamis, 17, 18

Santiago de Compostela, 83

Sartre, Jean-Paul, 258, 259, 260

Schiller, Friedrich, 221

Scrovegni, Enrico, 116

Sederunt principes, 107, 109

Seven Bridges of Königsberg, The, 194

Shakespeare, William, 165, 167, 168

Sic et non, 87

Sistine Chapel, 146

Slave Ship, The, 224, 226, 268

Smith, Adam, 206, 207, 211

Socrates, 23, 55

Song of Roland, 75, 77

Sophocles, 19, 21, 22, 31, 240

Spanish Inquisition, 130

St. Sernin de Toulouse, 84, 85

Sum of Logic, 128, 270

Summa Theologica, 110, 113

Sun King, 169

Ten Books of History, 57

Tetzel, Johannes, 154

Thermopylae, 17, 18

Tom Jones, 200, 203, 211, 266

Tristan, 106, 113, 266

Turner, William, 224, 225, 227, 235, 268

Two Treatises of Government, 188

Ulysses, 246, 247, 249, 260, 266

Uncertainty Principle, 251

Vasco da Gamba, 129

Velásquez, Diego, 178, 179, 191, 267

Vercingetorix, 37, 38

Versailles, 169, 198, 225

Vespasian, 45

Villon, François, 134, 135, 142

Virgil, 39, 40, 41, 250

Vitry, Philippe de, 136, 139

Wealth of Nations, The, 206

William of Normandy, 68, 72, 73, 74, 80, 115

William of Ockham, 121, 128

Zarlino. Gioseffo, 161

About the author

During his twenty-year career as a musicologist, Arthur Wenk published books on Claude Debussy (*Claude Debussy and the Poets; Claude Debussy and Twentieth-Century Music*) and music bibliography (*Analyses of Nineteenth- and Twentieth-Century Music; Musical Resources for the Revised Common Lectionary.*) Later he drew on his experiences as a university professor, church organist, choral conductor and concert pianist to produce a series of mystery novellas featuring musicologist Axel Crochet as sleuth: *The Quarter Note Tales; New Quarter Note Tales: Axel in Quebec; Axel Crochet: Musicologist-at-Large*; and *Quarter Note Tales #4: An Axel Crochet Trilogy.* Other books include *A Guide to the Bookstores of* Toronto, and *Camerata: A Guide to Organizing and Directing Small Choruses.* Dr. Wenk's subsequent careers as calculus teacher and psychotherapist have led to public lectures on graphing calculators, Geometer's Sketchpad, parenting and communication, separation and divorce, opera, western culture, and film. Since his retirement in 2014 Arthur Wenk lives in North Fort Myers, Florida and Lagoon City, Ontario.

CPSIA information can be obtained
at www.ICGtesting.com
Printed in the USA
LVHW080555270522
719857LV00012B/206